The Dolphin Writer, Book One

The Dolphin Writer, Book One

Building Sentences and
Composing Paragraphs

HOUGHTON MIFFLIN COMPANY   **Boston**   **New York**

Executive Publisher: Patricia Coryell
Editor-in-Chief: Carrie Brandon
Sponsoring Editor: Joann Kozyrev
Senior Marketing Manager: Tom Ziolkowski
Senior Development Editor: Judith Fifer
Project Editor: Shelley Dickerson
Art and Design Manager: Jill Haber
Cover Design Manager: Anne S. Katzeff
Senior Photo Editor: Jennifer Meyer Dare
Senior Composition Buyer: Chuck Dutton
New Title Project Manager: James Lonergan
Editorial Assistant: Daisuke Yasutake
Marketing Assistant: Bettina Chiu
Editorial Assistant: Anthony D'Aries

Cover image: Lisa Kreick—Ocean Eyes Photography; www.oceaneyesphotography.com

Printed in the U.S.A.

Library of Congress Control Number: 2007930111

Instructor's Annotated Edition ISBN 10: 0-618-37915-0
Instructor's Annotated Edition ISBN 13: 978-0-618-37915-6   302989
For ordering, use student text ISBNs
Student Edition ISBN 10: 0-618-37912-6
Student Edition ISBN 13: 978-0-618-37912-5

1 2 3 4 5 6 7 8 9–DOC–11 10 09 08 07

Brief Contents

Table of Contents

Part V   READING SELECTIONS

Each selection is followed by questions on Vocabulary, Checking Comprehension, Mode and Skill Check, and Questions for Discussion and Writing.

Preface

The Dolphin Writer

The Dolphin Writer is a three volume series that focuses on writing sentences to paragraphs (Book One), paragraphs to essays (Book Two), and essays (Book Three) in an easy-to-understand and affordable format. Each volume of the Dolphin Writer presents students with comprehensive yet approachable coverage of the writing process, from prewriting through peer evaluation through revision and preparation of the final paper. Book One includes complete coverage of sentence-to-paragraph issues such as grammar, mechanics, and usage, while Books Two and Three include a brief Handbook that contains this basic coverage. Each volume includes a readings section with ten level-appropriate readings.

The Dolphin Writer — Book One

Key features of the volume include:

- the same topics and content as do other comparable textbooks, but for a price that is more than a third less than that of similar books
- careful step-by-step explanations of each part of the writing process along with many student models; each of the Writing Process chapters includes a "Student Demonstration" of the process, as well as many shorter student samples throughout the chapter
- a multitude of practice exercises that permit students to practice each new concept
- carefully selected photos and other illustrations that enhance student understanding of the text and help students learn to understand and interpret visuals
- a focus on student success in all areas of reading, writing, and studying, with Writing for Success boxes that suggest ways to organize, manage, or implement techniques, including how to use a computer to assist in the writing process
- Web Work boxes at the end of each chapter provide suggestions for sites that provide additional help, exercises, or suggestions for further exploration

- definitions of difficult words as well as allusions in many of the examples, exercises, and readings appear as footnotes so that students do not have to look them up

- chapter pedagogy supports students in anticipating, learning, and reviewing key concepts, as well as providing suggestions for discussion and writing practice

- an ESL appendix in each of the texts focuses on areas of difficulty for multi-lingual students or students who need additional practice in standard English

- a student website that includes grammar practice exercises and live links to additional information and practice sites

Organization of the Text

Part I: Reading, Writing, and Thinking introduces students to the importance of developing the skills of reading, writing, and thinking critically, and encourages them to develop a positive attitude about writing.

Part II: Sentence Skills begins with an overview of the parts of speech (Chapter 2), elements of the basic sentence (Chapter 3), and then proceeds to in-depth coverage of verbs (Chapter 4), and modifiers (Chapter 5). Succeeding chapters deal with common problem areas, including subject-verb agreement (Chapter 6), pronouns and pronoun agreement (Chapter 7), and compound sentences, including a section on avoiding comma splices and run-on sentences (Chapter 8). Chapter 9, The Complex Sentence, includes a section on avoiding sentence fragments. Chapters 10 and 11 present the important concepts of parallelism and sentence combining. Chapters 12, 13, and 14 cover punctuation, capitalization, and spelling. Every chapter in Part II includes a pre-test (Test Yourself) and post-tests that help students assess their progress. In addition, a Part II Review provides mixed practice tests that focus on identifying and correcting common sentence errors.

In **Part III: The Writing Process** students learn the steps of the writing process, from prewriting through proofreading, editing, and preparing a final draft. Each of the chapters in Part III includes "A Student Demonstration," with student models of the techniques presented in the chapter.

Part IV: Common Strategies for Organizing Paragraphs introduces students to some basic methods of organizing, including time order (narration and process), space order (description), illustration, comparison/contrast, and order of importance (argument). "Writing for Success" features provide specific examples of how the modes can be used in various types of writing, including writing for the workplace.

Part V: Reading Selections provides ten brief readings on high-interest subjects; the readings are followed by vocabulary questions, comprehension questions, and mode and skill check questions that assess the student's understanding of the organizing principle, main idea, supporting details, tone, and inferences found in the reading. Questions for Discussion and Writing provide a transition to student writing practice.

An appendix, Additional Practice for Multilingual Writers, provides additional practice on areas of concern for ESL students; more interactive practice is found on the accompanying student website. An Index and a Rhetorical Index complete the text.

Ancillaries

For students

The accompanying student website offers 650 grammar practice exercises that provide immediate feedback and refer students back to specific text sections for review. Students can also find live links to websites that offer additional information and practice opportunities.

For instructors

An instructor's website for each of the volumes provides sample syllabi, additional writing suggestions, and chapter quizzes.

WriteSpace for Developmental English, Houghton Mifflin's Blackboard-enabled course management system, provides a rich assortment of exercises that can be linked to a gradebook, student model paragraphs and papers, tutorials on the writing process, and interactive multimedia modules that can be used as prompts for writing or for critically thinking about visuals and the media. WriteSpace allows an instructor to create a customized course with additional online components for students, gradebook capability, and HM Assess, a diagnostic tool that evaluates student problem areas and provides a customized study path for that student; instructors can also utilize Re:Mark, for online paper review and marking, and Peer Re:Mark, which allows students to review and comment on each other's papers.

Acknowledgments

Special thanks are owed to the reviewers of this series:

Sydney Bartman of *Mount San Antonio College*

Kathleen Beauchene of *Community College of Rhode Island*

Dawn L. Brickey of *Charleston Southern University*

Carol Ann Britt of *San Antonio College*

James W. Cornish of *McLennan Community College*

Ned Cummings of *Bryant & Stratton College*

Joli J. Dusk of *Lurleen B. Wallace Community College*

Donna Eisenstat of *West Virginia University Institute of Technology*

Grushenka Engelbrecht-Castanon of *Northwest College*

Matt Fox of *Monroe Community College*

Hank Galmish of *Green River Community College*

Mary Gross of *MiraCosta College*

Aileen Gum of *San Diego Community College District*

Toni Holloway of *Mountain View College*

Teresa S. Irvin of *Columbus State University*

Lilia A. Joy of *Henderson Community College*

Patsy Krech of *The University of Memphis*

Steven Lacek of *Southern West Virginia Community and Technical College*

Jill A. Lahnstein of *Cape Fear Community College*

James Landers of *Community College of Philadelphia*

Catherine A. Lutz of *Texas A&M Kingsville*

Patricia Maddox of *Amarillo College*

Teri Maddox of *Jackson State Community College*

Lisa Maggard of *Hazard Community & Technical College*

Patricia A. Malinowski of *Finger Lakes Community College*

Eugene Marino of *Monroe Community College*

Patricia McGraw of *Cape Cod Community College*

Carol Miter of *Riverside Community College, Norco Campus*

Theresa Mohamed of *Onondaga Community College*

Barbara E. Nixon of *Salem Community College*

Peggy Roche of *Community College of Allegheny County*

Sara Safdie of *Bellevue Community College*

James Scannell McCormick of *Rochester Community and Technical College*

Midge L. Shaw of *Rogue Community College*

Linda Spoelman of *Grand Rapids Community College*

Deborah Stallings of *Hinds Community College*

Karen Supak of *Western New Mexico University*

Linda Marianne Taylor of *Tri-County Technical College*

Dennielle True of *Manatee Community College*

Margaret Waguespcak of *Amarillo College*

Cody Yeager of *Central Oregon Community College*

Dana Zimbleman of *Jefferson College*

Improving Writing and Thinking

GOALS FOR CHAPTER 1

▶ Explain why "having nothing to say" is a temporary problem.

▶ Explain why writing is a mentally challenging activity.

▶ Explain the benefits of increasing your own knowledge about writing.

▶ Explain the benefits of getting feedback about your writing.

▶ Explain how your attitude affects your ability to learn about writing.

▶ Explain why it is important to read the writing of others.

Examining Your Feelings About Writing

Chances are good that you have already done at least some writing in your life. Take a moment to reflect on the things you have already written by completing the following exercise.

EXERCISE 1.1

In the following list, place a check mark beside every type of document you have already written at least once.

_____ A paper, such as an essay or summary, for a class

_____ A letter to a friend or relative

_____ An e-mail message

_____ A work-related document, such as a memo or business letter

_____ An entry in a journal or diary

_____ A letter of complaint

_____ A letter to the editor of a newspaper

_____ A speech

_____ A story

_____ A poem

_____ A thank-you note

_____ Other: _____

When you need to write a document like one of those you checked off in the list, how do you feel about the task? Are you eager to start getting your thoughts down on paper, or do you dread the process, perhaps putting it off as long as possible? As you complete the next exercise, spend a few moments considering your feelings about writing.

EXERCISE 1.2

On the following lines, write two or three sentences about your attitudes and feelings toward writing. For instance, you might say, "I love to write because I can express myself honestly" or "When I have to write, I do not enjoy it because I have nothing to say." There are no right or wrong answers in this exercise. Just be as specific as you can, and be honest!

_____

_____

_____

In Exercise 1.2, did you write about how much you enjoy writing? If you are like many students, you probably expressed a dislike for writing. You may have written that writing is distasteful to you because it is hard or because you seem to struggle with it more than anyone else you know. You may have written that writing makes you feel frustrated or even angry, so you try to avoid it as much as possible. You may have even written that you fear writing because you do not seem to "get it," so it makes you feel stupid. All of these reactions are common, especially among writers of varying skills and experiences.

But now stop and think about those two or three sentences you just wrote for Exercise 1.2. Did it not feel satisfying—and maybe even a little bit enjoyable—to be able to say exactly what you think about writing? If you did feel a small sense of satisfaction, you were experiencing the power of using writing as a tool for self-expression. Like most humans, you like to express what you think and believe. Writing gives you another avenue for that expression, so if you enjoyed your opportunity to state your feelings about writing in Exercise 1.2, you might enjoy opportunities to express in writing your thoughts and feelings about other topics as well.

Now, consider whether you had any trouble expressing your feelings about writing in Exercise 1.2. Did you struggle to find the words you were looking for, or was it pretty easy to write down your opinion? If you, like many people, have strong emotions about writing, it probably was not that difficult to write about your feelings. Perhaps, then, you might not struggle as much as you think you would to record your thoughts about other topics that concern you.

Therefore, Exercise 1.2 may have demonstrated to you that both power and pleasure are to be found in expressing yourself in writing. Nonetheless, you might be thinking, *Well, I still don't like it!* If that is still your response, your dislike is probably based on the following common objections:

1. "I really do not have much to say, so it is a struggle for me to write about anything."
2. "Writing is too hard. I just cannot remember all the 'rules' while I am writing."
3. "Other people—especially teachers—think I am a terrible writer. My papers are always covered with teachers' red corrections, proving that I have no idea what I am doing."

Do any of these statements sound like something you have said or thought before? Let us examine each one of these objections to writing.

"I really do not have much to say . . ."

If you have ever said something like this, you are forgetting that you, like everyone, have plenty of ideas, thoughts, feelings, and beliefs about the world you live in. Each of us is interested in various kinds of topics and activities, and each of us is concerned about something and/or someone. And, usually, we have plenty to say about the things that interest or trouble us. The next exercise will give you a chance to explore what some of those interests are.

 **EXERCISE 1.3**

Generate ideas for each of the following lists and record them on the blanks provided.

Three of my hobbies or interests

1. _____
2. _____
3. _____

Three people who have had an impact on my life

1. _____
2. _____
3. _____

Three topics I like learning more about

1. _____
2. _____
3. _____

Three of my goals

1. _____
2. _____
3. _____

Three problems that worry me

1. _____
2. _____
3. _____

Three things that make me angry

1. _____
2. _____
3. _____

If you were asked to write about one of the topics you listed in Exercise 1.3, you would probably have quite a lot to say about it. Of course, you might not be able to think of pages and pages of ideas all at once. But the ideas are there, and later in this book you will learn techniques for coaxing them out of your mind when you need them.

At this point, you might be thinking, *It would be great if I could write only about the things that matter most to me, but that does not happen, especially when I have to write papers for school.* It is true that your history teacher is going to be more interested in, say, your views about the Vietnam War than he or she is in your children or your love of motocross racing. And you are right: if you do not have much in your head about the Vietnam War, it is going to be pretty hard to write about it. However, do not make the mistake of thinking that "having nothing to say" is a permanent problem. Instead, it is a temporary obstacle that can be overcome by

1. Using techniques to discover what your mind already knows
2. Learning more information about the topic

3. Reflecting more on the information you already have about a topic

4. Finding some aspect of a topic that interests you

In other words, having "nothing to say" is a matter of needing to explore your own thoughts more and/or to learn more about your subject. It is easiest to write about the topics that interest us because we have already devoted a lot of thought to them. Once you think about and gather more information on just about any topic, you will have more to say about it. Also, later in the book, in Chapter 18, you will discover techniques for discovering an interesting aspect of any topic so that writing about it will be a more meaningful and rewarding experience.

EXERCISE 1.4

What do you have to say about the following photograph? Record your ideas on the blanks provided.

© Bruce Ayres/Getty Images

_____

_____

_____

_____

"Writing is too hard . . ."

When people say that writing is too hard, they usually mean one of several different things. Although writing involves much more than knowing where commas go, they may mean that they have a difficult time remembering all the rules for grammar and spelling as they are writing. They may mean that the "rules" that apply to writing seem hopelessly mysterious and impossible to understand. Or they may mean that the "rules" seem to keep changing or that there do not seem to be any real rules at all. As a result, for them writing every paper involves a lot of guesswork.

It is true that writing is a challenging activity. It requires thought, concentration, and effort. It asks you to engage in a variety of complex mental tasks such as logical reasoning and organization. These thinking skills tend to improve with practice and effort. The "rules," guidelines, techniques, or whatever you want to call them, however, just have to be learned. Therefore, if you feel as though you do not have a good grasp of them, or if they seem confusing or changeable or nonexistent, then you probably need to increase your knowledge of them. Trying to write without knowing much about the tools and techniques that are available to you is a lot like trying to hit a baseball by just swinging blindly. You might hit the ball once in a while. You might even hit it far every now and then. However, you will not hit it consistently well until you understand how to hold the bat, how to swing it, and how to keep your eye on the ball. Similarly, you are unlikely to write successful papers until you are aware of *what* you are doing and *how* you are doing it.

Fortunately, though, this lack of knowledge is another temporary problem. As with any other process, the more you learn about writing, the better—and more powerful—your writing is likely to be. Thus, this book offers you a valuable opportunity to learn the "rules," guidelines, techniques, or whatever you want to call them. The goals of this book are to increase your knowledge about writing and to give you opportunities to practice what you are learning. Part I, which covers sentence skills, will help you learn to write clear, sophisticated, grammatically correct sentences. Part II will illustrate the steps in the writing process and teach you about tools and techniques that will make this process more efficient and productive. Part III will demonstrate how to develop paragraphs with different rhetorical modes. Part IV offers additional reading selections to give you more opportunities to learn from the writing of others.

Therefore, if you decide to apply yourself to really learning something about writing, you will find that you may begin to dread writing a lot less. You will have learned some concepts and skills that will make your efforts more rewarding.

EXERCISE 1.5

Place a check mark on the blank beside every aspect of your writing that you would like to improve. Then, for each checked item, fill in the chapter number(s) of this book that contain information about those topics. Use this book's table of contents and index to help you identify chapter numbers.

_____ Overcoming writer's block (Chapter ___)

_____ Finding topics and ideas to write about (Chapter ___)

_____ Figuring out how to organize or determine the right order for ideas (Chapter ___)

_____ Writing clear sentences (Chapters _____)

_____ Spelling words correctly (Chapter ___)

_____ Making sentences grammatically correct (Chapters _____)

_____ Knowing where to put commas, semicolons, and other punctuation marks (Chapter ___)

_____ Developing, or explaining, ideas (Chapters _____)

_____ Knowing where to find information, or research (Chapters _____)

_____ Other: _____ (Chapter(s) _____)

"Other people—especially teachers—think I am a terrible writer . . ."

Are you one of those students who feel frustrated, angry, or depressed when they receive a graded, corrected paper back from a teacher? These feelings are perfectly valid, of course, but when you are feeling them, what do you do next? Do you carefully read the teacher's comments, trying to understand what you could improve upon? Do you discuss your paper with your teacher to make sure you know what to do differently next time? Or do you decide that you are just a bad writer—that's all there is to it—and put the paper someplace where you will never have to see it again?

One of the ways we learn to be better writers is to get feedback on our writing. But we have to take the time and make the effort to understand what the feedback means. Therefore, the next time you receive a graded paper, remind yourself that it presents a valuable learning opportunity. The vast majority of teachers who take the time to point out errors and make suggestions for improvement are trying to help you become a better writer. Use this help to discover how you can make changes that will improve your writing. Take advantage, too, of other opportunities for feedback; for example, ask your fellow students, friends, and family for their comments and suggestions.

EXERCISE 1.6

The following paper was written by a student who was assigned to write about a person who has impacted his life. This student wrote the paper and submitted it, and then his instructor graded the paper, adding comments and suggestions in red ink. Read over this graded paper and the teacher's comments, and answer the questions that follow.

A Person Who Has Impacted My Life

by Sam Ford

I would have to say that the person who has   *Clear thesis*

had the most impact on my life is my mom.

run-on sentence

Her name is Dolores she has been a single par-

apostrophe error

ent since my sister and I were young kids. She

comma error

is a nurse, who works very hard. I admire her

for what she's done.

For one thing, she is always trying to get

ahead so that our family can be better off

misspelling

finahcally. She rarely turns down a chance to

work overtime, even when she's tired. She has

been working on getting her bachelor's degree,   *Two effective supporting points*

taking night classes, so she can make more

money. It's hard on her to have to study and

work too, but she keeps doing it because she

knows it will pay off eventually. Even though

Develop this
second point
with more
detail in a
separate
paragraph

missing comma

she's busy she always finds time for me and my

give an example

sister. She has always been there for us. Her

apostrophe error

family is important to her, and she shows it.   *How?*

missing apostrophe

I think my mom is a good example of whats

important in life, and she has set a good exam-

hyphen error

ple by being a hard-worker and loving parent.

1. What is one thing that the instructor praised about this paper?

_____

_____

_____

2. What grammatical and mechanical concepts does the writer need to learn more about?

_____

_____

_____

3. What is the instructor's advice about the writer's second point?

_____

_____

_____

4. Where in this book could this student go for more instruction in each of the following? Write the chapter number(s) in the blanks provided.

Organizing ideas (Chapter ___)
Developing ideas with specific details (Chapters _____)
Commas (Chapter ___)
Run-on sentences (Chapters _____)
Spelling (Chapter ___)

EXERCISE 1.7

If you still have a paper you wrote that has been graded by a teacher, reread the teacher's comments. If you do not have a graded paper, try to remember comments and suggestions that you have received from instructors in the past. Answer the following questions by writing your responses on the blanks provided.

1. List two or three things teachers have identified as areas of your writing that need improvement.

    1. _____

    2. _____

    3. _____

2. What did you do in response to these suggestions? For example, did you attempt to correct your mistakes, or did you try to learn more about how and why you went astray? If you did not do anything, what could you have done to benefit more from this feedback?

    _____

    _____

    _____

    _____

3. List the names of two or three fellow students, friends, relatives, neighbors, or coworkers who could probably give you helpful feedback on your writing.

    1. _____

    2. _____

    3. _____

Attitude and Writing

Regardless of why you may dislike writing, remember that a positive attitude will help you open your mind to learning more about writing through your own efforts, through formal instruction in courses and books, and from those who offer you feedback. If you continue to tell yourself that you have nothing to say, that writing is too hard, or that other people do not like your writing, you are focusing on the negative. The more you focus on the negative, the harder it is to prepare your mind to learn. Begin to change your own attitudes, and you will find that you have removed some of the mental barriers to improving your own writing skills.

Reading About Writing

This chapter has covered several ways you can begin to improve your own writing right away:

1. Increase your knowledge about the tools and techniques of writing.
2. Practice writing.
3. Get feedback from others, and learn from it how to improve your next paper.

In addition to these approaches, there is a fourth way you can improve your writing skills: read the writing of others, and note what works and what does not work. Stephen King, a very successful writer of horror stories and nonfiction books, says in his book *On Writing,* "If you want to be a writer, you must do two things above all others: read a lot and write a lot." Not only do we learn to be better writers from practicing and getting suggestions from others, but we also hone our own skills by reading and studying what other writers do and how they do it. When you read someone else's writing, try to figure out exactly why it succeeds—or why it fails. Then apply these lessons the next time you sit down to write a paper of your own.

EXERCISE 1.8

The following excerpt is from a book entitled *Writing: My Worst Nightmare.* Read this excerpt, and then answer the questions by writing your responses on the blanks provided.

From "Writing: My Worst Nightmare"

by Christopher Lee and Rosemary Jackson*

Note: Despite severe learning disabilities, Christopher Lee managed to earn a degree from the University of Georgia.

1 Writing, like anything else, has many different aspects. The important aspect of writing is the substance, not the mechanics.[1] Writing is a form of communication,

1. **mechanics:** technical aspects, like grammar

**Source:* Reprinted by permission from *Faking It* by Christopher Lee and Rosemary Jackson. Copyright © 1992 by Christopher Lee and Rosemary Jackson. Published by Heinemann, a division of Reed Elsevier, Inc., Portsmouth, NH. All rights reserved.

and yet many people treat it as if it is a form of punishment. Writing is beautiful. It can express the depths of a person's soul. It is a way of talking without opening the mouth. Students with learning disabilities need to experience this.

2   I was in college before I discovered that even though the mechanics are very important, there comes a time when a person should just let go of the mechanics and write with feeling. If teachers wait to teach the communication and aesthetic[1] aspects of writing until their students are able to perfect the mechanics, their students may never experience the true pleasure of writing. When I let go of the mechanics and began to concentrate on what I was saying, I found that my writing improved, and in turn, my mechanics improved. Before college I hated writing because it was exposing and confronting a weakness and because it simply meant that I couldn't spell or correctly punctuate a sentence. I never once realized that writing was supposed to have meaning. As it turns out, writing is a joy.

3   My first insight into writing as it *should* be was in my first college English class. My teacher had us keep a weekly journal. Each week I could write about anything I wanted, and I was only supposed to take ten minutes. I was not supposed to worry about punctuation or spelling. At first, this assignment scared me. I knew I would have to put more than ten minutes into it simply to get a "Pass." In fact, I typically put three hours into each journal entry.

4   We could bare our souls about a serious problem, describe a pretty girl walking down the street, or just describe what we had for breakfast. The point of the journals was to get us to write without being encumbered by[2] any restraints. I found myself liking the idea of letting everything go, and even though I knew it was impossible for me to do that, I found a certain feeling of peace knowing that a grade would not be assigned to the thoughts I put on paper.

5   So I started to write my weekly journals. It was very hard at first. I found myself fighting to put my words on paper. I was fighting myself and the memory of years of discouragement. I did not like the fact that I had to struggle so hard and that it was so difficult to put things on paper. The freedom I longed for was not there. It was not as easy as the teacher had made it sound in class. What was supposed to be a ten-minute assignment turned out to be a week-long writing project. Then one day it happened. I was staring out the window of my dorm room and feeling sorry for myself when I saw two girls walking down the street. I had seen them around campus before. One of them was visually impaired. She had thick glasses and carried a cane. She always seemed to be smiling. She also always seemed to be alone. Walking beside her was another girl. She was a "little person" whom I had also seen around campus, also smiling. However, she, too, always seemed to be alone. I remember passing them individually on campus and trying not to feel sorry for them. I could not help thinking about how

1. **aesthetic:** concerning the appreciation of beauty

2. **encumbered by:** burdened by

lonely each girl must have been. I never saw them with anyone. Outside my window, walking down the chilly, lamplit street, under a starry sky, they had found each other. I realized that they were no longer alone. A warm feeling came over me, and I wanted to share it with someone.

6   There was no one around—only my pencil and paper. For the first time I wanted to put my thoughts down on paper. And I did. Forgetting about the structure, the organization, and yes, even the spelling, for the first time I was able to concentrate on the meaning. It was such a good feeling to see two people finding each other that it overrode any fear I had of writing. After I finished I realized I had written my first real paper. The paper was lousy, but I felt fantastic. Suddenly I realized the pleasure that came with putting my thoughts down in writing. For the first time I realized that, just as the blind girl had found her friend, I had found mine—writing. I was able to free my thoughts on paper. They had always been there, in my mind, but were bound by my lack of understanding of the mechanics. For the first time, the mechanics were not an obstacle. Now the thoughts were free. I had never before done this. The fact that my journal was full of errors meant nothing. I turned it in just as it was, hoping the teacher would say how good it was. She never did. But it did not matter, because it meant something special to me, and it opened up a new world.

1. Have you tended to view writing as a "form of communication" or as a "form of punishment" (paragraph 1)? Why?

_____

_____

_____

2. Do you, like the author, have a tendency to focus on the mechanics of writing (such as grammar, punctuation, and spelling) rather than on your meaning? Do you think that your writing would improve if you, like the author, could "let go of the mechanics and [begin] to concentrate on what [you are] saying" (paragraph 2)?

_____

_____

_____

3. Describe a time in your life when you, like the author, experienced pleasure in putting your thoughts down on paper. What were you writing about? Why? Who were you writing for or to?

_____

_____

4. The author found pleasure in writing a weekly journal. What have been your experiences with writing a journal or diary? Do you think that you, like the author, might benefit from writing down your thoughts and feelings in a journal?

_____

_____

_____

_____

5. In your opinion, what was the most interesting part of this excerpt? Why was it interesting to you? Try to determine *how* Christopher Lee made that part interesting.

_____

_____

_____

_____

CHAPTER 1 REVIEW

Fill in the blanks in each of the following statements.

1. Writing can be a powerful tool for _____.

2. If you feel as though you have nothing to say about a topic, you can _____ _____ and/or _____ about your subject.

3. If you believe that writing is too hard, you might need to increase your _____ about writing.

4. Another way we learn to be better writers is to learn from the _____ others give us.

5. Not only do we learn to write better by writing, but we also learn to write better by _____ the works of other writers.

6. You can make writing easier and get better results by changing your _____ about it.

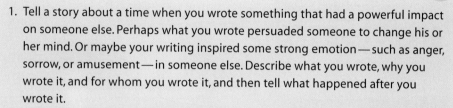

WRITING OPPORTUNITIES

1. Tell a story about a time when you wrote something that had a powerful impact on someone else. Perhaps what you wrote persuaded someone to change his or her mind. Or maybe your writing inspired some strong emotion—such as anger, sorrow, or amusement—in someone else. Describe what you wrote, why you wrote it, and for whom you wrote it, and then tell what happened after you wrote it.

2. Tell about something you have read that had a significant impact on you. Think of a book, article, or piece of writing that changed your behavior, your beliefs, your opinions, or your attitudes. Describe this written work, and explain how it affected you.

3. Christopher Lee tells about a time when he saw two girls walking and wanted to write down his feelings about them. Describe a powerful memory of your own, or tell a story about something meaningful that happened to you in the past.

WebWork

Go to the Nuts and Bolts of College Writing at **http://www.nutsandboltsguide .com/thinking.htm.** Read the information on this Web site, and then answer the following questions.

1. Do you write "because you have to" or "to show what you know"? What are other reasons why you write?

_____

2. What, according to the author of this Web site, is the best reason to write?

_____

3. What, in your opinion, will be some other short-term and long-term benefits of learning to write well?

_____

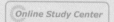 For more about improving writing and thinking, go to the Online Study Center that accompanies this book, at **http://www .college.hmco.com/pic/dolphinwriterone.**

2 Parts of Speech

▶ Define each of the following terms: *noun, pronoun, verb, adjective, adverb, preposition, conjunction,* and *interjection*.

▶ Identify each of the eight parts of speech in sentences.

✷ Test Yourself

Identify the part of speech of the bold word in each of the following sentences. On the blank beside each item, write *noun, pronoun, adjective, verb, adverb, preposition, conjunction,* or *interjection*.

_____ 1. He whistled **cheerfully** as he worked.

_____ 2. We were going to go to see a show **but** decided to stay home.

_____ 3. **You** said that we should see the movie.

_____ 4. Frank took **three** children to see *Stuart Little.*

_____ 5. Carrie does her work **enthusiastically.**

_____ 6. **Hey,** what's going on here?

_____ 7. The **tree** stood tall and straight.

_____ 8. I **enjoy** my dog and our long walks.

_____ 9. The book is **underneath** the sofa.

_____ 10. The hockey player was **stocky.**

As you work on the sentence skills in Part I of this book, you will need to know the eight different parts of speech. This chapter will provide you with a brief review of those parts of speech so that you will understand key terms as you work on improving your sentences in later chapters.

Every word in every sentence you write functions as a particular part of speech. A word can be different parts of speech depending on its *context,* or the other words around it. For example, the word *left* can be a noun, verb, adjective, or adverb:

Turn **left** at the stop sign. (adverb)
She writes with her **left** hand. (adjective)
I **left** her a message. (verb)
I live in the first house on the **left**. (noun)

In each sentence, the context determines the part of speech of this particular word.

Nouns

A **noun** is a word that names a person, place, thing, or idea: *nurse, school, nut, love*. Nouns are either common or proper. *Common nouns* refer to general people, places, or things: *boy, store, art*. *Proper nouns* name one specific person, place, thing, or idea, so they are capitalized:

Abraham Lincoln
Yellowstone National Park
Mercedes Benz

Collective nouns are those that refer to a group of people or things (*team, class, crowd, group, company, audience, family, jury, gang, faculty*).

To identify nouns in a sentence, ask yourself if a word names a person, place, thing, or idea.

common noun   common noun
Oranges are juicy **fruits.**

proper noun   common noun
Thomas Jefferson is my **hero.**

Also, look for the words *a, an,* and *the,* which always precede a noun.

common noun   common noun
The *monkey* ate **a** *banana.*

proper noun   common noun
A *Porsche* is **a** fast *car*.

NOTE: Adjectives, like the word *fast* in the second sentence, will often separate *a, an,* or *the* from the noun.

Nouns can be individual words, or they can be phrases. For example, read the following sentences:

Cleaning the bathroom is the chore I hate most.
She wants **to go to Mexico**.

These phrases function as nouns. In the first sentence, the phrase *Cleaning the bathroom* is a noun phrase that functions as the subject of the sentence. In the second example, *to go to Mexico* is a noun phrase that functions as the direct object.

 **EXERCISE 2.1**   **Identifying Nouns in Sentences**

Circle all of the nouns in each of the following sentences.

1. Rita swallowed a spoonful of the medicine.
2. Going to the mall is one of my favorite activities.
3. New York City is the greatest city on earth.
4. My daughter has long, beautiful hair.
5. Flying on airplanes makes some people very nervous.
6. The thing that makes Francine mad is lack of respect.
7. The zoo is Mark's favorite place.
8. *Catcher in the Rye* is a famous novel.
9. Using a handbook can help with writing.
10. The airport was crowded.

Writing REVIEW   **Using Nouns in Sentences**

Write ten sentences using a variety of nouns.

Pronouns

A **pronoun** is a word that is used in the place of a noun. For example, if you write one sentence that says, "Sally left the theater," the next sentence you write could substitute a pronoun instead of repeating the name *Sally*: "*She* did not like the movie." *She* is the pronoun used in place of the name *Sally*.

There are different kinds of pronouns. One kind refers to one or more specific persons or things.

I	you	she	they
me	yourself	her	them
myself	yourselves	herself	themselves
it	we	he	
itself	us	him	
	ourselves	himself	

We took **them** to see **him.**
She did **it herself.**

I, he, she, it, we, you, and *they* are the **personal pronouns.**

Other pronouns are called *indefinite* because they do not refer to any particular person, place, or thing:

all	both	many	someone
any	everybody	one	something
anybody	everyone	no one	several
anyone	everything	nothing	some
anything	few	somebody	

No one is sure what will happen.
She longs to tell **someone** her secret.

Another kind of pronoun points out specific things by referring to a certain noun; these are called **demonstrative pronouns.**

this
that
these
those

That is the best meal I have ever eaten.
This is my phone number.

NOTE: The pronouns *this, that, these,* and *those* also function as adjectives when they precede and point out a particular noun. For example, in the sentence

"These boots belong to Susan," the word *these* is an adjective that answers the question *Which boots?* For more on adjectives, see Chapter 5, page 73.

Some pronouns introduce questions:

who   what
whom   whose
which

What is the right answer?
Who is coming to dinner?

And finally, still other pronouns introduce dependent clauses, which you will learn more about in Chapters 11 and 12. These are the **relative pronouns.**

that   whose
what   whoever
which   whichever
who   whatever
whom

She is the one **who** loves to dance.
You know **that** I will be there.

For more about pronouns, see Chapter 7.

EXERCISE 2.2   **Identifying Pronouns in Sentences**

Circle all of the pronouns in the following sentences.

1. She told us the news.

2. Take care of her.

3. Did you go to the ballet with Marco or by yourself?

4. Nobody likes to be alone during the holidays.

5. This looks delicious, and we are ready to eat it.

6. To whom should I address the question?

7. He searched but could not find anything.

8. This is the reality show I told you about!

9. Make sure somebody takes care of the problem.

10. Does anyone know what time it is?

> *Writing* REVIEW   **Using Pronouns in Sentences**
>
> Write ten sentences using a variety of pronouns.

Adjectives

Adjectives modify (describe or limit) either nouns or pronouns. They tell *how many, what kind,* or *which one.*

> **four** friends
> **blue** ribbon
> **those** balloons
> a **snowy** day
> **few** people

Some adjectives introduce questions:

> **Which** one do you want?
> **Whose** ring is this?

An adjective can appear before or after the noun or pronoun it modifies:

> I will have **another** cup of **hot** tea.
> He is a man **possessed.**
> She is **tall** and **thin.**

One special class of adjectives includes the words *a, an,* and *the,* which are called *articles.* These words precede and point out specific people, places, or things.

> She ate **a** piece of cake.
> Tell me **the** truth.
> She took **an** aspirin to reduce **the** pain.

Like nouns, adjectives can be individual words, or they can be phrases:

> He made the decision **to go to Mexico.** (The phrase *to go to Mexico* modifies the word *decision* by answering the question *Which decision?*)
>
> **Trying to run,** she tripped and fell. (The phrase *trying to run* describes *she.*)

For more about adjectives, see Chapter 5.

EXERCISE 2.3   **Identifying Adjectives in Sentences**

Circle all of the adjectives in each of the following sentences.

1. She loves warm, tropical places.

2. Driving can be a challenge.

3. We decided to stay home and have a nice, long chat.

4. Hoping it would not rain, she planned an outdoor wedding.

5. Please pass me another piece of that delicious bread.

6. You should think happy thoughts!

7. They invited some friends over.

8. Red wine has been found to have health benefits.

9. You sound depressed.

10. Abraham Lincoln governed a nation divided.

Writing REVIEW   **Using Adjectives in Sentences**

Write ten sentences using a variety of adjectives.

Verbs

Verbs express either the action or state of being of the sentence's subject.

> The girl **jumped** into the pool. (action verb)
> They **understood** the directions. (action verb)
> I **am** a cheerleader. (being verb)
> He **was** twenty years old. (being verb)

Verbs can be in the *present tense,* expressing that the time of the action or state of being is occurring now:

> He **loves** to eat hotdogs.
> They **are** excited about the trip.
> She **teaches** third grade.

Verbs can also be in the *past tense,* expressing that the action or state of being occurred in the past:

> He **loved** to eat hot dogs.
> They **were** excited about the trip.
> She **taught** third grade.

Sometimes we indicate the past tense by adding *–d* or *–ed* to the end of the verb. For other verbs (like *break/broke* and *fly/flew*), the form of the word changes.

To express a verb's tense, one or more helping verbs are added to create verb phrases:

is	were	will
are	has	shall
am	had	could
be	have	would
was	might	may

> She **has written** to him three times.
> We **might be going** to France.
> They **will have been** in college for one year this August.

For more about verbs, see Chapter 4.

 **EXERCISE 2.4**   **Identifying Verbs in Sentences**

Circle the verb or verb phrase in each of the following sentences.

1. I am coming home tomorrow.

2. We are thrilled about the news.

3. Mary Anne enjoys her French class.

4. I am excited about going to the show this evening.

5. Jim might be joining us for dinner.

6. Kellie has decided on a career change.

7. She has been in her current job for three years.

8. I drove for three hours.

9. Carmen will be calling Juanita from the airport.

10. We dove off the side of the boat.

Writing REVIEW   **Using Verbs in Sentences**

Write ten sentences using a variety of verbs.

Adverbs

Adverbs modify verbs, adjectives, and other adverbs by telling *when, where, how,* or *to what degree* an action occurred. Many adverbs end in –*ly* (*certainly, hungrily, really*), but not all of them do. Adverbs can appear anywhere in a sentence.

> She **cheerfully** does her chores. (does *how?*)
> He is **very** sick today. (*how* sick?)
> We are going **tomorrow.** (are going *when?*)
> You should go **home.** (go *where?*)
> They were **completely** surprised. (surprised *to what degree?*)

Adverbs can be phrases as well as individual words:

> We threw her **into the pond.** (threw *where?*)
> I want an answer **by Monday.** (want *when?*)

NOTE: Answers to the question *What?* are direct objects, not adverbs.

>   *direct object*   *adverb*
> She stubbed her *toe*   **on the sidewalk.**

The question stubbed *what?* is answered by *toe,* which is the direct object. The question stubbed *where?* is answered by *on the sidewalk,* which is the adverb. For more on direct objects, see pages 40–41 in Chapter 3. For more about adverbs, see Chapter 5.

EXERCISE 2.5   **Identifying Adverbs in Sentences**

Circle all of the adverbs in each of the following sentences.

1. She pinched his face hard.

2. Jim will be leaving on Sunday.

3. The dog ran through the park quickly.

4. I dropped the ball in the street.

5. The baby cried loudly.

6. You clearly do not know the answer.

7. François will join you in a moment.

8. Unfortunately, I crashed the car into the building.

9. Merrily we roll along.

10. Peter sent the book to me.

Prepositions

Prepositions are words or groups of words that show how a noun or pronoun, called an *object,* is related to the rest of the sentence. Many prepositions show position or time orientation:

about	before	but	into	over
above	behind	by	like	past
across	below	despite	near	through
after	beneath	down	of	to
against	beside	during	off	toward
along	between	except	on	under
among	beyond	for	onto	underneath
around	in	unlike	until	up
from	on	upon	at	with
without	out	outside		

Others are phrases:

according to	ahead of	along with
as far as	as well as	aside from
because of	in back of	in case of
in front of	in spite of	instead of
on account of	together with	with respect to

A **prepositional phrase** consists of a preposition, its object (which is always a noun or a pronoun), and the object's modifiers. For example, look at this prepositional phrase:

preposition   *object*

behind the tall *tree*

modifiers

In sentences, prepositional phrases can function as either adjectives or adverbs.

Adverb: It broke **into two pieces.** (broke *how?*)
Adjective: The woman **with the flowers** is my mother. (*which* woman?)

EXERCISE 2.6   **Identifying Prepositions in Sentences**

In the following sentences, circle the prepositions and underline the objects of prepositions.

1. He went to the beach last week.
2. Ben is not from New Jersey.
3. According to Anya, daylight-saving time was started in 1918.
4. Until now, there has been no snow.
5. Despite my best efforts, the cake burned in the oven.
6. That goal is beyond my reach.
7. Between the two of you, you will discover a solution.
8. Look for the dog books in the front of the library.
9. What is a little joking among friends?
10. The restroom is the first door on your left.

Writing REVIEW   **Using Prepositions in Sentences**

Write ten sentences using a variety of prepositions.

Conjunctions

Conjunctions connect and show relationships between words, phrases, or clauses. The seven conjunctions that can link any type of elements together are

and	yet
but	so
or	for
nor	

this **and** that (words)
by land **or** by sea (phrases)
We are out of money, **so** we cannot go to the movies. (clauses)

Some conjunctions come in pairs. They are called the **correlative conjunctions.**

both/and	just as/so
neither/nor	whether/or
either/or	not only/but also

Both the teacher **and** the students look forward to summer break.
Either you go with us, **or** you ride with them.

Other conjunctions link dependent clauses to independent clauses. A *clause* is a group of words with a subject and a verb. An *independent clause* can stand alone as a complete sentence, but a *dependent clause* cannot. The following list contains conjunctions that link dependent and independent clauses and show their relationship to one another. They are called **subordinating conjunctions.**

after	because	provided	where
although	before	since	whereas
as	but that	so that	wherever
as if	if	until	while
as long as	in order that	when	notwithstanding
as soon as	whenever		

conjunction
While I waited, she ran into the store.

dependent clause   *independent clause*

conjunction

We canceled the picnic **because** it was raining.

*independent
clause*

*dependent
clause*

NOTE: You probably noticed that some of the words in the list of conjunctions can also be prepositions. To tell them apart, determine whether the word is part of a phrase or a clause.

She finished **before** lunch. (preposition)
She had finished **before** we ate lunch. (conjunction)

 **EXERCISE 2.7**   **Identifying Conjunctions in Sentences**

Circle all of the conjunctions in each of the following sentences.

1. She considered marrying him but decided against it.

2. Before you do that, consider the consequences.

3. We waited until eight o'clock so that Janice could join us.

4. Whenever you go to that store, pick me up some bagels.

5. I will support you as long as you agree with all of my advice.

6. Pat will go to Greece, and you will go to Ireland.

7. Neither Chris nor Frank will enjoy his vacation.

8. We do not have a lot of cash, yet we still go out to dinner often.

9. Not only does Juanita make straight A's, but she also wins chess tournaments.

10. We will get to your house by train or by bus.

Writing REVIEW   **Using Conjunctions in Sentences**

Write ten sentences using a variety of conjunctions.

Interjections

Interjections are words or phrases that express emotion or surprise.

> **Oh,** you scared me.
> **Drat!** We lost again.
> **Wow!** He looks great.

Because of their informality, interjections are rarely appropriate in academic and professional writing.

CHAPTER 2 REVIEW

Fill in the blanks in each of the following statements.

1. _____ determines a word's part of speech.

2. A _____ is a word that names a person, place, thing, or idea.

3. _____ nouns name general people, places, or things; _____ nouns name one specific person, place, or thing.

4. Nouns can be individual words, or they can be _____.

5. A _____ is a word that is used in the place of a noun.

6. _____ pronouns do not refer to any particular person, place, or thing.

7. _____ modify (describe or limit) either nouns or pronouns.

8. Like nouns, adjectives can be individual words, or they can be _____.

9. _____ express either the action or the state of being of the sentence's subject.

10. Verbs can be in either the _____ tense or the _____ tense.

11. _____ modify verbs by telling when, where, how, or to what degree.

12. _____ are words or groups of words that show how a noun or pronoun called an *object* is related to the rest of the sentence.

13. A _____ consists of a preposition, an object, and the object's modifiers.

14. Prepositional phrases can function as either _____ or _____.

15. _____ show relationships between words, phrases, or clauses.

16. A _____ is a group of words with a subject and a verb.

17. An _____ clause can stand alone as a complete sentence.

18. A _____ clause cannot stand alone; it must be linked to an independent clause.

19. _____ are words or phrases that express emotion or surprise.

CHAPTER 2: TEST 1

On the blank provided, write the part of speech of the bold word or words.

_____ 1. He misses her **terribly**.

_____ 2. **Either** you are crazy, **or** I do not understand what you are doing.

_____ 3. **Driving my sports car** is a relaxing activity.

_____ 4. **They** seem very happy to see him.

_____ 5. The school is located at the **end** of Gerston Drive.

_____ 6. Put that hammer **on** the table.

_____ 7. **This** television show is Jane's favorite.

_____ 8. He **was changing** his tire in the driveway.

_____ 9. **Together with** Jack, we tackled the homework.

_____ 10. **Whether** we go **or** not should be of no concern to you.

_____ 11. Max arrived **after** dinner.

_____ 12. Max arrived **after** we had eaten dinner.

_____ 13. Michael wants **to leave town**.

_____ 14. He was changing his tire **in the driveway**.

_____ 15. **Look** for the tulips behind the roses on the second shelf.

A. In the following sentences, circle all of the nouns and underline all of the adjectives.

 1. A rich aunt sends me fifty dollars every Christmas.

 2. I have five friends but just one best buddy.

 3. Where on earth did you get this wonderful cheese?

 4. Abbie was lucky to get a fabulous balloon kit from friends in California.

 5. The lot adjacent to that house is vacant.

B. In the following sentences, circle all of the verbs and underline all of the adverbs.

 1. I will e-mail you soon.

 2. Jean made these Valentine's tarts happily.

 3. The cat jumped into the birdbath.

 4. She accepted the job on Monday.

 5. Carlos always sings with passion.

C. In the following sentences, circle all of the pronouns and underline all of the prepositions.

 1. You must not leave the keys in the door.

 2. Above all, I must remember the lock's combination.

 3. In spite of Jason's warnings, she went to the club.

 4. If you are looking for him, he is under the bed.

 5. Until today, she had always ignored them.

D. In the following sentences, circle all of the conjunctions and underline all of the interjections.

 1. Oh! It's a phone and a camera.

 2. I love him, and darn it, I miss him.

 3. When it rains, I feel sad.

 4. We want to go to Dallas, but we cannot afford the trip.

 5. Hey, you look great in either blue or green.

WRITING ASSIGNMENT

What advice would you give someone just starting college? What have your experiences been? Write a paragraph that includes all of the parts of speech covered in this chapter.

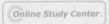

WebWork

For more practice identifying parts of speech, go to the Guide to Grammar and Writing Web site at **http://grammar.ccc.commnet.edu/grammar/index.htm.** Find the section of the Web site that defines and illustrates the parts of speech. Then review the eight parts of speech and complete a quiz for each one.

Online Study Center. For additional information and practice with parts of speech, go to the Online Study Center that accompanies this book, at **http://www.college.hmco.com/pic/dolphinwriterone.**

The Basic Sentence

GOALS FOR CHAPTER 3

▶ Define the term *simple sentence*.

▶ Define the term *independent clause*.

▶ Define the terms *subject* and *verb*.

▶ Identify the subjects of sentences.

▶ Define the terms *simple subject* and *complete subject*.

▶ Identify complete subjects of sentences.

▶ Define the term *compound subject*.

▶ Identify compound subjects in sentences.

▶ Distinguish subjects from objects of prepositions.

▶ Define the term *compound verb*.

▶ Identify verbs in sentences.

▶ Define the terms *direct object, indirect object, modifiers,* and *appositives*.

▶ Identify direct objects, indirect objects, modifiers, and appositives in simple sentences.

Test Yourself

A. Circle the simple subject and underline the verb in each of the following sentences.

1. The cowgirl with the red hair has performed that trick before.

2. *Monsters, Inc.,* is a great movie for kids.

3. Are you at home today?

4. I am going to France in the spring.

5. There are two good reasons for my choice.

B. Identify the function of the bold word in each of the following sentences. On the blank beside each sentence, write *direct object, indirect object, adjective, adverb,* or *appositive.*

_____ 1. The car, a silver **Mercedes,** was a gift from her father.

_____ 2. He gave **her** the car for her birthday.

_____ 3. The chef made us a **delicious** dinner.

_____ 4. The chef **cheerfully** made us a delicious dinner.

_____ 5. The chef made **dinner.**

Now that you have reviewed the eight parts of speech, you can begin to see how words are put together to form sentences. Once you learn about basic sentences in Chapters 3–7, you can begin to understand how to make your own sentences interesting, sophisticated, and grammatically correct.

A **simple sentence**[1] is defined as one independent clause only. An *independent clause*[2] is a group of words that can stand alone as a separate sentence because it contains both a *subject*[3] (a noun or pronoun that causes the action or is in some state of being) and a *verb.*[4] A simple sentence can also contain other parts of speech, such as adverbs or prepositions, but it includes just one subject-verb relationship.

subject verb

We   ate   beans.

subject   verb

The **actor**   **walked**   across the stage.

1. **simple sentence:** one independent clause
2. **independent clause:** a group of words that can stand alone as a separate sentence; contains a subject and a verb
3. **subject:** a noun or pronoun that causes the action or is in some state of being
4. **verb:*** a word that shows action or expresses a state of being

*Chapter 4 will cover verbs in more detail.

Subjects

The **subject** of a sentence is always a noun or pronoun, so when you are trying to identify the subject, find all of the nouns and pronouns first. Next, find the verb, the word or words that express action or state of being. (Verbs are discussed in detail in Chapter 4.) Then, ask yourself, *Who or what is performing the action or expressing some state of being?* For example, look at the following sentence:

She called her father on his cell phone.

There are two nouns and one pronoun in this sentence.

pronoun   *noun*   *noun*
She called her **father** on his cell **phone.**

Therefore, the subject of the sentence is either *she, father,* or *phone.* Now, what is the action being performed? The past tense verb in this sentence is *called.* Who is doing this calling? It is *she,* so *she* is the subject of the sentence.

Can you identify the subjects in the following sentences?

The lawnmower broke yesterday.
History is my favorite subject.
I cannot find my sock.

In the previous sentences, the subjects are *lawnmower, history,* and *I.*

Locations of Subjects

You have probably noticed that subjects often appear at or near the beginning of sentences. However, they can also follow the verb:

verb   *subject*
Here is an example. (In this sentence, *here* is an adverb, not the subject.)

verb   *subject*
In the car sat the suspect.

In questions, too, the subject may follow the verb or part of the verb.

verb   *subject*   *verb*
Can   you   go with us tomorrow?

To determine the subject in questions, you can mentally rearrange the sentence so that it is a statement:

subject   verb

You   can go   with us tomorrow.

Now it is easier to see that the subject is *you*.

In sentences that make commands or requests, the subject may not be stated. Instead, it is implied:

Go get my shoes.
Please come home.

The subject of both these sentences is *you*. Although the word does not appear in either sentence, it is understood that the person to whom the sentence is directed is to perform the action.

EXERCISE 3.1   **Identifying the Subjects of Sentences**

Circle the subject in each of the following sentences. If the subject is implied, write the implied subject beside the sentence.

1. Coffee is my favorite drink.

2. Frank seems angry.

3. Do you see him?

4. Does Pottery Barn sell candles, too?

5. Please do not say that!

6. Jaime has many children.

7. What did he think of my research paper?

8. My car was rear-ended on the Whitestone Bridge.

9. Here is my monkey.

10. Mind your own business.

Simple and Complete Subjects

So far, you have been identifying just the simple subject of a sentence. The **simple subject** is a single noun or pronoun. A **complete subject,** on the other hand, is the subject along with all of its modifiers (the articles and adjectives that limit or describe).

Our wonderful vacation included a trip to Sea World.

In this sentence, *vacation* is the simple subject, and *our wonderful vacation* is the complete subject.

A desire to help people led him to become a firefighter.

In the previous sentence, *desire* is the simple subject, and *a desire to help people* is the complete subject.

Do not forget that a noun phrase can be the subject of a sentence:

Going to the moon was an incredible achievement.

To review noun phrases, see Chapter 2.

EXERCISE 3.2   **Identifying Complete Subjects in Sentences**

Circle the complete subject in each of the following sentences.

1. The two playful puppies licked his face.
2. My phone has an annoying ring.
3. Learning to drive was one of her major goals.
4. Do you enjoy the movies?
5. Swimming with dolphins must be fun.
6. This fabulous meal would not have been possible without Chef Mario.
7. Legos are my son's favorite toys.
8. Cooking dinner is Fran's least favorite activity.
9. A miniature schnauzer makes a great pet.
10. Owning a dog requires a lot of patience.

Compound Subjects

A **compound subject** is defined as two or more subjects joined by the words *and,* *or,* or *nor.*

subject   *subject*

The **doctor** and her **husband** are going to Spain.

subject   *subject*

Jack   or   **I** will pick you up.

subject   *subject*

Neither the **ostrich** nor the **penguin** can fly.

 **EXERCISE 3.3**   **Identifying Compound Subjects in Sentences**

Circle all of the compound subjects in the following sentences.

1. At the top of the page are the title and the author's name.
2. Neither the phone nor the beeper was working properly.
3. Do you or Luiz ski?
4. At the side of my house are a garden and a driveway.
5. Seeing the Eiffel Tower and visiting the Leaning Tower of Pisa are two goals of my vacation.
6. Where are Rose and Rich going for dinner?
7. Baiting the hook and unhooking the fish are my least favorite parts of fishing.
8. Patricia or Charles picked up the mail.
9. Ice, hail, and snow are to be blamed for many accidents.
10. Sunbathing and swimming are enjoyable summer activities.

Writing REVIEW   **Using Subjects in Sentences**

Write ten sentences of your own that include simple subjects and compound subjects. When you are finished, go back and circle all of the complete subjects in each of your sentences.

Subjects Versus Objects of Prepositions

Often, it can be easy to confuse a subject with the object of a preposition. The object of a preposition cannot be the subject of a sentence, so you might want to identify all prepositional phrases before you decide what the subject is.

One of the students in the class is on the football team.

The nouns in this sentence are *one, students, class,* and *team.* To identify the ones that are objects of prepositions, draw parentheses around all of the prepositional phrases.

One of the students in the class is on the football team.

Now it is much easier to see that *One* is the simple subject of the sentence. Refer back to Chapter 2 for a list of the prepositions.

 **EXERCISE 3.4**   **Identifying Subjects Among Prepositional Phrases**

In each of the following sentences, put parentheses around all of the prepositional phrases and then circle the simple subject.

1. The ride to the cabin was very bumpy.
2. Flying in a snowstorm is dangerous.
3. Two of my friends go to this school.
4. Several of you can ride with us.
5. The girl with the dogs walks in the park on Wednesdays.
6. Driving to school in the downpour was treacherous.
7. On the cover of the book is a photo of a motorcycle.
8. In the grass lay a blue Easter egg with yellow stripes.
9. I danced with joy in the rain.
10. In a moment, the woman in the box will disappear.

Other Elements of Simple Sentences

As mentioned earlier, a simple sentence must contain both a subject and a verb. It can also include a direct object, an indirect object, modifiers, and an appositive.

Verbs

In Chapter 2, a **verb** was defined as a word or phrase that expresses action or a state of being. Verbs will be discussed in detail in Chapter 4. Note, however, that verbs—like subjects—can be **compound.**

They **ate** a picnic lunch and **played** Frisbee.

In this sentence, the subject, *They,* is performing two actions, so there are two verbs.

EXERCISE 3.5   **Identifying Verbs in Sentences**

Circle all of the verbs and verb phrases in the following sentences. Watch for compound verbs, and make sure that you circle both.

1. New York is a very crowded city.
2. They walked through the snow and skated across a pond to get here.
3. Ann lives next to a golf course.
4. We ate and talked throughout the dinner.
5. What is the answer to this question?
6. I drove very carefully in the hailstorm.
7. This is a boring town.
8. Her children fight and argue much of the time.
9. We jumped and swam through the waves to get ashore.
10. Think about going to the concert.

Direct Objects

A simple sentence may or may not include a direct object. A **direct object** is a noun or pronoun that answers the question *whom?* or *what?* for an action verb.

verb   direct object

He **lost** his   **keys.**   (Lost *what?*)

To find the direct object in a sentence, you will need to locate the verb first.

She typed the message with tears in her eyes.

In this sentence, the verb is *typed*. Now, ask the question typed *what?* The answer is *message,* which is the direct object.

> We thanked her for the gift.

In this sentence, the verb is *thanked.* Ask the question thanked *whom?* The answer is *her,* which is the direct object.

Direct objects can be compound, just as subjects and verbs can.

> *direct object*   *direct object*
> He wrote **poems** and **plays.**

> *direct object*   *direct object*
> She set the **groceries** and the **mail** on the table.

EXERCISE 3.6   **Identifying Direct Objects in Sentences**

Circle the direct object(s) in each of the following sentences.

1. You sang that song beautifully.
2. She sings opera and jazz.
3. Carrie loves movies.
4. The lawyer settled the case.
5. I studied English in college.
6. Esteban enjoys cooking and wrestling.
7. The church collected money for the new air conditioner.
8. Please mail this letter.
9. Lee sent an e-mail message to me.
10. Check your voice mail for messages.

Indirect Objects

A simple sentence may or may not include an indirect object. An **indirect object** answers the question *to whom, for whom, to what,* or *for what?* for an action verb.

> *indirect object*
> He sent his **friend** an e-mail.   (Sent *to whom?*)

To find the indirect object, locate the verb first.

My sister gave me her truck.

In this sentence, the verb is *gave*. To find the direct object, you ask, *gave what?* The answer is *truck*. To find the indirect object, ask, *gave to whom?* The answer is *me*, which is the indirect object.

Like direct objects, indirect objects can be compound:

indirect object   indirect object

My grandfather left his **grandchildren** and his **nephew** all of his money.

 **EXERCISE 3.7**   **Identifying Indirect Objects in Sentences**

Circle the indirect object(s) in each of the following sentences.

1. I brought my aunt an orchid.

2. Marie wrote Frank a letter.

3. Dede told me her secret.

4. Ann prepared Abbie and Ben lunch and dinner.

5. I paid her fifty dollars.

6. The nurse handed the doctor a sponge.

7. Please give Mary Jo and Pat your answer before Friday.

8. They sent the teacher a get-well card.

9. We found the dog a home.

10. The customer left the waitress a big tip.

Writing REVIEW   **Using Verbs, Direct Objects, and Indirect Objects in Sentences**

Write ten sentences of your own that include verbs, direct objects, and indirect objects. When you are finished, go back and circle all of the complete verbs, direct objects, and indirect objects in each of your sentences.

Modifiers

A simple sentence may include modifiers, which are adjectives or adverbs. You learned in Chapter 2 that adjectives, which modify nouns or pronouns, can be single words or phrases:

adjective

She broke up with her **unfaithful** boyfriend. (*Unfaithful* describes the noun *boyfriend*.)

adjective

The cast **of the show** took a bow. (The prepositional phrase *of the show* answers the question *which cast?*)

Adverbs, which modify verbs, adjectives, or other adverbs, can also be single words or phrases:

adverb

He can run **fast**. (The adverb *fast* answers the question *can run how?*)

adverb

She studied **until dawn**. (The prepositional phrase *until dawn* answers the question *studied when?*)

adverb

He was **very** sick. (*Very* is an adverb that modifies the adjective *sick*.)

For more about modifiers, see Chapter 5.

 **EXERCISE 3.8**   **Identifying Adjectives and Adverbs in Sentences**

Circle the adjectives and underline the adverbs in the following sentences.

1. A cold rain fell this morning.
2. The old secretary types slowly.
3. The overworked waitress limped into the kitchen.
4. Quickly I ran past the abandoned bus depot.
5. This diet works well.
6. Unfortunately, the festive holiday party was canceled.
7. A wise student studies every day.

8. Twelve unhappy people attended the town board meeting and angrily voiced dissenting opinions.

9. Do you have a carefully thought-out plan?

10. The weekly newsletter includes very important articles on health.

Appositives

Simple sentences might include appositives. An *appositive* is a noun or noun phrase that follows a noun or pronoun and renames it.

> *appositive*
>
> Our neighbor, **Mrs. Jones,** rides a motorcycle. (*Mrs. Jones* renames *neighbor.*)

An appositive phrase includes the appositive and all of its modifiers:

> *appositive*
>
> John, **the best player on our team,** just broke his leg.

In this sentence, *player* is the appositive that renames *John,* and the other words in the phrase modify the word *player.*

EXERCISE 3.9   **Identifying Appositives in Sentences**

Circle the appositive or appositive phrase in each of the following sentences.

1. Richard Gere, my favorite actor, was in that movie.

2. Wayne Gretzky, the greatest hockey player of all time, scored the most goals of anyone on the ice.

3. My friend, Mary Alice, attends weekly meetings at the church.

4. *Chicago,* a musical, is up for many awards.

5. September 11, the day of the terrorist attacks, is a sad anniversary.

6. Pinot noir, an Oregon wine, is very popular in the East.

7. My favorite restaurant, La Fortuna, serves veal scaloppini.

8. Sunday, the Christian Sabbath, is a day for churchgoing.

9. *Survivor,* one of the first reality TV shows, is still the most popular.

10. Do you, a marathon winner, recommend running daily?

> *Writing* REVIEW **Using Modifiers in Sentences**
>
> Write ten sentences of your own that include modifiers and appositives. When you are finished, go back and circle all of the complete modifiers and appositives in each of your sentences.

Avoiding Sentence Fragments

To be complete, a sentence must contain a subject and a verb. When either is lacking, a sentence fragment results. Notice how both of the following examples lack subjects:

> Made her sad.
> Found my keys in the car.

Adding subjects, though, will make them complete:

> *subject*
> The romantic **movie** made her sad.

subject
> I **found** my keys in the car.

The following examples lack verbs:

> Only one of the dishes.
> Mr. Kaplan, my favorite neighbor.

Adding verbs will make them complete.

> *verb*
> Only one of the dishes **broke.**

> *verb*
> Mr. Kaplan, my favorite neighbor, **is moving.**

For information about avoiding other types of sentence fragments, see pages 75, and 141.

CHAPTER 3 REVIEW

Fill in the blanks in each of the following statements.

1. A simple sentence is defined as one _____ only.

2. An independent clause contains both a _____ and a ____ and can stand alone as a complete sentence.

3. A _____ is a noun or pronoun that causes the action or is in some state of being.

4. A ____ is a word that shows action or expresses a state of being.

5. The subject of a sentence can appear near the beginning of the sentence, or it can follow the ____.

6. The _____ subject is a single noun or pronoun, and the _____ subject is the subject along with all of its modifiers.

7. A ____ phrase can be the subject of a sentence.

8. A _____ is defined as two or more subjects joined by the words *and*, *or*, or *nor*.

9. The subject of a sentence cannot be the _____ of a preposition.

10. A _____ verb is defined as two or more verbs joined by *and*, *or*, or *nor*.

11. A _____ is a noun or pronoun that answers the question *Whom?* or *What?* for an action verb.

12. An _____ answers the question *To whom?* for an action verb.

13. Modifiers are _____ and _____.

14. _____ are words or phrases that modify nouns or pronouns.

15. _____ are words or phrases that modify verbs.

16. An _____ is a noun that follows a noun or pronoun and renames it.

Circle the complete subject of each of the following sentences.

1. Going to sleep was difficult last night.

2. Skating and biking are good forms of exercise.

3. On top of my dresser is *are* some cash and the tickets.

4. My friends like to go shopping every weekend.

5. Does the restaurant serve vegetarian dishes?

6. There is no way out.

7. Can your son read yet?

8. My brother and I are identical twins.

9. Winning the lottery is everyone's hope.

10. Is the weekend here yet?

A. In the following sentences, circle the complete subject(s) and underline the verb(s). If the subject is implied, write the implied subject beside the sentence.

1. My dog ate my homework.

2. Her cat tracked mud through the house.

3. Does Crate and Barrel sell furniture?

4. Patrick ran home.

5. Hand me that hammer.

B. In the following sentences, circle the direct object(s) and underline the indirect object(s).

1. I send him my love.

2. She loaned us the car.

3. They sent their grandparents and their uncle a cheeseball.

4. The trainer threw the seal a fish.

5. I gave Sammy money for gas.

C. In the following sentences, circle the adjective(s), underline the adverb(s), and put parentheses around the appositive phrases.

1. Lisa, the new employee, is very smart.

2. The last boss, a bad-tempered man, yelled at me daily.

3. Dessert, a chocolate pie with whipped cream, was simply delicious.

4. The plane, a large and expensive aircraft, belonged to an unbelievably rich businessman.

5. Unfortunately, the local supermarket is being replaced by a dry-cleaning business.

WRITING ASSIGNMENT

Write about a favorite childhood memory. What you write about can include a favorite trip or vacation, a memory that includes a relative or friend, or a holiday that was special. When writing, use complete subjects and verbs that convey the feeling that you had. When you are done, go back and review all of the subjects, verbs, direct and indirect objects, modifiers, and appositives that you used.

WebWork

For more practice in identifying the elements of simple sentences, go to the Guide to Grammar and Writing Web site at **http://grammar.ccc.commnet.edu/grammar/index.htm.** Find the section called "Sentence Parts/Functions" and complete one of the Sentence Parts quizzes for practice.

Online Study Center   For additional information and practice with the basic sentence, go to the Online Study Center that accompanies this book, at **http://www.college.hmco.com/pic/dolphinwriterone.**

Verbs

GOALS FOR CHAPTER 4

▶ Define the terms *action verb* and *linking verb*.

▶ Identify action verbs and linking verbs in sentences.

▶ Define the terms *tense, present tense,* and *past tense*.

▶ Use the correct forms of past and present verbs in sentences.

▶ Define the term *future tense*.

▶ Define the term *helping verbs*.

▶ Identify verb phrases in sentences.

▶ Explain the difference between *regular* and *irregular verbs*.

▶ Use the correct forms of irregular verbs in sentences.

▶ Define the terms *verbal, infinitive, gerund,* and *participle*.

▶ Identify verbals in sentences.

▶ Rewrite passive voice sentences using active voice.

▶ Rewrite sentences to substitute strong verbs for weaker ones.

▶ Revise sentences for consistency in verb tense.

Test Yourself

A. In each of the following sentences, circle the verb and write on the blank whether it is an *action verb* or a *linking verb*.

_____ 1. They are businessmen from China.

_____ 2. We discussed the topic.

_____ 3. I ran to the store.

———————— 4. We were happy about the change.

———————— 5. We went to Janis's house.

B. In each of the following sentences, write the form of the verb contained in parentheses that expresses the correct tense.

1. Next year, they ———————— on an African safari. (*go*)

2. Mary ———————— this with her husband now. (*discuss*)

3. Michael ———— all night to get here in time. (*drive*)

4. When the phone rang, I ————. (*awake*)

5. She ———— three bunches of flowers last week. (*buy*)

C. Circle the verbals in each of the following sentences.

1. He hoped to get a raise soon.

2. To leave now would be a disaster.

3. Drafting a new amendment will take time.

4. Arising at seven is a hardship for me.

5. I want to make the right decision.

In Chapters 2 and 3, you learned that a verb is the word (or words) in a sentence that expresses the subject's action or state of being. In this chapter, you will examine in more detail the various features of verbs. Knowing how to use verbs correctly will strengthen your writing significantly.

Action Verbs and Linking Verbs

There are two kinds of verbs, action verbs and linking verbs. **Action verbs** express action of some kind:

She **read** the magazine.
He **thought** about her night and day.
They **surfed** in Hawaii.

Linking verbs express some state of being:

am	appear
is	seem
are	become
was	grow
were	remain

I **am** lucky. (*lucky* describes *I*)
That man **is** a vacuum cleaner salesman. (*salesman* renames *man*)
They **appear** exhausted after the long trip. (*exhausted* describes *they*)

NOTE: The verbs *am, is, are, was,* and *were* can also be helping verbs that accompany action verbs. Helping verbs are discussed later in this chapter.
　　Linking verbs can also relate to the senses:

look	sound
smell	feel
taste	

Her perfume **smells** terrible.
I **feel** lonesome tonight.
The chocolate cake **tastes** good.

 **EXERCISE 4.1**　　**Identifying Action Verbs and Linking Verbs in Sentences**

In each of the following sentences, circle the verb and write on the blank whether it is an *action verb* or a *linking verb*.

_____ **1.** She bowls every Friday night.

_____ **2.** Ed is sad about his team's loss.

_____ **3.** That radio sounds terrible.

_____ **4.** I feel happy.

_____ **5.** Donald jogs all the way to school.

_____ **6.** Dee cleans my kitchen.

_____ **7.** I am dismayed by your actions.

_____ **8.** She dances in a chorus line.

_____ **9.** Marie grows weary of his antics.

_____ **10.** He speaks at church every Sunday.

Verb Tense

Verbs always express time, which is called **tense.** Two of the basic tenses, or simple tenses, are present tense and past tense. (The other is future tense, which will be discussed later in this chapter.) **Present tense verbs** indicate that the action or state of being is occurring now or is ongoing:

I **am** hungry.
They **adore** green beans.
He **wants** to marry her.
She **cooks** dinner every night.

The form of a present tense verb often changes based on whether the subject is *singular* (meaning that it refers to just one person or thing) or *plural* (referring to more than one thing):*

Singular	*Plural*
I stop	we stop
you stop	you stop
he, she, it stops	they stop

Notice that the singular form that goes with *he, she,* and *it* has an –*s* on the end. The other forms do not. This is the case with many verbs that are *regular,* or conform to predictable patterns. Here are a few more regular verbs that add an –*s* to certain forms:

I love, he loves
You trade, she trades
I jump, it jumps

*For more on subject-verb agreement, see Chapter 6.

Past tense verbs indicate that the action or state of being happened completely in the past:

> I **was** hungry.
> They **adored** green beans.
> He **wanted** to marry her.
> She **cooked** dinner every night.

To form the past tense of regular verbs, you add *–ed, –d,* or *–ied,* depending on how the base form ends. Here are some examples:

Base Form	*Past Tense*
learn	learned
bat	batted
cope	coped
worry	worried

When the base form of the word ends in a consonant, you will usually add *–ed* to form the past tense.

Base Form	*Past Tense*
track	tracked
rest	rested
lean	leaned

Sometimes forming the past tense requires doubling the verb's final consonant and then adding *–ed.*

Base Form	*Past Tense*
jog	jogged
stop	stopped
rub	rubbed

For regular verbs that end in *e,* you will usually add just a *–d.*

Base Form	*Past Tense*
like	liked
hope	hoped
change	changed
file	filed

For regular verbs that end in *–y*, you will usually drop the *–y* and add *–ied*.

Base Form   *Past Tense*
cry   cried
carry   carried
satisfy   satisfied

 **EXERCISE 4.2**   **Using the Correct Forms of Past and Present Tense Verbs**

In each of the following sentences, write on the blank the correct form of the verb contained in parentheses.

1. Yesterday, I _____ to call you. (*try*)
2. When she worked there, she _____ the floor every day. (*mop*)
3. She _____ in the chorus line when she was in her twenties. (*dance*)
4. He _____ about you when you are gone. (*worry*)
5. Last night, she _____ a perfect game. (*bowl*)
6. I _____ you would stop by before you go home. (*wish*)
7. The dog _____ constantly while his owner is away. (*bark*)
8. The cat _____ my face, and I went to the doctor. (*scratch*)
9. I _____ the eggs for hours before I removed them from the pot. (*boil*)
10. Right now, I _____ chocolate. (*crave*)

Helping Verbs

Past and present are two of the basic tenses. A third basic tense is the **future tense,** which indicates that the action or state of being will occur in the future. To indicate the future tense, as well as more specific types of the other two simple tenses, helping verbs are added to the main verb. The **helping verbs** are

is	be	may	would
am	can	might	has
are	could	must	have
was	do	shall	
were	does	should	
been	did	will	

The following chart adds the future tense to the lists:

Base Form	Past Tense	Future Tense
like	liked	will like
hope	hoped	will hope
change	changed	will change
file	filed	will file
cry	cried	will cry
carry	carried	will carry
satisfy	satisfied	will satisfy

Different combinations of helping verbs and main verbs allow speakers of English to indicate different times and qualities of verbs. In particular, some of these helping verbs allow speakers to express twelve different verb tenses, which are summarized in the following table.

Present	I work He works They work
Past	I worked He worked They worked
Future	I **will** work He **will** work They **will** work
Present Perfect	I **have** worked He **has** worked They **have** worked
Past Perfect	I **had** worked He **had** worked They **had** worked
Future Perfect	I **will have** worked He **will have** worked They **will have** worked
Present Progressive	I **am** working He **is** working They **are** working
Past Progressive	I **was** working He **was** working They **were** working

Future Progressive	I **will be** working He **will be** working They **will be** working
Present Perfect Progressive	I **have been** working He **has been** working They **have been** working
Past Perfect Progressive	I **had been** working He **had been** working They **had been** working
Future Perfect Progressive	I **will have been** working He **will have been** working They **will have been** working

Other helping verbs express different qualities of the action (such as ability, possibility, or necessity) or are used to form questions.

> She **can work** tomorrow.
> They **do** not **work** as hard as she does.
> **Do** you **work** on Tuesdays?
> He **could be** at work.
> You **should have been working.**
> **May** I **work** with you?

The main verb along with its helping verb is called a **verb phrase.**

Writing REVIEW   **Writing Sentences Using Verbs in the Past and Present Tense and Helping Verbs**

Write ten sentences of your own that include verbs in the past tense and present tense. Some sentences should have helping verbs.

 **EXERCISE 4.3**   **Identifying Verb Phrases in Sentences**

In each of the following sentences, circle the verb phrase.

1. She has been flirting with him off and on.

2. Will he be following your progress?

3. She will help you get a job.

4. Did he revise his resumé?

5. We can depend on Yolanda.

6. They have been playing poker for two hours.

7. Should we talk about this later?

8. Do the girls attend private school?

9. Frances is watching her favorite show.

10. Shall we dance?

Irregular Verbs

So far, you have focused only on regular verbs, the verbs that change forms according to predictable patterns. However, there is another category of verbs called irregular verbs. **Irregular verbs** are those verbs that change form in different tenses and when forming the *past participle,* the form of the verb that is used with the helping verbs *has, have,* or *had.* Whereas the past participle form of regular verbs is usually the same as the past tense form (He *worked;* he has *worked*), the past participle form of irregular verbs differs from the past tense form (It *flew;* it has *flown*). The following list includes many common irregular verbs:

Base Form	Present Tense	Past Tense	Past Participle
arise	arises	arose	arisen
be	is	was/were	been
bear	bears	bore	borne
begin	begins	began	begun
bite	bites	bit	bitten/bit
blow	blows	blew	blown
break	breaks	broke	broken
bring	brings	brought	brought
buy	buys	bought	bought
catch	catches	caught	caught
choose	chooses	chose	chosen
come	comes	came	come
creep	creeps	crept	crept
dive	dives	dived/dove	dived
do	does	did	done
draw	draws	drew	drawn
dream	dreams	dreamed/dreamt	dreamt
drink	drinks	drank	drunk
drive	drives	drove	driven
eat	eats	ate	eaten

Base Form	Present Tense	Past Tense	Past Participle
fall	falls	fell	fallen
fight	fights	fought	fought
fly	flies	flew	flown
forget	forgets	forgot	forgotten
forgive	forgives	forgave	forgiven
freeze	freezes	froze	frozen
get	gets	got	got/gotten
give	gives	gave	given
go	goes	went	gone
grow	grows	grew	grown
hang	hangs	hung	hung
hide	hides	hid	hidden
know	knows	knew	known
lay	lays	laid	laid
lead	leads	led	led
lie	lies	lay	lain
light	lights	lit	lit
lose	loses	lost	lost
prove	proves	proved	proved/proven
ride	rides	rode	ridden
ring	rings	rang	rung
rise	rises	rose	risen
run	runs	ran	run
see	sees	saw	seen
seek	seeks	sought	sought
set	sets	set	set
shake	shakes	shook	shaken
sing	sings	sang	sung
sink	sinks	sank	sunk
sit	sits	sat	sat
speak	speaks	spoke	spoken
spring	springs	sprang	sprung
steal	steals	stole	stolen
sting	stings	stung	stung
strike	strikes	struck	struck/stricken
swear	swears	swore	sworn
swim	swims	swam	swum
swing	swings	swung	swung
take	takes	took	taken
tear	tears	tore	torn
throw	throws	threw	thrown
wake	wakes	woke/waked	woken/waked/woke
wear	wears	wore	worn
write	writes	wrote	written

 **EXERCISE 4.4**   **Using the Correct Forms of Irregular Verbs**

In each of the following sentences, write on the blank the correct form of the verb contained in parentheses.

1. You have _____ this all out of proportion. (*blow*)

2. He has _____ the entire glassful. (*drink*)

3. We _____ out all of the spoiled food yesterday. (*throw*)

4. She had _____ on that rope before. (*swing*)

5. Lee had ____ all night long. (*run*)

6. You ____ two feet last year? (*grow*)

7. Janice _____ me a letter just last month. (*write*)

8. She was _____ by that dog. (*bite*)

9. I _____ Karate classes in 2005. (*teach*)

10. Have you _____ that sweater before? (*wear*)

Writing REVIEW   **Writing Sentences with Irregular Verbs**

Using the previous list of irregular verbs, write ten sentences of your own that include irregular verbs.

Verbals

As you are learning to identify verbs in sentences, you will need to watch for words called **verbals** that look like verbs but function as other parts of speech in sentences. There are three kinds of verbals: *infinitives, gerunds,* and *participles*.

An **infinitive** is composed of the word *to* plus a verb. Infinitives often act as nouns in sentences:

He wanted **to fish.** (The infinitive *to fish* is a direct object that answers the question *wanted what?*)

To win was her only desire. (*To win* is the subject of the sentence.)

Infinitive phrases include the infinitive along with its modifiers, objects, and/or complements.

> He wanted **to fish all day long.**

> **To win the contest** was her only desire.

A **gerund,** which is a verb with *–ing* on the end, functions as a noun.

> **Choosing** wasn't easy. (*Choosing* is the subject of this sentence.)

> He loved **going.** (*Going* is the direct object.)

A gerund phrase includes the gerund along with its modifiers, objects, and/or complements.

> **Choosing just one dessert** was not easy.

> He loved **going on safari.**

Participles are verbs that end in *–ed* or *–ing*. They function as adjectives in sentences.

> **Slipping,** he fell and broke his leg. (*Slipping* is an adjective that describes *he.*)

> I caught her **lying.** (*Lying* is an adjective that describes *her.*)

> He was a fugitive **wanted** in three states. (*Wanted* is an adjective that modifies *fugitive.*)

As you see in the last example, a participial phrase consists of a participle along with its modifiers, objects, and/or complements. Modifiers in participial phrases can be prepositional phrases:

> **Slipping on the ice,** he fell and broke his leg.

> I caught her **lying about her age.**

 **EXERCISE 4.5**   **Identifying Verbals in Sentences**

In each of the following sentences, circle the verbal and write on the blank whether it is an *infinitive,* a *gerund,* or a *participle.*

_____ 1. The girl skiing behind the boat hit a wave and wiped out.

_____ 2. Swimming is my passion.

_____ 3. To go with you would be my dream.

_____ 4. He wanted to leave.

_____ 5. He was a chef desired by every restaurant in New York City.

_____ 6. Painting well is one of Fred's goals.

_____ 7. Diving can be dangerous.

_____ 8. Tom finished reading the book.

_____ 9. She hopes to find the treasure.

_____ 10. My father is the man sitting in the front row.

> *Writing* REVIEW **Writing Sentences with Verbals**
>
> Write ten sentences of your own that include verbals.

Writing Better Sentences

You can write better, more interesting sentences of your own by paying more attention to your choice of verbs. In particular, avoid using too many passive voice verbs, choose strong verbs over weaker ones, and make sure the tense of your verbs is consistent.

Passive Versus Active Voice

We can write sentences in either of two basic ways. The first uses **active voice,** in which the subject of the sentence is the performer of the action:

subject verb   direct object

Aiko mowed the **lawn.**

The active voice, which shows the subject performing an action, is clear and direct. In passive voice sentences, on the other hand, the *receiver* of the action (the direct object in the active voice sentence), instead of the performer, is the subject. The performer of the action is now the object of the preposition.

subject   verb   object of preposition

The **lawn was mowed** by   **Aiko.**

In this version, the reader has to wait until the end of the sentence to find out who performed the action. This type of sentence is less interesting and less energetic than an active voice sentence. It also tends to include unnecessary words.

There are some occasions when the passive voice is appropriate. If you do not know who the performer of the action is, the passive voice permits you to leave out that information.

The window was broken sometime during the night.

In addition, if you need to omit the subject to conceal who was responsible for an action, then the passive voice may be appropriate.

The hospital agreed that mistakes had been made.

The point is that the passive voice should be used intentionally rather than accidentally. In most instances, if the subject is known, the active voice is the better, more interesting choice.

 **EXERCISE 4.6**   **Rewriting Passive Voice Sentences**

On the blanks provided, rewrite each of the following sentences, changing passive voice to active voice.

1. All of the shrimp were eaten by the girls.

   _____

2. The piano was played by Patrick.

   _____

3. The test was taken by all of the students.

   _____

4. The spaghetti was cooked by Jimmy.

   _____

5. The damage was done by the dogs.

   _____

6. The skating party was enjoyed by the children.

   _____

7. The birthday cake was eaten by the guests.

   _____

8. The TV show *Power Rangers* is watched by my son.

   _____

9. The story was read by me.

_____

10. The house was painted by Chris.

_____

Strong Verbs Versus Weak Verbs

Clear, interesting writing always includes strong action verbs. The more descriptive the verb, the sharper the image it produces in the reader's mind. Compare these next two sets of examples:

Weak:	At our bake sale, we **will have** free samples.
Strong:	At our bake sale, we **will give** away free samples.

Weak:	He **comes** in every morning.
Strong:	He **saunters** in every morning.

In the second sentence of the first set of examples, a more action-oriented verb brings more vitality to the sentence. In the second sentence of the second set of examples, a more specific verb conveys more information about _how_ the subject moves.

As you write, you may tend to choose weaker verbs because they may be the first ones that occur to you. Using _to be_ and _to have_ verbs, in particular, often drains the life from a sentence.

Weak:	He **was** sick to his stomach.
Strong:	He **vomited** on the rug.

Weak:	He **has** a great fondness for redheads.
Strong:	He **adores** redheads.

Notice how the second sentence of each pair conveys the same information as the first sentence but does so with more action and energy. Also avoid writing too many sentences that begin with _There is/are_ or _It is_. Although this can sometimes be an appropriate way to begin a sentence, the sentence will automatically include a weak _to be_ verb. Notice how each of the following revisions improves the sentence:

Weak:	There are many reasons why I am leaving.
Strong:	I am leaving for many reasons.

> *Weak:*   It is important that we stop spending so much money.
> *Strong:*   We must stop spending so much money.

When you begin to see sentences in your own writing that begin with *There is/are* or *It is,* try to rewrite them to eliminate those phrases and substitute stronger verbs.

As you are evaluating the strength of your verbs, be aware that the best verb can be lurking elsewhere in the sentence as another part of speech:

> We **have been having** quite a few calls of complaint.

This sentence relies on a weak *to have* verb. But notice the word *calls,* which is functioning as the direct object, as well as the word *complaint,* which is hiding in a prepositional phrase at the very end of the sentence. Either one of these words is a better verb for this sentence, which needs a little rewriting:

> People **are calling** often to complain.
> Callers **are complaining** often.

Now look at the sentence that follows. Which word in this sentence would actually be the best verb?

> We will have a short meeting to get organized.

If you said that the word *meeting* should be the verb, you are right. We could rewrite this sentence to read: *We will meet briefly to get organized.*

Also, ask yourself if you are overusing adjectives and adverbs in place of strong verbs. For example, read the next sentence:

> He walked quickly into the room.

The adverb *quickly* tells how he walked, but you could replace the phrase *walked quickly* with one strong verb, such as *strode, jogged,* or *trotted.* Here is another example:

> Her hair was very pretty and shiny in the sunlight.

You could substitute strong verbs for the weak verb *was* and the adjectives *pretty* and *shiny:*

> Her hair shone and sparkled in the sunlight.

EXERCISE 4.7   **Rewriting Sentences to Include Stronger Verbs**

On the blank provided, rewrite each of the following sentences to include a stronger verb.

1. There was a cool breeze blowing in from the ocean.

   _____

2. She is very fond of him.

   _____

3. We took an airplane to get to Paris.

   _____

4. There were dolphins swimming in the tank.

   _____

5. There are a lot of things that we will discuss at the meeting.

   _____

6. She cried hard and very loudly when she heard the news.

   _____

7. It is important that you try to listen to what I am saying.

   _____

8. He was dishonest when he completed his homework.

   _____

9. The star looked bright and glowing in the dark sky.

   _____

10. There are many reasons for you to agree to this deal.

   _____

Writing REVIEW   **Writing Sentences Using Active, Strong Verbs**

Write ten sentences of your own that include active, strong verbs.

✦ **EXERCISE 4.8**   **Using Strong Verbs**

Using strong verbs, describe the action in the following photograph. Tell what each of the people in the photograph is doing.

© David Woolley/Getty Images

_____

_____

_____

_____

_____

Consistency in Verb Tense

As you write, you will want to make sure that you use verb tenses consistently. Mixing past and present tenses inappropriately is confusing to readers. Note the shift in verb tense in the following sentence:

present tense   *past tense*

　　We **go** to the store today, and I **asked** for a refund.

The first verb, *go*, should be in the past tense, *went*. We may shift tenses like this in casual conversation, but we should not write this way. If you start out in the past tense, remain in the past tense throughout the sentence and/or paragraph. If you start out in the present tense, remain in the present tense.

✳ **EXERCISE 4.9**   **Correcting Errors in Verb Tense Consistency**

In each of the following sentences, underline the two verbs. Then, correct the second verb so that its tense matches that of the first verb. Write the corrected verb on the blank following the sentence.

1. Last summer, the sharks were everywhere, but my friend goes into the surf anyway. _____

2. We left for vacation, and the mailman delivers our mail. _____

3. Every morning, I brush my teeth and dressed for the day. _____

4. During the lecture, Ang listened attentively, but May twiddles her thumbs. _____

5. Ben helped mix the paint, but Abbie does not do anything. _____

6. Martha invested in many stocks, but Stuart decides against it. _____

7. This time of year, the trees are in bloom, and the birds chirped. _____

8. She sold her house and buys a new car. _____

9. Every time you make a decision, you changed your mind. _____

10. We went shopping together, and my friend leaves me to hang out with other people. _____

✳

CHAPTER 4 REVIEW

Fill in the blanks in each of the following statements.

1. A ____ is the word (or words) in a sentence that expresses the subject's action or state of being.

2. One kind of verb is the _____ verb, which expresses action of some kind.

3. Another kind of verb is the _____ verb, which expresses some state of being. This type of verb can also relate to the _____.

4. The time expressed by verbs is called _____.

5. _____ verbs indicate that the action or state of being is occurring now or is ongoing.

6. The form of a present tense verb depends on whether the subject is _____ or _____.

7. _____ verbs indicate that the action or state of being happened in the past.

8. To form the past tense of regular verbs, you add ___, __, or ____, depending on how the base form ends.

9. Another basic verb tense, in addition to past and present, is _____ tense.

10. _____ verbs are words that are added to a main verb to express different tenses, to express different qualities of the action, or to form _____.

11. The main verb along with its helping verbs is called a _____.

12. _____ verbs are those verbs that change forms in different tenses and when forming the past participle.

13. _____ are words that look like verbs but function as other parts of speech in sentences.

14. An _____ is composed of the word *to* plus a verb. Infinitives act as _____ in sentences.

15. A _____ is a verb with an *–ing* ending that functions as a _____.

16. _____ are verbs that end in *–ed* or *–ing*. They function as _____ in sentences.

17. In _____ voice sentences, the subject of the sentence is the performer of the action.

18. In _____ voice sentences, the direct object (the *receiver* of the action) becomes the subject.

19. Clear, interesting writing always includes _____ action verbs.

20. Verb tense should be _____ throughout sentences and paragraphs.

A. In each of the following sentences, circle the verb and write on the blank whether it is an *action verb* or a *linking verb*.

_____ 1. She frowned at him.

_____ 2. You sound happy.

_____ 3. She feels sad.

_____ 4. I swam across the pool.

_____ 5. Bill Clinton was president in the 1990s.

B. In each of the following sentences, write on the blank the correct form of the verb contained in parentheses.

1. Six months from now, she _____ from college. (*graduate*)

2. Since they met, he _____ fond of her. (*grow*)

3. Before I found you, I _____ lonely. (*be*)

4. Before the argument started, she already _____ the party. (*leave*)

5. At this moment, we _____ a DVD. (*watch*)

C. In each of the following sentences, circle the verbals.

1. Confused by his response, she asked him to explain.

2. To leave now would be an insult.

3. I wonder if she wants to go.

4. Hoping for the best, she walked out on the stage.

5. It would not be in your best interest to start an argument.

Rewrite each of the following sentences to eliminate the passive voice, substitute a stronger verb, and/or correct errors in verb tense consistency.

1. It is so typical of her to ignore me.

_____

2. The video was returned by Sara.

_____

3. The miniature poodle was bought by Joan and her husband.

_____

4. She is very good at singing and dancing.

_____

5. The tree was damaged by the storm.

_____

6. During the bad weather, Jim shoveled, and I throw down ice melt.

_____

7. On their walk, Sean saw a bluebird, and Kelly notices a hawk.

_____

8. At the same time, the rain fell and thunder booms.

_____

9. There are several home improvements I would like to make.

_____

10. He moved past her at a rapid rate of speed.

_____

WRITING ASSIGNMENT

Think about your first day of college and write about any emotions you felt on that day. Were you scared? Excited? Overwhelmed? Use the different types of verbs you have learned about in this chapter to make your story more interesting.

WebWork

For more practice with the active and passive voice, go to **http://www2.gsu.edu/ ~accerl.** Review the information about the passive voice and then complete the self-tests provided.

For more practice with the various features of verbs, go to the Guide to Grammar and Writing Web site at **http://grammar.ccc.commnet.edu/grammar/verbs.htm.** Review the information and test your understanding by completing the computer-graded quizzes provided.

Online Study Center For additional information and practice with verbs, go to the Online Study Center that accompanies this book, at **http://www.college.hmco.com/pic/dolphinwriterone.**

5

Modifiers: Adjectives and Adverbs

GOALS FOR CHAPTER 5

▶ Define the term *modifier*.

▶ Define the term *adjective*.

▶ Define the term *article*.

▶ Identify adjectives in sentences.

▶ Define the terms *comparative* and *superlative*.

▶ Use comparative and superlative adjective forms correctly in sentences.

▶ Punctuate adjectives correctly in sentences.

▶ Define the term *adverb*.

▶ Identify adverbs in sentences.

▶ Define the term *double negative*.

▶ Rewrite sentences to correct adverb errors.

▶ Explain three ways to improve writing with adjectives and adverbs.

Test Yourself

A. In each of the following sentences, circle the words or phrases that are functioning as adjectives, and underline the words or phrases that are functioning as adverbs.

1. The young man was driving too fast.

2. That car moves quickly.

3. Mary's young daughter is very intelligent.

4. The man rowing the boat speaks with an accent.

5. The experienced mechanic diagnosed the problem immediately.

B. **In each of the following sentences, circle the adjective(s) or adverb(s) that is (are) used incorrectly.**

1. I did not bring no cash.

2. Jake had the most best time of all.

3. Nancy speaks English very good.

4. I can't hardly wait for spring.

5. She handled that situation bad.

In Chapters 2 and 3, you learned that **modifiers** are either adjectives or adverbs. In this chapter, you will explore both kinds of modifiers in more detail.

Adjectives

Adjectives are words that describe or limit nouns. They tell how many, what kind, or which one:

red shoes (*what kind?*)
fifth chapter (*which one?*)
that team (*which one?*)
six dollars (*how many?*)
several people (*how many?*)

The **articles**—*a, an,* and *the*—are special kinds of adjectives that point out nouns:

the window
a cat
an octagon

Adjectives can come before the noun, or, in a sentence with a linking verb, they can follow the verb:

> She looks **beautiful.**
> He is **tall, dark,** and **handsome.**

EXERCISE 5.1   **Identifying Adjectives in Sentences**

Circle the adjectives in each of the following sentences.

1. She wore a huge, sparkling diamond.
2. The silver gown glistened.
3. A big red fire engine was there.
4. Was that shaggy dog outside?
5. Are those gold coins valuable?
6. The president looks old and tired.
7. Mrs. Franks is a beautiful woman.
8. The loud motorboat stopped.
9. Mr. Dinger is a lab technician.
10. The white terrier bites.

Phrases That Function as Adjectives

Adjectives can be single words, or they can be phrases. Prepositional phrases, which you learned about in Chapter 2, can function as adjectives:

> the man **in the photo**   (the phrase describes *man*)
> fudge **with nuts**   (the phrase describes *fudge*)
> the quilt **on the bed**   (the phrase describes *quilt*)

Participial phrases, too, function as adjectives in sentences. A participle is a verb that ends in *–ed* or *–ing.*

> **Limping slowly,** the player headed for the bench.
> The hotdog, **topped with cheese and chili,** was delicious.
> The dog **barking its head off** belongs to me.

Notice that phrases that function as adjectives can come before or after the nouns they modify.

 **EXERCISE 5.2**　**Identifying Phrases Functioning as Adjectives**

Circle the phrases functioning as adjectives in each of the following sentences.

1. Everyone in the crowd was smiling.

2. The boy in front of me smiled.

3. Skating quickly, the hockey players made a line change.

4. The ice cream covered in whipped cream and chocolate sauce is mine.

5. The little girl crying in the parking lot is sad.

6. Singing loudly, the chorus sounded joyful.

7. The man next to the door is my husband.

8. The smoked salmon swimming in dill sauce looks unappetizing.

9. Stopped for speeding, the man looked nervous.

10. The hamster running around like a lunatic is cute.

Avoiding Sentence Fragments

Prepositional and participial phrases cannot stand alone; they must be attached to an independent clause or they become sentence fragments. For example, read the following sentences:

> *sentence fragment*
>
> **Dialing the phone slowly.** Joe attempted to remember the number.

> *sentence fragment*
>
> She sat beside her ailing husband. **All through the day.**

Both of these sets of sentences must be combined to eliminate the fragments. For information about avoiding other types of sentence fragments, see pages 45, 75, and 141.

Misplaced or Dangling Modifiers

In a sentence, an adjective modifier must be placed next to the word it describes. If a modifier is not next to the word it describes, it is called a **misplaced modifier,** and it can cause confusion:

> **Lying in a puddle,** George saw his morning newspaper.

In this sentence, the phrase *lying in a puddle* modifies *George* because that is the closest word to the phrase. Therefore, this sentence is saying that George was lying in a puddle. Actually, though, it was the newspaper that was in a puddle. To correct this sentence, rewrite it so that the modifier is next to the word it modifies:

George saw his morning newspaper **lying in a puddle.**

Misplaced modifiers can be phrases or single words. The word *only*, for example, is commonly misplaced:

She **only** brought chips to the party.

In this sentence, the word *only* is modifying the verb, but it should be modifying the word *chips*. Thus, it needs to be moved:

She brought **only** chips to the party.

If the word the modifier is supposed to be describing is not in the sentence at all, the error is called a **dangling modifier.**

Walking home yesterday, the rain came down hard.

At age six, my parents divorced.

In the first sentence, the modifier *walking home yesterday* is incorrectly describing *rain*. It is not the rain that walked home but rather the person or people who made the journey. In the second sentence, the modifier *at age six* is incorrectly describing *my parents*. It is not the parents who were six years old but rather the speaker of the sentence. To correct these errors, rewrite the sentences to add the missing information:

Walking home yesterday, **Sharon and Marge** were drenched by a hard rain.

At age six, **I** experienced my parents' divorce.

 **EXERCISE 5.3**   **Identifying Misplaced and Dangling Modifiers**

On the blank, write *Misplaced* if the sentence contains a misplaced modifier, *Dangling* if the sentence contains a dangling modifier, or *Correct* if all modifiers are correctly placed.

_____   1. After making the wrong turn, the area was totally unfamiliar.

_____   2. Dialing carelessly, the caller punched in the wrong number.

_____   3. Lost in space, the scientists got no response from the robot probe.

_____ 4. Fortunately, they only lost possessions in the fire.

_____ 5. On the way home from work, Ted spotted an owl.

_____ 6. While writing the paper, errors were included.

_____ 7. Overspending with credit cards, the debt increased.

_____ 8. They watched the grazing cows sitting on a park bench.

_____ 9. Sleeping soundly, a warm blanket covered the infant.

_____ 10. The roofing company fixed the damage caused by the storm.

 **EXERCISE 5.4**   **Revising Misplaced and Dangling Modifiers**

Select five of the sentences in Exercise 5.3 that you labeled _misplaced_ or _dangling_.
Then rewrite each of these sentences to eliminate the misplaced or dangling modifier.

Comparative and Superlative Forms of Adjectives

Most adjectives have two additional forms. One of them, the **comparative** form,
is used to compare two things. The other, the **superlative** form, is used to compare
three or more things.

Adjective	_Comparative_	_Superlative_
pretty	prettier	prettiest
young	younger	youngest
smart	smarter	smartest
dull	duller	dullest
hungry	hungrier	hungriest

Thus, we would say, for example, that the rose is _prettier_ than the daisy. But we
would say that the rose is the _prettiest_ flower in the whole bouquet.

As you can see in the previous list, we usually add _–er_ to the end of the adjective to form the comparative form. We add _–est_ to the end to form the superlative form. However, other adjectives stay the same and add the word _more_
to form the comparative and _most_ to form the superlative.

Adjective	_Comparative_	_Superlative_
grateful	more grateful	most grateful
foolish	more foolish	most foolish
determined	more determined	most determined
gorgeous	more gorgeous	most gorgeous

Still other adjectives are irregular and change forms altogether.

Adjective	Comparative	Superlative
good	better	best
bad	worse	worst
little	less	least
much, many, some	more	most
far	farther	farthest

 EXERCISE 5.5   **Using the Correct Forms of Adjectives in Sentences**

On the blank in each sentence, write the correct form of the adjective contained in parentheses.

1. Of all of the cars I have driven, my Honda is _____. (*good*)

2. The _____ amount of money to be donated is three dollars. (*little*)

3. The West Highland Terrier was the _____ of the two dogs. (*lively*)

4. The _____ thing that could happen has occurred. (*bad*)

5. You look _____ than a summer's day. (*lovely*)

6. Hank is the _____ person I have ever met. (*foolish*)

7. Of the two girls, Dawn is the _____ skater. (*good*)

8. She was _____ from home than he was. (*far*)

9. That's the _____ thing I have ever seen. (*dumb*)

10. Albert Einstein was the _____ man who ever lived, in my opinion. (*smart*)

Punctuating Adjectives

When you describe a noun with more than one adjective, you may need to separate the adjectives with a comma:

> She gazed out at the **calm, blue** sea.
> The **tall, thin** tree swayed in the breeze.

However, no comma is necessary in this sentence:

> We should get some **delicious Thai** food.

To decide whether or not to include a comma, you mentally insert the word *and* between the two adjectives. If the sentence still makes sense, you will need to add a comma.

> She gazed out at the calm **and** blue sea.
> The tall **and** thin tree swayed in the breeze.

Both of these sentences require a comma between the two adjectives.

You can also try to reverse the two adjectives. If the sentence still makes sense, insert a comma.

> She gazed out at the **blue, calm** sea.

Notice that the adjectives in this sentence cannot be reversed; thus, no comma is added:

> We should get some **Thai delicious** food.

 **EXERCISE 5.6**   **Punctuating Adjectives in Sentences**

In each of the following sentences, circle the adjectives (but not the articles) and add a comma between them if necessary. If no comma is necessary, write *No comma needed* beside the sentence.

1. The balloon rose into the light blue sky.

2. We need a dependable trustworthy car.

3. He is a smart friendly dentist.

4. I bought a long, thin French bread.

5. The abused scared dog ended up in the pound.

6. The bright red ball disappeared in the woods.

7. The midterm chemistry exam was difficult.

8. The patients appreciated the nurse's gentle soft touch.

9. He could not climb the barbed wire fence.

10. The tall Gothic church rose up over the skyline.

Writing REVIEW   **Writing Sentences with Adjectives**

Write ten sentences of your own that include adjectives.

Adverbs

Adverbs are words that describe or limit verbs, adjectives, or other adverbs. They tell where, when, how, and to what degree:

Please put it **there.**	(put *where?*)
They will arrive **tomorrow.**	(will arrive *when?*)
She screamed **loudly.**	(screamed *how?*)
It is **very** beautiful.	(beautiful *to what degree?*)

Many adverbs end in *–ly* (*gracefully, terribly, poorly*), but others do not (*soon, later, so, here*).

Adverbs can appear anywhere in a sentence:

Recently I gave blood.
He is **usually** punctual.
I picked up the broken glass **carefully.**

EXERCISE 5.7   **Identifying Adverbs in Sentences**

Circle the adverbs in each of the following sentences.

1. I will be there soon.
2. Regretfully, he left yesterday.
3. They will arrive later.
4. I will be outside today.
5. Merry blew the horn loudly.
6. We drove too slowly.
7. I am extremely tired.
8. They are very lovely people.
9. Put that very hot pot there.
10. She does her homework cheerfully.

Phrases That Function as Adverbs

Adverbs, like adjectives, can be single words, or they can be prepositional phrases, which you learned about in Chapter 2.

The party begins **at six o'clock.**   (begins *when?*)
He walked **around the block.**   (walked *where?*)
She danced **with joy.**   (danced *how?*)

 **EXERCISE 5.8**   **Identifying Phrases Functioning as Adverbs**

Circle the phrases functioning as adverbs in each of the following sentences. Beware of phrases that are functioning as adjectives, and do not circle those by mistake.

1. The cat with green eyes ran under the bed.
2. Patrick starts school on Monday.
3. We went to the store.
4. The power plant is located on the river.
5. I clapped my hands with glee.
6. She attends church every Sunday.
7. He eats with gusto!
8. I drove around the block.
9. On Thursdays we go to the park.
10. She sings with passion.

Comparative and Superlative Forms of Adverbs

Like adjectives, some adverbs can have comparative and superlative forms. Usually we add the word *more* to form the comparative and *most* to form the superlative.

Adverb	*Comparative*	*Superlative*
bravely	more bravely	most bravely
quick	more quickly	most quickly
rudely	more rudely	most rudely

Of all the soldiers, John behaved **most bravely.**
This plant blooms **more quickly** than that plant does.

Avoiding Double Negatives

Certain adverbs, those which express the negative, should not be used together in the same sentence. These words include

no	never
not	hardly
none	barely
nothing	scarcely

Notice how double negatives are corrected in the following sentences:

Double negative: I have **hardly never** been sick.
Corrections: I have hardly ever been sick.
      I am never sick.

Double negative: There is **not no** butter for the bread.
Corrections: There is not any butter for the bread.
      There is no butter for the bread.

Using Adjectives and Adverbs Correctly

Certain adjectives and adverbs are easily confused if you are unsure which is which. The words *good* and *well, bad* and *badly,* and *real* and *really* are the three pairs that are most often misused in sentences.

The adverbs in these pairs are *well, badly,* and *really.* The last two are easy enough to remember because they both end in –*ly,* like many other adverbs.

You sang **well** last night. (**not** you sang *good*)
He dances **badly.** (**not** he dances *bad*)
She is **really** tired. (**not** she is *real* tired)

The adjectives are *good, bad,* and *real.* They all describe nouns, but they are often misused with linking verbs:

He feels **bad** today. (**not** he feels *badly*)
The soup tastes **good.** (**not** the soup tastes *well*)

Notice how the meaning changes in the following sentences, depending on whether you use an adjective or an adverb:

He smells bad.
He smells badly.

In the first sentence, the adjective *bad,* which follows a linking verb, communicates that the subject is the source of a foul odor. In the second sentence, the word *smells* is an action verb, and the word *badly* is an adverb. Therefore, the sentence indicates that the subject's nose is not functioning properly.

 **EXERCISE 5.9**   **Correcting Adverb and Adjective Errors**

Rewrite each of the following sentences to correct adverb errors. Check for the correct use of comparative and superlative forms, double negatives, and adjectives incorrectly used as adverbs. If the sentence needs no correction, write *No correction needed* beside it.

1. He looks well in his new suit.

_____

2. There is not nothing we can do about this.

_____

3. She is real pretty.

_____

4. He acts bad when things do not go his way.

_____

5. She sings well.

_____

6. That player pitches the ball good.

_____

7. There is not hardly any milk left.

_____

8. That is not no way to talk about that topic!

_____

9. He types very bad.

_____

10. He feels badly about his mistake.

_____

Writing REVIEW   **Writing Sentences with Adverbs**

Write ten sentences of your own that include adverbs.

Writing Better Sentences

There are three ways to improve your writing with adjectives and adverbs:

1. Use them to add descriptive detail.
2. Do not overuse them.
3. Do not substitute them for strong verbs.

Adjectives and adverbs help create mental images in your readers' minds. Notice the difference between the following sets of sentences:

Our front porch was cool.
Our wide, shady front porch was cool and inviting on a hot summer day.

The leaves drifted down to the ground.
The red, yellow, and gold leaves drifted gently to the ground.

The second sentence of each pair, which includes more adjectives and adverbs, provides more descriptive details that help readers form a sharper mental picture. Especially when you are describing something such as an object, a person, or a place, make sure that you are adding adjectives and adverbs to bring your description to life.

However, beware of overusing adjectives and adverbs. You do not want to load your sentences with too many of them, for an excess can slow the pace of your sentences and bog down your ideas with unnecessary information.

Too many modifiers:	The young man in his early twenties was handsome and very desirable to young ladies his own age.
Revision:	The ladies desired the handsome young man.
Too many modifiers:	He quickly threw the ball hard, fast, and with a lot of power to first base.
Revision:	He threw the ball hard and fast to first base.

Check to make sure each adjective or adverb offers essential information, and make sure they are not simply repeating each other.

If you have a tendency to use too many modifiers, you might also be using adjectives and adverbs to convey meaning that is more effectively delivered by your verbs.

Too many adjectives:	We went for miles and miles down the long, lonely stretch of deserted highway.
Revision:	The lonely highway **stretched** for miles before us.

Too many adjectives: He was in the deep snow, struggling to walk.
Revision: He **trudged** through deep snow.

EXERCISE 5.10   **Revising Sentences to Improve Use of Adjectives and Adverbs**

Rewrite each of the following sentences to add modifiers, eliminate modifiers, or strengthen verbs as appropriate.

1. Her speech is soft and difficult to hear.

_____

2. They are a merry, happy, laughing, fun-loving bunch of people.

_____

3. He whistled merrily, with great happiness and joy etched on his face.

_____

4. Full of energy and life, the little dog jumped in a lively manner.

_____

5. We are in admiration of the one with the trophy in his hands.

_____

CHAPTER 5 REVIEW

Fill in the blanks in the following statements.

1. _____ are either adjectives or adverbs.

2. _____ are words that describe or limit nouns; they tell how many, what kind, or which one.

3. The _____—*a, an,* and *the*—are special kinds of adjectives.

4. _____ phrases and _____ phrases can function as adjectives in sentences.

5. The _____ form of an adjective is used to compare two things.

6. The _____ form of an adjective is used to compare three or more things.

7. Sometimes, you will need to separate two or more adjectives with a _____.

8. _____ are words that describe or limit verbs, adjectives, or other adverbs; they tell where, when, how, and to what degree.

9. _____ phrases can function as adverbs in sentences.

10. To form the comparative form of an adverb, add the word _____.

11. To form the superlative form of an adverb, add the word _____.

12. _____ adverbs, such as *no, not, hardly,* and *barely,* should not be used together in the same sentence.

13. The words *well, badly,* and *really* are all _____.

14. The words *good, bad,* and *real* are all _____.

15. To improve your writing, include adjectives and adverbs to provide _____ detail, but do not overuse them.

16. Make sure you are not substituting adjectives and adverbs for strong _____.

CHAPTER 5: TEST 1

In each of the following sentences, circle the words or phrases that are functioning as adjectives, and underline the words or phrases that are functioning as adverbs.

1. This morning I ate a delicious blueberry muffin with butter.

2. On Sunday the old church filled with song.

3. We happily went to the beach every June.

4. Tomorrow Nathan will join the talented cast of this show.

5. The heated debate began at seven o'clock.

6. The old man walks around the mall every day.

7. The rotted tree trunk is home to large squirrels this year.

8. You will find the warm fleece blanket under the bed.

9. On Thursday we will attend the peace rally.

10. I go to the high school only on Fridays.

Rewrite each of the following sentences to correct adjective and adverb errors.

1. That player hits the ball real bad.

   _____

2. I had the bestest time at that party.

   _____

3. Jim hardly never goes grocery shopping anymore.

   _____

4. The patient took a very long time to move very slowly down the corridor toward her hospital room.

   _____

5. You are a real good dancer.

   _____

6. Her face suddenly became a bright red color.

   _____

7. There is not never anyone to talk to.

   _____

8. He is the most bravest firefighter in our town.

   _____

9. She sees poor after dark.

   _____

10. The sky grew blacker and blacker until finally big, fat raindrops fell to the ground.

    _____

WRITING ASSIGNMENT

Look out the window closest to you. What do you see? Using a variety of adjectives and adverbs, describe the view. Pay close attention to how you punctuate your sentences using adjectives and adverbs.

**Web**Work

For more practice with modifiers, go to the Guide to Grammar and Writing Web site at **http://grammar.ccc.commnet.edu/grammar/index.htm** and complete the quizzes on adjectives and adverbs.

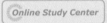Online Study Center   For additional information and practice with modifiers, go to the Online Study Center that accompanies this book, at **http://www.college.hmco.com/pic/dolphinwriterone.**

Subject-Verb Agreement

GOALS FOR CHAPTER 6

▶ Define the terms *singular* and *plural*.

▶ Choose the verb that agrees with the subject of a sentence.

▶ Make subjects and verbs agree in sentences in which prepositional phrases intervene between the subject and the verb.

▶ Make subjects and verbs agree in sentences with inverted word order.

▶ Make verbs agree with subjects that are indefinite pronouns.

▶ Make verbs agree with compound subjects.

▶ Make verbs agree with singular subjects that end in –*s*.

▶ Make verbs agree with collective nouns.

▶ Make verbs agree with titles and proper nouns.

Test Yourself

In each of the following sentences, circle the verb that agrees with the subject.

1. A list of needed items (is, are) posted on the bulletin board.

2. What (do, does) you want for dinner?

3. Frank (spend, spends) a lot of time on the computer.

4. They (enjoy, enjoys) their children.

5. Where (is, are) the library?

6. Where (is, are) your shoes?

7. The beach and the mountains (is, are) very relaxing vacation spots.

8. How many speeches (has, have) you given?

9. Everyone (loves, love) a good movie.

10. One of the players (is, are) almost seven feet tall.

The Basics of Subject-Verb Agreement

In Chapter 3, you learned that a basic sentence contains both a subject and a verb. This subject and verb must agree in number; that is, if the subject is singular (one person, place, thing, or idea), then the verb in the sentence must be in its singular form. If the subject is plural (more than one person, place, thing, or idea), then the verb in the sentence must be in its plural form.

singular   singular

The **bell**   **rings** at noon.

plural   plural

The **bells**   **ring** at noon.

The third person singular forms of regular verbs (see Chapter 4) end in *–s.*

She **sings.**
The flag **waves.**
The audience **claps.**

Irregular verbs (such as the *to be* and *to have* verbs) have different singular and plural forms.

I **am.**
They **are.**
He **has.**
We **have.**

 **EXERCISE 6.1**   **Making Subjects and Verbs Agree**

In each of the following sentences, underline the simple subject. Then, circle the verb that agrees with that subject.

1. The children (play, plays) in the backyard.

2. The cat (tangle, tangles) the yarn.

3. The protesters (march, marches) on Broadway.

4. I (walk, walks) my dogs every day at noon.

5. (Do, does) you travel often?

6. The singers (perform, performs) tonight.

7. Eileen (is, are) a great teacher.

8. The players (roll, rolls) the dice.

9. Several staff members (commute, commutes) on the Hudson Line train.

10. The sleeping bag (roll, rolls) out to a flat square.

Trickier Subject-Verb Agreement Situations

Basic subject-verb agreement is relatively straightforward. However, you will be writing sentences that will present you with trickier subject-verb agreement situations. They might be tricky because the subject is more difficult to find. Or they may be tricky because you are not sure if the subject is singular or plural. The remainder of this chapter covers the kinds of sentences that will make choosing the correct verb a little more challenging.

Intervening Prepositional Phrases

Sometimes a prepositional phrase will separate the subject and the verb of a sentence, causing confusion about what the subject of such a sentence really is. As you learned in Chapter 3, the object of a preposition cannot be the subject of a sentence. Therefore, before you attempt to determine the right verb, you may want to physically or mentally cross out the prepositional phrase or phrases that intervene between the subject and the verb.

One of the boys **eats** pizza every day.

In this example, it might be tempting to conclude that *boys* is the subject of the sentence. But *boys* is the object in a prepositional phrase, and *One* is actually the subject. If you use the plural form of the verb (*eat*) to make it agree with *boys*, then your sentence will contain a subject-verb agreement error. The singular subject *One* must be matched with the singular verb *eats*.

Cross out the intervening prepositional phrases in the following sentences and decide whether or not the verbs agree.

People with experience **is** exactly what we need.
The lines on her face **makes** her look wise.
Men in uniform **are** very handsome.

In the first sentence, the subject is *People* (not *experience*, which is the object of the preposition). The subject is plural and the verb *is* is singular, so the sentence contains a subject-verb agreement error. The verb should be *are*. In the second sentence, *lines* is the subject and *face* is the object of the preposition. The singular verb *makes* does not agree with the plural subject, so it should be changed to *make*. In the last sentence, both the subject (*men*) and the verb (*are*) are plural, so the sentence is correct.

 **EXERCISE 6.2**   **Making Subjects and Verbs Agree in Sentences with Intervening Prepositional Phrases**

In each of the following sentences, draw parentheses around prepositional phrases that intervene between the subject and the verb. Then circle the verb that agrees with the subject.

1. Citizens of this country (elects, elect) a president every four years.
2. These cartons of milk (is, are) cold.
3. The price of strawberries (has, have) increased.
4. The people in our group (meet, meets) on Saturdays.
5. The sound of ocean waves (soothe, soothes) her.
6. The children in this class (like, likes) their teacher.
7. The reasons for her choice (seems, seem) logical.
8. A flock of geese (fly, flies) over my house every autumn.
9. The smell of the baking cookies (make, makes) my mouth water.
10. This box of chocolates (is, are) for you.

Inverted Word Order

Another type of sentence that makes the subject more difficult to discern is one with inverted word order. In a sentence with inverted word order, the subject comes *after* the verb. In sentences that begin with *there* or *here,* for example, the subject follows the verb:

> *verb*   *subject*
>
> Here **are** two *dollars* for your lunch.

The subject of this sentence is the plural *dollars.* The word *Here* is an adverb, and the word *lunch* is the object of a preposition. Therefore, if you were to write *Here **is** two dollars for your lunch,* the sentence would be incorrect.

In questions, too, inverted word order can make determining the subject more challenging:

> *verb*   *subject*
>
> Where **are** my *shoes?*

In this sentence, the verb (*are*) must agree with the plural subject *shoes. Where* is an adverb. Therefore, writing *Where is my shoes?* would be incorrect.

Finally, there are other cases of inverted word order:

> *verb*   *subject*
>
> In the boat **were** two *fish* on ice.

In the boat and *on ice* are prepositional phrases, so cross them out. Then you can see that *fish* (plural) is the subject, so the verb must be plural, too.

 **EXERCISE 6.3**   **Making Subjects and Verbs Agree in Sentences with Inverted Word Order**

In each of the following sentences, underline the subject and then select the verb that agrees with that subject.

1. There (is, are) banging noises coming from the basement.

2. On my kitchen table (is, are) the newspaper.

3. Under the bed (is, are) two pairs of boots.

4. Here (comes, come) the judge.

5. Where (is, are) my eyeglasses?

6. (Is, Are) there any meatballs?

7. In the closet (hangs, hang) a raincoat.

8. Into the pot (goes, go) the lobster.

9. On the driveway (sits, sit) four raccoons.

10. (Was, Were) you going to the store?

Indefinite Pronouns

In the remaining tricky sentences, the subject is not necessarily difficult to find, but you might not be sure whether it is singular or plural. For example, you may wonder whether some of the indefinite pronouns are singular or plural. As you learned in Chapter 2, indefinite pronouns do not refer to any particular person, place, or thing.

> **Everybody** loves ice cream.
> **Something** is going to happen.

The indefinite pronouns become more specific when a prepositional phrase is added.

> **One** *of my friends* won the tournament.
> **No one** *in the class* is prepared for the test.

However, each indefinite pronoun is either singular or plural, regardless of the phrase that modifies it. The singular indefinite pronouns are

one	nobody	nothing	each
anyone	anybody	anything	either
someone	somebody	something	neither
everyone	everybody	everything	

singular   *singular*

> **Each** *of my classes* **challenges** me in a different way.

singular   *singular*

> **Everyone** *in the United States* **attends** elementary school.

The indefinite pronouns that are plural include

both	many
few	several

plural   *plural*

> **Both** of my legs **were** broken.

plural   *plural*

> **Several** of his reasons **are** good ones.

But perhaps the trickiest of the indefinite pronouns are the ones that can be singular or plural, depending on the noun or pronoun to which they refer. These pronouns are

all	most
any	none
more	some

Notice the difference in the following examples:

singular singular

Most of the *cake* **is** gone.

plural plural

Most of my *friends* **know** how to dance.

singular singular

All of the *book* **is** interesting.

plural plural

All of her *relatives* **plan** to attend the reunion.

 **EXERCISE 6.4** **Choosing Verbs That Agree with Indefinite Pronoun Subjects**

In each of the following sentences, circle the verb that agrees with the subject.

1. Each of the contestants (is, are) talented.

2. Everyone (needs, need) a pencil.

3. Most of the students (arrive, arrives) on time.

4. All of the milk (has, have) spoiled.

5. None of us (go, goes) to that church.

6. Several of the cats (has, have) fleas.

7. Most of the writing (was, were) error-free.

8. Both of her sons (join, joins) the Boy Scouts every year.

9. Every one of us (agree, agrees) this movie is great.

10. Some of the members (has not, have not) paid their dues.

Compound Subjects

You learned in Chapter 3 that a compound subject consists of two or more subjects joined by a coordinating conjunction (*and, or, either/or, neither/nor*). This conjunction determines whether you use the singular form of the verb or the plural form of the verb. If the word *and* joins the two subjects, they are plural, and you use the plural form of the verb:

> The stars *and* the moon **are** beautiful tonight.
> My son *and* I **like** to ride skateboards.

If the subjects are joined by *or, either/or,* or *neither/nor,* the verb agrees with the subject that is closest to the verb.

> *singular subject*   *plural subject*
> The **babysitter** *or* the **children** always **eat** the ice cream.

> *singular subject*   *plural subject*
> *Either* **Jay** *or* his **sisters** **clean** the pool every day.

> *plural subject*   *singular subject*
> *Neither* the **stars** *nor* the **moon** **is** visible tonight.

 **EXERCISE 6.5**   **Choosing Verbs That Agree with Compound Subjects**

In each of the following sentences, circle the verb that agrees with the subject.

1. Either the cheerleaders or the mascot (get, gets) the fans clapping.

2. Neither the chickens nor the goats (has, have) been fed.

3. The parents and their children (attend, attends) swimming lessons.

4. Francine and her daughter (enjoy, enjoys) cooking.

5. Either red or pink (is, are) the best color for the couch.

6. The principal or the school secretary (unlocks, unlock) the door every morning.

7. Mary Jo and her family (move, moves) often.

8. Flowers or a box of chocolates (makes, make) a nice gift.

9. Neither Jim nor his parents (is, are) willing to give in.

10. The copyeditor and the proofreader (find, finds) errors in books.

Singular Nouns That End in –s

Some nouns end in –s like plural nouns, but they are nevertheless considered singular because they refer to a single thing. The following list includes some examples of these words.

physics   series
news   politics
economics measles

The news **is** not good.
The series **starts** tonight on public television.

Collective Nouns

Collective nouns are those that refer to a group of people or things (*team, class, crowd, group, company, audience, family, jury, gang, faculty*). If the subject of the sentence is a collective noun and the group is acting together as one unit, then use a singular verb:

The team **practices** every day.
The audience always **laughs** at that joke.

However, if the members of the group are acting individually, use a plural verb:

The team **disagree** about the new uniforms.
The family **go** their separate ways after dinner.

Sums of money and measurements are also considered to be singular when they are one unit.

Two dollars for a tasty lunch **is** a good deal.
Fourteen blocks **is** the length of the island.

Titles and Other Proper Nouns

Titles of poems, novels, short stories, plays, films, and other works are always considered to be singular.

The Adventures of Huckleberry Finn **is** Mark Twain's best book.
"The Flintstones" **is** my favorite cartoon.

A proper noun, such as the name of a person, place, or thing, is also considered to be singular.

McDonald's **is** open until midnight.
The southern United States **lies** in the hurricane's path.
Warner Brothers **is** releasing the film this summer.

 **EXERCISE 6.6**   **Making Verbs Agree with Singular Nouns That End in –s, Collective Nouns, and Proper Nouns**

In each of the following sentences, circle the verb that agrees with the subject.

1. Mathematics (is, are) a challenging subject for me.
2. The Academy Awards (is, are) the biggest event in Hollywood.
3. Children (enjoy, enjoys) going to the park.
4. Los Angeles (is, are) home to many movie stars.
5. Sixteen pounds (is, are) her total weight loss.
6. The House of Representatives (meet, meets) many times throughout the year.
7. That group (take, takes) too long for lunch.
8. The editorial staff (make, makes) decisions about book content.
9. Gymnastics (tone, tones) your muscles.
10. The *Times* (arrive, arrives) at six in the morning.

Writing REVIEW   **Writing Sentences with Proper Subject-Verb Agreement**

Write ten sentences of your own using proper subject-verb agreement. For variety, review what you learned in this chapter and use different types of subjects and verbs, making sure that they agree within the sentences.

Fill in the blanks in the following sentences.

1. The subject and verb of a sentence must _____ in number; that is, if the subject is singular, the verb must be in its _____ form, and if the subject is plural, the verb must be in its _____ form.

2. An intervening prepositional phrase often separates the _____ and the _____ of a sentence.

3. The object of a preposition cannot be the _____ of a sentence.

4. In a sentence with _____ word order, the subject comes *after* the verb.

5. Indefinite pronouns, such as *everyone, nothing,* and *each,* must be matched with the _____ form of the verb.

6. Indefinite pronouns such as *both, many,* and *few* must be matched with the _____ form of the verb.

7. Some indefinite pronouns, including *all* and *most,* can be singular or plural, depending on the _____ to which they refer.

8. A compound subject joined by the word *and* needs a _____ verb.

9. A compound subject joined by *or, either/or,* or *neither/nor* needs a verb that matches the subject that is _____ to the verb.

10. Some nouns that end in *–s,* such as *physics, series,* and *sports,* are matched with the _____ form of the verb.

11. Collective noun subjects that act as a unit need a _____ verb.

12. Titles and other proper nouns, such as names of businesses, are considered to be _____.

CHAPTER 6: TEST 1

In each of the following sentences, circle the verb that agrees with the subject.

1. The man with the trained monkeys (entertains, entertain) the crowd.

2. Your friend with the blue eyes (drive, drives) like a maniac!

3. Here (is, are) the beach umbrella you wanted.

4. Neither these markers nor this pen (writes, write) very well.

5. That group (debate, debates) serious issues.

6. My class (go, goes) to lunch at eleven thirty.

7. The President of the United States (make, makes) very important decisions.

8. Everyone at Jim's school (take, takes) Latin.

9. Rose and Richard (travel, travels) all summer.

10. The family (eat, eats) dinner together every night.

11. Do you (has, have) any eggs?

12. Hockey and baseball (is, are) Pat's favorite sports.

13. The Croton Aqua Ducks (is, are) the name of Dan's softball team.

14. The manager or the assistant manager (hires, hire) new employees.

15. Either the congregation or the choir members (sing, sings) the first hymn.

CHAPTER 6: TEST 2

In each of the following sentences, circle the verb that agrees with the subject.

1. Everyone in this department (is, are) trying to increase sales.

2. Most of the weekend (flies, fly) by.

3. All of Barbara's daughters (go, goes) to the elementary school in town.

4. Christine and her brothers (have, has) red hair.

5. Wendy's (offer, offers) chocolate shakes at a discount before noon.

6. (Is, Are) you going to Canada this winter?

7. Here (is, are) the dollar I owe you.

8. How many cats (live, lives) here?

9. Potatoes or applesauce (go, goes) well with pork.

10. Either the piano or the violins (is, are) out of tune.

11. The flags on the roof (flap, flaps) in the breeze.

12. In my bathroom (is, are) two new toothbrushes.

13. The people at the parade (watch, watches) every float go by.

14. This company (needs, need) more employees.

15. Neither the stove burners nor the oven (is, are) working properly.

WRITING ASSIGNMENT

Think of a gathering you participate in on a regular basis. Are you a member of a club or organization? A church group? Or do you often gather with friends for some specific purpose? Write a paragraph to describe what you usually do when you get together with this group. Then, review your writing to make sure that all subjects and verbs agree.

WebWork

For more practice with making subjects and verbs agree, go to the Guide to Grammar and Writing Web site at **http://grammar.ccc.commnet.edu/grammar/sv_agr.htm** and complete the quizzes on subject-verb agreement.

Online Study Center For additional information and practice with subject/verb agreement, go to the Online Study Center that accompanies this book, at **http://www.college.hmco.com/pic/dolphinwriterone.**

7

Pronouns and Pronoun Agreement

▶ Explain the difference between the subjective and objective pronoun case, and list the subjective and objective pronouns.

▶ Choose the correct subjective and objective pronouns for sentences.

▶ Define the three different points of view.

▶ Correct pronoun consistency errors within sentences.

▶ Define the term *antecedent*.

▶ Rewrite sentences to correct unclear pronoun reference.

▶ Choose pronouns that agree with the gender and number of antecedents.

Test Yourself

In each of the following sentences, circle the correct pronoun.

1. Just between you and (I, me), I'm planning to dye my hair red.

2. That breed of dog is famous for (its, their) long, wavy hair.

3. You are smarter than (I, me).

4. In a contest between you and (I, me), you would win.

5. To (who, whom) should I address this speech?

6. We ordered the vegetables because (we, you) have to eat a well-balanced meal.

7. Each of the boys played with (his, their) own bat.

8. Everyone thinks that (he or she is, they are) the smartest person in the room.

9. The women are preparing (her, their) quilt for the auction right now.

10. Someone should speak up and put in (his or her, their) two cents!

In Chapter 2, you learned that a pronoun is a word that is used in the place of a noun. In this chapter, you will learn how to choose the correct pronouns for your sentences.

Pronoun Case

The **case** of a pronoun refers to its function in a sentence. A pronoun that functions as a subject or refers back to the subject is in the **subjective case.** The subjective pronouns are

I	we
he	they
she	who
it	whoever
you	

In the following sentences, the subjective pronouns are functioning as subjects:

You and **I** should have lunch.
We hope to win the lottery.
Who is on the phone?

A subjective pronoun can also follow the word *than* or *as* in a comparison:

You are stronger than **I.** (The word *am* is implied after the word *I*.)

We are as knowledgeable about the subject as **they.** (The word *are* is implied after the word *they*.)

We do not usually speak this way, though, so you will often hear, "You are stronger than *me.*" However, this usage is incorrect in writing.

In the next set of examples, the pronouns are referring to the subject, so they, too, are subjective:

We players are collecting money.
The rest of us—Jim, Jose, and **I**—will gather firewood.

The **objective pronouns** function as direct objects, indirect objects, or objects of prepositions, or they refer back to objects. The objective pronouns are

me	us
him	you
her	them
it	whom, whomever

direct object

I saw **him** in class this morning.

indirect object

The baby gave **me** a big smile.

object of preposition

Give the tickets to **her.**

object of preposition

To **whom** did you send the letter?

refers to direct object

They sent **us** boys to Room 101.

Therefore, if you figure out the part of speech of a pronoun, you can determine whether you should use the subjective or objective case. For example, look at the following sentence. What function does the pronoun in question serve?

Mr. Smith and (I, me) presented the information to the team.

This sentence has a compound subject, and the pronoun is the second half of that subject. Therefore, we must choose the subjective case pronoun, *I*. Now read another example:

For (he, him) and (I, me), this is a dream come true.

In this sentence, the two pronouns are objects of the preposition *for*. Thus, we must use the objective case pronouns, *him* and *me*. Here is one final example:

(We, Us) students want to go home early.

In this sentence, the pronoun refers to the subject *students*, so it must be the subjective *We*. If you pretend the word *students* is not there, you can see that "We want to go home early" is correct.

Of all of these pronouns, *who* and *whom* tend to be two of the most confusing. The difference between these two words will be discussed later, in Chapter 11.

EXERCISE 7.1   **Choosing the Correct Pronoun Case**

In each of the following sentences, circle the correct pronoun.

1. She and (I, me) love to go shopping.

2. Marion and (I, me) are not friends.

3. The relationship between Dan and (I, me) is over.

4. (We, Us) citizens have a right to vote on this issue.

5. (She, Her) and (I, me) will be going to Quebec this summer.

6. The dog bit (me, I).

7. I called (her, she) on the phone.

8. The vacation was relaxing for (she, her) and (I, me).

9. Paula gave (me, I) a five-dollar bill for my birthday.

10. They made (us, we) girls go first.

The **possessive pronouns** indicate possession, or ownership. The possessive pronouns are

my	our
mine	ours
your	your
yours	yours
his	their
her	theirs
hers	
its	

Julie has finished writing **her** paper.
Hernando gave me **his** granola bar, and I gave him **my** pear.

Writing REVIEW **Writing Sentences with Pronouns**

Write ten sentences of your own that include pronouns.

Pronoun Consistency

When you write, you take a certain **point of view,** or perspective. In *first person* point of view, you use the pronouns *I* and *we* because you describe the events from your own perspective. In *second person* point of view, you use the pronoun *you* because you are usually directing the reader to do something. In instructions, for example, you would write "You do this" and "You do that." In *third person* point of view, you use *he, she, they,* and *it,* and you avoid the first and second person pronouns.

If you start out in one point of view, remain consistently within that point of view, and do not shift from one to the other. Notice how the point of view changes in the following sentences:

first person   *second person*

When **I** registered for classes, **you** had to stand in line for hours.

first person   *first person*   *second person*

Although **we** dislike getting sweaty, **we** signed up for P.E. because **you** have to take it.

second person   *first person*

You do not want to pet a dog until **we** find out if it is friendly.

To remain consistent, change the *you* to *I* in the first sentence and the *you* to *we* in the second sentence. In the third sentence, you can change the *you* to *we* or the *we* to *you.*

EXERCISE 7.2   **Revising Inconsistent Pronouns**

In each of the following sentences, cross out the pronoun that is inconsistent, and write the correct pronoun above it.

1. They know about her bad temper, so you do not want to make her mad.

2. We are joining the health club because you have to exercise.

3. If you know that a dog bites, he should not go near it.

4. We like swimming in the ocean, but you really need to be careful of the undertow.

5. Although we do not know how to cook, we signed up for a cooking class so I can learn the basics.

Clear Pronoun Reference

Another pronoun problem is unclear reference. A pronoun always refers to a noun, and this noun is called an **antecedent.** If a pronoun's antecedent is not clear, confusion can result:

Bob told his father that **he** had behaved like a fool.

In this sentence, does the pronoun *he* refer to Bob or to his father? Is Bob criticizing his father's behavior, or is Bob assessing his own actions? Because there are two possible antecedents for the pronoun, the meaning of this sentence is in question. To correct it, you would probably have to rewrite the sentence:

> Bob said to his father, "I behaved like a fool."

Here is another sentence that contains an unclear reference:

> The boy on the bicycle ran into the stop sign, but **it** was barely scratched.

In this sentence, the pronoun *it* could refer to the bicycle or the stop sign. To correct the unclear reference, rewrite the sentence:

> The boy ran into the stop sign, but his bicycle was barely scratched.

Possessive pronouns, too, can be unclear:

> She let her daughter wear **her** dress to the dance.

Does the dress belong to the mother or daughter? The pronoun *her* does not make the meaning clear. Here is one way to correct the problem:

> She wore her mother's dress to the dance.

Be aware, too, of including a pronoun that has no antecedent at all:

> I took my car to be repaired, and **they** said I need a new transmission.

Who is *they* in this sentence? We can infer that this pronoun refers to the mechanics who examined the car, but we cannot be sure. To correct the unclear reference, rewrite the sentence, eliminating the unclear pronoun altogether if necessary:

> I took my car to be repaired, and the mechanics said I need a new transmission.

 **EXERCISE 7.3**   **Eliminating Unclear Pronoun Reference**

Rewrite each of the following sentences to eliminate unclear pronoun reference.

1. Tonya told her neighbor that her grass needs to be mowed.

_____

2. The car hit the wall, but it was dented only slightly.

_____

3. He let his son ride his bicycle.

_____

4. I wanted to get my watch repaired, but they said it could not be fixed.

_____

5. Beth told her daughter that she needed a haircut.

_____

6. He took his son to the library so that he could check out a book.

_____

7. Jim told his brother that his car needed gas.

_____

8. The girl hit the glass with her arm, but it did not break.

_____

9. Jane wanted to make an appointment to see the doctor, but they said there were not any available.

_____

_____

10. I made a motion to the board, but they said that it was not valid.

_____

Writing REVIEW **Writing Sentences with Clear and Consistent Pronouns**

Write ten sentences of your own that include pronouns. When you are done, review your sentences to make sure that all of the pronouns are clear and consistent within individual sentences.

Pronoun Agreement

A pronoun must agree with, or match, the gender and the number of its antecedent. **Gender** refers to whether the antecedent is masculine (he/him/his), feminine (she/her/her), or neutral (it/it/its). In the following sentences, notice how the gender of the pronoun matches the gender of the italicized antecedent:

His _wife_ gave **her** solemn promise.
The _man_ driving the bus said that **he** was tired.
The _horse_ bruised **its** leg when **it** tried to jump the fence.

Number refers to whether the antecedent is singular or plural. If the antecedent is singular, use a singular pronoun, and if the antecedent is plural, use a plural pronoun:

    singular   *singular*

The *teacher* dropped **his** book.

    plural   *plural*

The *women* are packing **their** bags right now.

   singular   *singular*

Her *hair* has lost **its** shine.

Basic pronoun agreement is relatively straightforward. However, you will be writing sentences that will present you with trickier pronoun agreement situations. They are usually tricky because you may not be sure if the antecedent is singular or plural. The remainder of this chapter covers the kinds of sentences that will make choosing the correct pronoun a little more challenging.

Indefinite Pronouns

In Chapter 6, you learned that the indefinite pronouns can make subject-verb agreement more tricky. When an indefinite pronoun is an antecedent, choosing the pronoun that agrees with it is more challenging. However, you can apply what you learned about indefinite pronouns in Chapter 6 to pronoun agreement.

Most of the indefinite pronouns are singular:

one	nobody	nothing	each
anyone	anybody	anything	either
someone	somebody	something	neither
everyone	everybody	everything	

Therefore, you will use a singular pronoun to match an antecedent that is one of the indefinite pronouns in the previous list. When you know the gender of the antecedent, choose the appropriate singular pronoun:

Each of the men flexed **his** muscles.
Neither of the girls knows where **she** stands.

To avoid gender bias when the gender of the indefinite pronoun is either unknown or mixed, writers often use the phrases *he or she* and *his or her*:

Everyone thinks **he or she** would love to win the lottery.
One of the students forgot to write **his or her** name on the paper.

In spoken conversation, you will often hear (and say), "Each of the men flexed *their* muscles" and "Everybody paid *their* dues on time." However, both of these sentences contain pronoun-agreement errors, so we do not write this way. If you think that writing *he or she* or *his or her* is cumbersome, then rewrite the sentence to have a plural subject. Then, you can use *they* or *their* as the pronoun:

All *people* think **they** would love to win the lottery.

The indefinite pronouns that are plural include

both	many
few	several

You use plural pronouns with these subjects:

Both of the ladies wore **their** red boots.
Few remembered what **they** were supposed to be doing.

Finally, remember that some indefinite pronouns can be singular or plural, depending on the noun or pronoun to which they refer. These pronouns are

all	most
any	none
more	some

Most of the *books* are missing **their** covers.
Most of the *soil* had lost **its** ability to support plant life.

 **EXERCISE 7.4**   **Making Pronouns Agree with Indefinite Pronoun Antecedents**

In each of the following sentences, underline the antecedent. Then, circle the pronoun that agrees with that antecedent.

1. Somebody left (his or her, their) umbrella on the bus.

2. Everybody misses (his or her, their) train now and then.

3. Neither of the boys found (his, their) baseball glove.

4. Everybody thinks that (he or she, they) is a great driver.

5. Most of us like to think that (we know, he or she knows) best.

6. Her dog has lost (her, its) collar.

7. She keeps (its, her) day planner on her desk.

8. One of the Marines has lost (his, their) knife.

9. Each of the women got (her, their) work done on Saturday.

10. Everybody in our family pays (his or her, their) taxes on time.

Compound Subjects

As with subject-verb agreement, if the word *and* joins two antecedents, they are plural, and you use the plural form of the pronoun:

> Todd *and* the rest of the class brought in presents for **their** teacher.
> The doctor *and* the nurse looked at **their** watches.

If the antecedents are joined by *or, either/or,* or *neither/nor,* the pronoun agrees with the antecedent that is closest to it:

> *plural antecedent   singular antecedent   singular pronoun*
> *Neither* the **macaws** *nor* the   **parrot**   would stop **its** squawking.

Collective Nouns

Collective nouns are those that refer to a group of people or things (*team, class, crowd, group, company, audience, family, jury, gang, faculty*). If the antecedent is a collective noun and the group is acting together as one unit, then use a singular pronoun:

> The *herd* fixed **its** attention on the busload of tourists.

However, if the members of the group are acting individually, use a plural pronoun:

> The *herd* scattered in different directions to save **their** own skins.

 **EXERCISE 7.5**   **Making Pronouns Agree with Compound Subjects and Collective Nouns**

In each of the following sentences, underline the antecedent. Then, circle the pronoun that agrees with that antecedent.

1. The jury will deliver (its, their) verdict in the morning.

2. Antoinette and the group brought cookies in for (her, their) class.

3. The House of Representatives will unveil (its, their) plan later today.

4. The boy and his little brother do not know (his, their) cousins.

5. The groupies and the one other fan assembled near (her, their) favorite band at the outdoor concert.

6. The town trustees decided to let the townspeople know about (its, their) decision.

7. The school board makes (its, their) decision based on the majority rule.

8. The swim team and soccer team practice at (its, their) own facility.

9. The maintenance committee has a lot on (its, their) plate in terms of repairs to the school.

10. That species is known for (its, their) ferocious roar.

Writing REVIEW **Writing Sentences with Indefinite Pronoun Antecedents, Compound Subjects, and Collective Nouns**

Write ten sentences of your own that include indefinite pronoun antecedents, compound subjects, and collective nouns.

CHAPTER 7 REVIEW

Fill in the blanks in each of the following statements.

1. The _____ of a pronoun refers to its function in a sentence.

2. A pronoun that functions as a subject or refers back to the subject is in the _____ case.

3. The _____ pronouns function as direct objects, indirect objects, or objects of prepositions, or they refer back to objects.

4. If you figure out the _____ of a pronoun, you can determine whether you should use the subjective or objective case.

5. The three different points of view are _____ (I, we), _____ (you), and third person (he, she, they, it).

6 Pronouns are said to be inconsistent when the writer shifts from one _____ _____ to another.

7. The noun to which a pronoun refers is called an _____.

8. If a sentence contains unclear pronoun reference, there is more than one possible _____.

9. The _____ of a pronoun refers to whether it is masculine, feminine, or neutral.

10. The _____ of a pronoun refers to whether it is singular or plural.

11. Pronouns must agree in gender and number with their _____.

12. Indefinite pronouns such as *everyone, nothing,* and *each* must be matched with a _____ pronoun.

13. Indefinite pronouns such as *both, many, few,* and *several* must be matched with a _____ pronoun.

14. Some indefinite pronouns, including *all* and *most,* can be singular or plural, depending on the _____ to which they refer.

15. A compound antecedent joined by the word *and* needs a _____ pronoun.

16. A compound antecedent joined by *or, either/or,* or *neither/nor* needs a pronoun that matches the part of the antecedent that is _____ to the pronoun.

17. Collective noun antecedents that act as a unit need a _____ verb.

CHAPTER 7: TEST 1

In each of the following sentences, circle the correct pronouns.

1. There is a bond developing between (I, me) and (she, her).

2. (She, her) and (I, me) have a special bond.

3. To (who, whom) should I send this e-mail message?

4. (Who, Whom) is coming to dinner?

5. Everyone on the team—Nancy, Anna, and (me, I)—will participate in the fundraiser.

6. (She, Her) and Mary will make the presentation.

7. Can you guess (who, whom) is coming to our party?

8. (We, Us) members are not pleased with this decision.

9. For (her, she) and (I, me), this money is a wonderful thing.

10. The date between John and (I, me) did not go very well.

CHAPTER 7: TEST 2

A. **Rewrite each of the following sentences to correct unclear pronoun reference.**

1. I will not shop there anymore because their prices are too high.

   _____

2. You should not buy that breed of dog until you find out if they are calm.

   _____

3. Barbara told her sister that she had a great personality.

   _____

4. I do not worship there because they are always asking for money.

   _____

5. Andrea removed her daughter from the nursery school because their philosophy was not a good one.

   _____

   _____

B. **In each of the following sentences, correct errors in consistency and agreement by crossing out the incorrect pronoun and writing the correct one above it.**

1. Everyone should bring their own towel.

2. I do not like getting my hair done at the salon, but I went on Saturday because you want to look nice when you go to a wedding.

3. The bride and the groom said his vows.

4. One member of the team should agree to be their spokesperson.

5. The male nurse said that she felt like he was having a heart attack.

6. The students in the class are getting its books right now.

7. Her pocketbook is in their usual place by the door.

8. Neither of the girls understands their French homework.

9. The bus is leaving their space in the depot right now.

10. I go to that supermarket because you want to buy fresh produce.

WRITING **ASSIGNMENT**

Write a paragraph about your classmates in one of your classes, using the variety of pronouns you learned about in this chapter.

For more practice with pronouns, complete these quizzes in the Guide to Grammar and Writing Web site: "Quiz on Pronoun Usage" at **http://grammar.ccc.commnet.edu/ grammar/cgi-shl/quiz.pl/pronoun_quiz.htm**, and "A Second Quiz on Pronoun Forms" at **http://grammar.ccc.commnet.edu/grammar/quizzes/pron2_quiz.htm**.

Online Study Center For additional information and practice with pronouns and pronoun agreement, go to the Online Study Center that accompanies this book, at **http://www.college.hmco.com/pic/dolphinwriterone**.

8

The Compound Sentence

GOALS FOR CHAPTER 8

▶ Identify compound elements in sentences.

▶ Define the term *compound sentence*.

▶ Describe three ways to form compound sentences.

▶ List the seven coordinating conjunctions.

▶ Choose the correct coordinating conjunctions to connect independent clauses.

▶ Write and correctly punctuate compound sentences with coordinating conjunctions.

▶ Choose the correct conjunctive adverbs to connect independent clauses.

▶ Write and correctly punctuate compound sentences with conjunctive adverbs.

▶ Write and correctly punctuate compound sentences with just a semicolon.

▶ Distinguish compound sentences from simple sentences with compound elements.

▶ Define the term *comma splice*.

▶ Identify and correct comma splices in sentences.

▶ Define the term *run-on sentence*.

▶ Identify and correct run-on sentences.

Test Yourself

A. In each of the following sentences, circle the subject(s) and underline the verb(s). Then, add any needed punctuation.

1. Spring is a beautiful time of year, but people with allergies often suffer through it.

2. Some people use eyedrops for allergy relief, but others fear side effects.

3. Some allergy medications cause dry mouth and sleepiness; they produce headaches, too.

4. Most people take allergy medicines; as a result, they can go outdoors without sneezing.

5. Those without allergies are lucky; they should be grateful!

B. Rewrite each of the following sentences so that they are compound sentences free of comma splices and run-ons.

1. Thomas Jefferson is her hero, she admires his accomplishments.

   _____

2. I do not like broccoli, it does not taste good to me.

   _____

3. Do not put that book on the table that is not its place.

   _____

4. Cooking is an enjoyable hobby, I like to do it.

   _____

5. He is not short at all he is actually quite tall.

   _____

In Chapters 3 through 7 of this book, you worked on mastering the simple sentence, an independent clause with only one subject-verb relationship. In Chapters 8 and 9, you will focus on the compound sentence, which has two or more subject-verb relationships. Learning to use compound sentences correctly will help you elevate the complexity and sophistication of your writing.

Compound Elements

In previous chapters, as you learned about the elements of the basic sentence, you encountered various kinds of compound elements. As you recall, *compound* means more than one. Thus, subjects are compound if there are two or more nouns or pronouns performing the action or existing in some state of being:

subject   subject verb

Joe and his **brother** *ride* motorcycles every weekend.

A verb is compound if the subject is performing more than one action:

subject verb   *verb*

   She **dusted** the furniture and **swept** the floor.

Likewise, direct objects, indirect objects, antecedents of pronouns, and other elements can be compound.

   In the next sections, you will see how sentences can be compound, and you will learn to distinguish compound sentences from compound elements in a simple sentence.

EXERCISE 8.1   **Identifying Compound Elements in Sentences**

In each of the following sentences, circle the two words that form a compound element. Then, on the blank, identify the element as *CS* (compound subject) or *CV* (compound verb).

___ **1.** The children screamed and hid under the bed.

___ **2.** My sister and I went to the Jersey Shore.

___ **3.** Dogs and cats do not get along usually.

___ **4.** We skied and snowboarded for two weeks in Aspen.

___ **5.** Mark reads and writes better than most children his age.

___ **6.** Marissa paints and dances very well.

___ **7.** John and Mary Beth are very close.

___ **8.** The dog ran and jumped into the fallen leaves.

___ **9.** My father and brother are very tall.

___ **10.** Music and art are two of my hobbies.

Writing REVIEW   **Writing Sentences Using Compound Elements**

Write ten sentences using compound subjects or compound verbs.

Three Kinds of Compound Sentences

Compound sentences contain at least two different subject-verb relationships:

subject   verb   *subject verb*

The   **piranha**   *bit*   his finger, so   **he**   *threw*   it back into the river.

subject   verb   *subject   verb*

He   *proposed*   to her;   **she**   *said*   yes.

subject   verb   *subject   verb*

She   *dislikes*   rap music; however,   **she**   *went*   to the concert anyway.

A group of words that can stand alone as a complete sentence because it contains a subject and a verb is called an **independent clause.** A compound sentence contains at least two independent clauses.

EXERCISE 8.2   **Identifying Subjects and Verbs in Compound Sentences**

In each of the following compound sentences, circle the subjects and underline the verbs.

1. Rhonda majored in accounting at first, but then she changed her major to business.

2. We went to the movies; they went to the mall.

3. I had my hair done before the wedding; it looked nice.

4. The car sputtered, for it was out of gas.

5. Andrew trimmed the trees in the backyard; some branches had died during the winter.

6. We went to the coffee shop, and we talked for two hours.

7. James traveled to Canada; he brought back lots of souvenirs.

8. Your dog needs an identification tag on her collar, or she will get lost.

9. The plates are in the cupboard, and the silverware is in the drawer.

10. I need a piece of furniture for my glass collection; I like to display it.

Because there are two separate independent clauses, a compound sentence can form two complete sentences that could each stand alone:

The piranha bit his finger. He threw it back into the river.

He proposed to her. She said yes.

She dislikes rap music. However, she went to the concert anyway.

However, the two independent clauses are combined to form one longer compound sentence because there is some relationship between the two of them. In the first previous example, for instance, the first event is the *cause* of the second event, so they are linked together with a coordinating conjunction (*so*) to indicate this relationship. We could separate these two independent clauses and write them as two simple sentences, but linking them together increases the sophistication of the writing. It also prevents readers from having to determine on their own if or how the two clauses are related.

There are three ways to form compound sentences. You can join independent clauses with a comma and a coordinating conjunction, with a semicolon and a conjunctive adverb, or with a semicolon only.

Independent Clauses Joined by a Coordinating Conjunction

The first way to form a compound sentence is to join two independent clauses with a coordinating conjunction. You learned in Chapter 1 that the conjunctions *and, or, for, but, so, nor,* and *yet* link together words, phrases, clauses, and sentences. These words are known as the **coordinating conjunctions** because they join coordinate, or equal, elements. Two coordinate, independent clauses can be joined with these conjunctions:

subject   verb   subject   verb

We *stopped* at the bank, <u>and</u> then **we**   *went*   to the post office.

subject   verb   subject   verb

I   *want*   to have a garden, <u>but</u> **I**   *know*   nothing about plants.

subject   verb   subject   verb

You   *can   spend* your money now, <u>or</u> **you**   *can   save* it for something better.

Each of the coordinating conjunctions indicates a certain type of relationship.

Addition: *and*
Cause or effect: *for, so*
Contrast: *but, yet*
Choice or alternative: *or, nor*

 **EXERCISE 8.3**   **Using Coordinating Conjunctions to Indicate Relationships**

On the blank in each of the following sentences, insert the word *and, or, for, but, so, nor,* or *yet* to indicate the relationship between the two independent clauses.

1. I do not feel very well, ____ I am not going to work.

2. Fred does not drive, ____ he takes the bus to work every day.

3. Rose does not like baseball, ____ she bought a ticket to the baseball game.

4. We went to the gift shop, ____ we also went to the mall.

5. He will not take the medicine, ____ will he follow the doctor's instructions.

6. Either you are with us on this deal, ____ you are against us.

7. I will not be driving to Ohio, ____ I will still make the trip.

8. The rain kept us from the yard work, ____ it was far too wet.

9. I will try my best to get you the job, ____ I cannot promise anything.

10. Would you like paper, ____ would you like plastic?

When you join two independent clauses with a coordinating conjunction, notice that you add a comma *before* (and not after) the conjunction.

    Incorrect: The sun is shining and, the birds are singing.
    Correct: The sun is shining, and the birds are singing.

 **EXERCISE 8.4**   **Writing and Punctuating Compound Sentences with Coordinating Conjunctions**

On the following blanks, write compound sentences that are correctly punctuated.

1. _____ and _____ .

2. _____ so _____ .

3. _____ but _____ .

4. _____ or _____ .

5. _____ for _____ .

6. _____ nor _____ .

7. _____ yet _____ .

Independent Clauses Joined by a Semicolon and Conjunctive Adverb

The second way to join two independent clauses involves adding a semicolon and a conjunctive adverb. Some of the most common **conjunctive adverbs** are

also	moreover
as a result	nevertheless
consequently	next
finally	now
furthermore	on the other hand
hence	otherwise
however	similarly
in addition	soon
indeed	still
in fact	then
instead	therefore
likewise	thus
meanwhile	

He is very intelligent; **in fact,** he graduated at the top of his class.
The temperature dropped below freezing; **as a result,** the pipes burst.
They sold their house; **then,** they bought a motor home.

Like coordinating conjunctions, conjunctive adverbs signal different relationships between the two independent clauses. The adverbs _as a result, consequently, therefore,_ and _thus_ all indicate a cause/effect relationship. The adverbs _however, instead, nevertheless,_ and _on the other hand_ signal contrast. The adverbs _finally, next,_ and _soon_ indicate a time order relationship.

Your choice of a conjunctive adverb matters, for you can change the meaning of a sentence by changing just the conjunctive adverb:

They married young; **later,** they divorced.

In this sentence, the word _then_ indicates only a time relationship between the two clauses. Notice how the meaning changes in the next compound sentence:

They married young; **consequently,** they divorced ten years later.

In this sentence, the word _consequently_ suggests that marrying young was the _cause_ of the breakup.

EXERCISE 8.5   Using Conjunctive Adverbs to Indicate Relationships

On the blank in each of the following sentences, insert one of the conjunctive adverbs in the list on page 122 to indicate the relationship between the two independent clauses.

1. She wants to compete in the Olympic Games; _____ , she is training hard every day.

2. We were not able to attend the seminar; _____ , we knew little about the topic.

3. I know you cannot make it to our next meeting; _____ , you should come to the one in May.

4. In this bad economy, you should not sell your house; _____ , you should not buy a new car.

5. Please come to the party; _____ , it will not be any fun!

6. The church is holding a silent auction to raise money; _____ , the temple will have a casino night fundraiser.

7. We could make a decision now; _____ , there is no harm in waiting.

8. Eating carrots is good for your eye health; _____ , they are packed with beneficial vitamins.

9. Land prices have fallen in the past two years; _____ , a $100,000 piece of property is now worth half!

10. I did not attend the meeting; _____ , I did not know the committee's decision.

When you join independent clauses with a conjunctive adverb, notice that you add a semicolon *before* the conjunctive adverb and a comma *after* it:

Incorrect: The sculpture is strange, nevertheless, I like it.
Correct: The sculpture is strange; **nevertheless,** I like it.

Do not make the mistake of using a comma in place of the semicolon, or you will create an error called a *comma splice*, which will be discussed later in this chapter.

Writing and Punctuating Compound Sentences with Conjunctive Adverbs

Write ten compound sentences, each of which joins two independent clauses with a different conjunctive adverb. Make sure you punctuate each sentence correctly.

Independent Clauses Joined by a Semicolon

The third way to form a compound sentence is to join independent clauses with just a semicolon:

> We have to leave now; it is time for our lunch break.

> He did not want to hurt her feelings; he fibbed about liking her new hairstyle.

Notice than when only a semicolon joins independent clauses, the second clause begins with a lowercase letter.

Before you link two independent clauses, make sure the two ideas they express are closely related. One sentence may show a cause and the other an effect. The two ideas may be contrasting. There could be a time relationship, and so on. Then, consider whether you should provide a conjunctive adverb that more explicitly states the relationship. Your reader may or may not discern the relationship you mean to suggest, so providing an adverb will remove the guesswork:

> He did not want to hurt her feelings; **therefore,** he fibbed about liking her new hairstyle.

With the addition of the conjunctive adverb *therefore,* this sentence now makes the relationship between the two clauses more clear.

Writing REVIEW **Writing and Punctuating Compound Sentences with Semicolons**

Write ten compound sentences that are joined with only a semicolon. Make sure the two independent clauses express ideas that are closely related.

Distinguishing Compound Elements from Compound Sentences

At the beginning of this chapter, you reviewed compound elements such as compound subjects, compound verbs, and compound direct objects. Now that you know how to write compound sentences, you can practice distinguishing them from a basic, or simple, sentence with a compound element. Knowing the difference will ensure that you punctuate your sentences correctly.

Notice the difference between the following sentences:

> *subject   verb*   *verb*
> The   **day**   *started*   out sunny but then *turned* cloudy.

> *subject   verb*   *subject   verb*
> The   **day**   *started*   out sunny, but then the   **sky**   *turned*   cloudy.

Should the first sentence have a comma after the word *sunny* and before the coordinating conjunction *but?* No, it should not; the first sentence is not a compound sentence. It contains a compound verb: the subject is *day,* and the two verbs are *started* and *turned.* Because it does not contain two different subject-verb relationships, we do not add a comma before the conjunction.

 **EXERCISE 8.6**   **Distinguishing and Punctuating Compound Sentences and Compound Elements**

For each of the following sentences, write *CS* on the blank if the sentence is compound. Write *CE* on the blank if the sentence contains a compound element but is not a compound sentence. Then, add missing punctuation as needed.

_____ **1.** Juan studied hard and made a perfect score on the test.

_____ **2.** The supervisor thanked her for her hard work and promoted her.

_____ **3.** Jorge tried but could not get there on time.

_____ **4.** We voted for him and he won.

_____ **5.** He parked illegally and his car was towed.

_____ **6.** She walks but does not jog.

_____ **7.** This might be the place but I'm not sure.

_____ **8.** We either mow the grass or pull weeds every evening.

_____ **9.** The professor lectured and the students took notes.

_____ **10.** Either they are running late or they are lost.

Writing REVIEW	**Writing Sentences with Coordinating Conjunctions and Conjunctive Adverbs**

Write ten sentences using coordinating conjunctions and conjunctive adverbs.

Avoiding Comma Splices and Run-ons in Compound Sentences

Now that you have learned how to write the three different kinds of compound sentences, you can learn to recognize two serious errors—the comma splice and the run-on sentence—that occur when compound sentences are not correctly punctuated.

The Comma Splice

A **comma splice** occurs when a comma is used where a semicolon should be:

> He is holding four aces, he definitely has the winning hand.

> She made the salad, meanwhile, he set the table.

In both of these sentences, only a comma separates the two independent clauses. A comma is appropriate if the clauses are joined with a coordinating conjunction; however, neither of these two includes a conjunction. In the first sentence, the comma must be replaced with a semicolon:

> He is holding four aces; he definitely has the winning hand.

In the second example, which includes the conjunctive adverb *meanwhile,* the first comma must be changed to a semicolon:

> She made the salad; meanwhile, he set the table.

You can also correct a comma splice by replacing the incorrect comma with a period and creating two separate sentences. However, the comma error is usually an indication that the two independent clauses are related, so it is often more appropriate to link them in some type of compound sentence.

EXERCISE 8.7   **Identifying and Correcting Comma Splices**

On the blank before each of the following sentences, write *CS* if the sentence contains a comma splice and *Correct* if it is correct. In those sentences you have labeled *CS,* circle each comma that must be changed to a semicolon.

_____   1. The car will not start, the battery is dead.

_____   2. The beginning scene of the book was interesting, but I lost interest in the story.

_____ **3.** The time for change is now, so you should make a decision.

_____ **4.** The grill is ready, put on the hamburgers.

_____ **5.** _Trading Spaces_ is my favorite show, do you watch it?

_____ **6.** It is beginning to look like snow, get out your shovels!

_____ **7.** I buy my plants around Mother's Day, that is the best time to buy.

_____ **8.** The garbage needs to go out, for it smells in here.

_____ **9.** I need to change the litter box, and you need to bathe the cat.

_____ **10.** The lawnmower needs repair, it is making a weird noise.

The Run-on Sentence

A **run-on sentence,** which is also known as a _fused_ sentence, occurs when there is no punctuation at all between two independent clauses:

> We could go fishing we could go swimming.
> She would love to visit Paris she cannot afford the trip.
> Pizza is his favorite food he eats it often.

These three sentences contain two independent clauses that are run together without any punctuation.

We can correct them in one of three ways. First of all, we could simply add a semicolon between the two independent clauses:

> We could go fishing; we could go swimming.
> She would love to visit Paris; she cannot afford the trip.
> Pizza is his favorite food; he eats it often.

Or we could add a comma and an appropriate coordinating conjunction:

> We could go fishing, **or** we could go swimming.
> She would love to visit Paris, **but** she cannot afford the trip.
> Pizza is his favorite food, **so** he eats it often.

A third way to correct a run-on sentence is to add a semicolon and an appropriate conjunctive adverb followed by a comma:

> We could go fishing; **on the other hand,** we could go swimming.
> She would love to visit Paris; **however,** she cannot afford the trip.
> Pizza is his favorite food; **therefore,** he eats it often.

EXERCISE 8.8   **Identifying and Correcting Run-on Sentences**

For each of the following run-on sentences, write three different corrections on the blanks provided. Make sure you add the necessary punctuation to your corrected sentences.

1. She asked for a raise her boss agreed to pay her more.

_____

_____

_____

2. My house needs a paint job it has not had one in three years.

_____

_____

_____

3. Jim's car broke down he needs to buy a new one.

_____

_____

_____

4. She needs a haircut he needs a shave.

_____

_____

_____

5. Your dog has been digging holes in my garden my tomato plants are all dead.

_____

_____

_____

Fill in the blanks in each of the following statements.

1. The word _____ means more than one.

2. Compound sentences contain at least two different _____ relationships.

3. There are three ways to form compound sentences; you can join independent clauses with a comma and a _____, with a semicolon
   and a _____, or with a _____ only.

4. The words *and, or, for, but, so, nor,* and *yet* are the _____,
   which join coordinate elements in sentences.

5. Each of the coordinating conjunctions indicates a certain type of _____:
   addition, cause or effect, contrast, or choice or alternative.

6. When you join two independent clauses with a coordinating conjunction,
   place the comma _____ the conjunction.

7. Expressions like *as a result, however, similarly,* and *therefore* are called
   _____.

8. Like coordinating conjunctions, conjunctive adverbs signal different
   _____ between two independent clauses.

9. When you join independent clauses with a conjunctive adverb, add a _____
   before the conjunctive adverb and a _____ after it.

10. Independent clauses can be joined with a _____ only.

11. In a basic sentence with a compound element, do not place a _____ before
    the coordinating conjunction as you would in a compound sentence.

12. A _____ occurs when a comma is used where a semicolon should be.

13. A _____ occurs when there is no punctuation at all between two
    independent clauses.

14. You can correct a run-on sentence by adding a _____ between the in-
    dependent clauses, by adding a comma and an appropriate _____
    _____, or by adding a semicolon and an appropriate _____
    followed by a comma.

CHAPTER 8: TEST 1

In each of the following sentences, circle the subject(s) and underline the verb(s). Then, add any needed punctuation.

1. I dislike spiders but I fear snakes even more.

2. They went out to dinner and then danced until dawn.

3. I participated in a review of the latest action movie but the director ignored my advice about the ending.

4. The weather is bad therefore many softball games have been canceled.

5. We went to Palm Springs and played a lot of golf.

6. He went to a community college she attended a four-year university.

7. She dislikes the ballet nevertheless she joined Fran for a performance of *Swan Lake*.

8. The sun's rays are strong so it is very hot outside.

9. The drought is severe therefore our garden is dead.

10. We went to Barbados and then we went to Miami.

CHAPTER 8: TEST 2

On the blank provided for each sentence, write *CS* if the sentence contains a comma splice, *RO* if the sentence is a run-on sentence, or *Correct* if the sentence contains no errors. In those sentences labeled *CS*, circle the incorrect comma. In those sentences labeled *RO*, add the missing punctuation.

_____ 1. That cut looks deep, he may need stitches.

_____ 2. She tried to pay him for the work he wouldn't accept any money.

_____ 3. My cat has fleas they are now in my rug.

_____ 4. She told me that she was coming, she did not arrive at all.

_____ 5. My birthday is in August, can you come to my pool party?

_____ 6. This book is taking a long time to write when will we be done?

_____ 7. I will pick you up at eight, so be ready when I get there.

_____ 8. The bag of equipment is arriving today, we can have our first practice tomorrow.

_____ 9. The meeting is scheduled for Wednesday, you can come early to get a seat.

_____ 10. The bag is heavy we should take some things out to make it lighter.

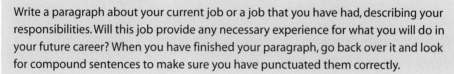

WRITING ASSIGNMENT

Write a paragraph about your current job or a job that you have had, describing your responsibilities. Will this job provide any necessary experience for what you will do in your future career? When you have finished your paragraph, go back over it and look for compound sentences to make sure you have punctuated them correctly.

For more practice with correcting comma splices and run-on sentences, go to the Guide to Grammar and Writing Web site and complete the quizzes at **http://grammar.ccc.commnet.edu/grammar/runons.htm**.

Online Study Center For additional information and practice with compound sentences, go to the Online Study Center that accompanies this book, at **http://www.college.hmco.com/pic/dolphinwriterone**.

9

The Complex Sentence

▶ Define the terms *dependent clause* and *complex sentence*.

▶ Define the term *subordinating conjunction*.

▶ Recognize subordinating conjunctions and dependent clauses in sentences.

▶ Complete complex sentences by adding dependent and independent clauses.

▶ Correctly punctuate dependent clauses in sentences.

▶ Define the term *relative clause*.

▶ Recognize relative clauses in sentences.

▶ Punctuate essential and nonessential relative clauses correctly.

▶ Use the relative pronouns *that, which, who,* and *whom* in sentences correctly.

▶ Correct dependent clause and relative clause sentence fragments.

Test Yourself

In the following sentences, add missing commas, circle inappropriate relative pronouns, and write *Fragment* if the item is a sentence fragment.

1. After she looked up the definition.

2. Mrs. Reynolds who delivers the mail is sick with the flu.

3. The girl who I adore just agreed to go out with me.

4. Even though it was dark.

5. *Gladiator* which is my favorite movie is on cable television tonight.

6. The cat which lives in the house next door scratches at Fran's back door.

7. When I decided to stay.

8. Frank's sister, that he writes often, lives in France.

9. The Browns who live in Pennsylvania visit New York City every year.

10. Unless you have a good reason.

In Chapter 8, you learned about the compound sentence, which links related ideas together to make their relationships clearer to readers. In this chapter, you will learn about increasing the clarity and sophistication of your writing by creating complex sentences, which are combinations of dependent and independent clauses.

Dependent Clauses

As you recall from Chapter 3, an *independent clause* is a group of words that can stand alone as a separate sentence because it contains both a subject and a verb, along with their modifiers and objects. Likewise, a **dependent clause** is a group of words that contains both a subject and a verb and their modifiers and objects. However, a dependent clause cannot stand alone; in order to make sense, it must be attached to an independent clause. Hence a dependent clause *depends* upon an independent clause to complete its meaning. Notice how the following dependent clauses express thoughts that are incomplete:

> Because she did not study
> When you get to the convenience store
> Unless you plan to be home

However, when these dependent clauses are added to independent clauses, their meaning becomes complete and clear:

> *dependent clause*   *independent clause*
> *Because she did not study,* she failed the exam.

> *dependent clause*   *independent clause*
> *When you get to the convenience store,* call me.

independent clause   *dependent clause*

I will lock the door *unless you plan to be home.*

Combining one or more dependent clauses with an independent clause creates a **complex sentence.** A **compound-complex sentence** contains two or more independent clauses and one or more dependent clauses.

Subordinating Conjunctions

When you learned about compound sentences, you saw that their independent clauses are linked together with coordinating conjunctions. These conjunctions indicate that both clauses are *coordinate,* or equal. The clauses in a complex sentence, however, are not equal. One of them is dependent on, or subordinate to, the other. Thus they are linked together with **subordinating conjunctions,** words that indicate this subordinate relationship. By adding one of the following words or phrases to the beginning of a clause, you make it dependent, or subordinate.

after	unless
although	until
as	what
because	whatever
before	when
even if	whenever
even though	where
how	whereas
if	whether
in order that	whichever
since	while
though	whoever

Notice how adding one of these words to an independent clause instantly creates a dependent clause that requires the addition of an independent clause to complete its meaning:

Independent clause:	We lost the game.
Dependent clause:	**After** we lost the game
Dependent clause:	**Even though** we lost the game
Dependent clause:	**When** we lost the game

These subordinating conjunctions not only point out which idea is subordinate but also indicate the relationship (time order, cause or effect, contrast, and so on) between the two ideas.

 **EXERCISE 9.1** **Recognizing Subordinating Conjunctions and Dependent Clauses in Complex Sentences**

In each of the following complex sentences, circle the subordinating conjunction and underline the entire dependent clause.

1. When we get home, I am going to take out the trash.

2. Because I do not have any money, I need to go to the ATM machine.

3. Frank closed the windows because it was raining.

4. Mindy will stay with the kids unless she finds a babysitter.

5. When you are finished with the exam, tell the teacher.

6. Whenever you hear that song, think of me.

7. We should go skiing even though the snow is not deep.

8. We should not have dinner until the other couple arrives.

9. They will have dessert after they eat dinner.

10. If you decide to stay, let me know.

EXERCISE 9.2 **Completing Complex Sentences**

Complete each of the following complex sentences by adding either a dependent clause or an independent clause, as appropriate.

1. If you want to retire rich, _____.

2. I cannot buy the car I really want _____.

3. _____, read this magazine.

4. _____, I am going to go.

5. I think you made the right decision _____.

6. Call your father _____.

7. Whenever you can, _____.

8. Although it is raining, _____.

9. _____ because there is no traffic.

10. Since he decided to go back to college, _____.

Punctuating Dependent Clauses

When a dependent clause that begins with a subordinating conjunction starts a sentence, the dependent clause is followed by a comma:

> *dependent clause*   *independent clause*
> *Because she suffers from allergies,* she cannot have a cat.

> *dependent clause*   *independent clause*
> *Since she came to work here,* the office is more organized.

If the dependent clause *follows* the independent clause, you usually do not need a comma.

> *independent clause*   *dependent clause*
> She cannot have a cat *because she suffers from allergies.*

> *independent clause*   *dependent clause*
> The office is more organized *since she came to work here.*

EXERCISE 9.3   **Punctuating Dependent Clauses**

In each of the following sentences, underline the dependent clause and add a comma to the sentence if one is needed. If no comma is needed, write the word *Correct* beside the sentence.

1. She did not renew her license until it expired.

2. Even though she kept the secret he guessed it anyway.

3. The trees have a lot of buds because it has rained so much this spring.

4. Even though we lost the championship game we got a trophy anyway.

5. Unless you change your mind I will assume that you are not coming.

6. We will wait for you until you arrive.

7. Wherever he goes he takes his lucky coin.

8. They will not play the game if you do not.

9. Let Glenn know when you plan to arrive.

10. It has been a long time since I last called you.

Writing REVIEW   **Writing Sentences with Subordinating Conjunctions and Dependent Clauses**

Write ten sentences of your own that include subordinating conjunctions and dependent clauses. Make sure your sentences are punctuated properly.

Relative Clauses

The **relative clause** is a type of dependent clause that begins with a relative pronoun such as *that, which, who,* or *whom.*

> Children **who walk to school** benefit from the exercise.

> The dish **that fell and broke** was an antique.

This type of clause functions in a sentence as either a noun or an adjective:

noun (direct object)

> He confessed **that he committed the crime.** (The clause is a direct object that answers the question *confessed what?*)

adjective

> The file **that he requested** is missing. (The clause is an adjective that answers the question *which file?*)

adjective

> Her essay, **which she wrote in an hour,** earned a C. (The clause is an adjective that modifies the word *essay.*)

 **EXERCISE 9.4**   **Recognizing Relative Clauses in Sentences**

In each of the following sentences, underline the relative clause.

1. The historic figure whom I admire most is Dr. Martin Luther King Jr.

2. The car, which belonged to Mrs. Sweeney, was damaged in the accident.

3. The soup that I bought was cold.

4. The Goldbergs, who live on Van Wyck Street, have three children.

5. The tree that I just planted is turning yellow.

6. The person whom you should call is the director.

7. The house that has the most Christmas lights is the most beautiful.

8. My brother, who races cars, is fearless.

9. The air conditioner, which broke last week, is too old to fix.

10. The cake that she made fell on the floor.

Punctuating Relative Clauses

You may have noticed by now that some of this chapter's example sentences have included commas around relative clauses and that some have not. Whether a relative clause is separated from the rest of the sentence by commas depends on whether the clause is essential or nonessential. The nonessential relative clause adds information that is not necessary to knowing which person or thing the writer means:

Mr. Rodriguez, *who owns this restaurant,* is very wealthy.

In this sentence, the relative clause *who owns this restaurant* is not essential to knowing who the subject is. Therefore, the clause is not essential; it could be eliminated without any loss of meaning. As a result, it is separated from the rest of the sentence by a comma before and a comma after.

Sometimes, however, a relative clause offers information that is essential to knowing which person or thing the writer means:

The man *who owns this restaurant* is very wealthy.

In this sentence, we do not know which man the writer means without the information in the relative clause. Therefore, the clause is essential, and it is *not* enclosed within commas.

Using *That, Which, Who,* and *Whom* Correctly

Writers often confuse the relative pronouns *that, which, who,* and *whom.* They cannot be used interchangeably, so you will need to learn to distinguish them from one another.

First of all, the relative pronouns *that* and *which* refer to things and animals whereas the relative pronouns *who* and *whom* refer to humans.

Incorrect: A woman **that** inspires me is Oprah Winfrey.

Correct: A woman **who** inspires me is Oprah Winfrey.

Next, you will need to distinguish between *that* and *which*. *That* begins *essential* relative clauses whereas *which* begins nonessential relative clauses.

essential relative clause

The dish **that I love the most** is spaghetti and meatballs.

nonessential relative clause

I eat spaghetti and meatballs, **which is my favorite dish,** at least once a week.

Therefore, relative clauses beginning with *that* will not be enclosed in commas. Relative clauses beginning with *which* offer information that is not essential, so they are set off with commas from the rest of the sentence.

Finally, learn the difference between *who* and *whom*. In Chapter 7, you studied the subjective and objective forms of pronouns. The relative pronoun *who* is the subjective form. Therefore, it is the correct pronoun to use when it is immediately followed by a verb:

verb

The person **who** *eats* the most hotdogs wins the contest.

As you recall from the previous section about punctuating essential and nonessential relative clauses, you will separate any *who* clause that offers nonessential information with commas from the rest of the sentence:

Her cousin, *who arrived yesterday*, plans to stay a week.

The relative pronoun *whom* is the objective form. Therefore, it is the appropriate form to use when it is immediately followed by a noun or a pronoun:

noun

The girl **whom** the *judges* chose cried tears of joy.

Use commas before and after a *whom* clause if the information it offers is not essential:

nonessential relative clause

His wife, **whom he adores,** is his best friend.

EXERCISE 9.5   Using *That, Which, Who,* and *Whom* Correctly in Sentences

In each of the following sentences, circle the correct relative pronoun. Use the punctuation in each sentence for clues about the right choice.

1. The teacher (who, whom) taught us the most was Mrs. Jones.

2. An animal (which, that) scares me is the bat.

3. My best friend, (who, whom) I love like a sister, lives far away.

4. *Terms of Endearment* is the only movie (that, which) makes her cry.

5. *Terms of Endearment,* (that, which) is my favorite movie, makes me cry.

6. The man (who, whom) called says he is our cousin.

7. The message (that, which) I left you is incorrect.

8. The person (who, whom) wins our game of musical chairs gets a prize.

9. The glass (that, which) broke belongs to Mr. Perry.

10. Her fiancé, (who, whom) she plans to marry next year, is an engineer.

EXERCISE 9.6   Punctuating Sentences with Relative Clauses

Add necessary commas to each of the following sentences. Use the relative pronouns in the sentences as clues. If no commas should be added, write the word *Correct* beside the sentence.

1. The class that challenged him the most was Calculus I.

2. *Toy Story* which is a great movie is my son's favorite.

3. The Dickersons who are my next-door neighbors have two cats.

4. The basketball team that is his favorite is the Milwaukee Bucks.

5. His girlfriend was the only one whom he could trust.

6. The sandwich that I ordered was supposed to be chicken salad.

7. My sandwich which was supposed to be chicken salad arrived with turkey.

8. The mail that was supposed to arrive at ten arrived at one.

9. People who exercise regularly are better off than people who do not.

10. My driving test which I took on April 4 was a disaster.

> *Writing* REVIEW   **Writing Sentences with Relative Clauses**
>
> Write ten sentences of your own that include relative clauses. When you are done, review the sentences to make sure they are punctuated properly.

Avoiding Sentence Fragments

You learned at the beginning of this chapter that dependent clauses cannot stand alone. A dependent clause must be attached to an independent clause that completes its meaning. Therefore, if a dependent clause ends with a period, it becomes a type of **sentence fragment**:

Sentence fragment: Although he loves to exercise.
Sentence fragment: That she plans to install herself.

In the next sections, you will learn methods for correcting these fragments.

Correcting Dependent Clause Sentence Fragments

Dependent clause sentence fragments are those that begin with a subordinating conjunction and end, incorrectly, with a period:

Sentence fragment: **Even though** he is eighteen years old.
Sentence fragment: **Because** the hotel does not allow pets.

This type of fragment can be corrected in one of two ways. First of all, you can simply remove the subordinating conjunction, which would make the clause independent:

He is eighteen years old.
The hotel does not allow pets.

The second way to correct a dependent clause fragment is to add the independent clause that completes its meaning. This independent clause is often the sentence that comes immediately before or after the fragment:

Even though he is eighteen years old, he is still relatively immature.

I will have to board my dogs at the kennel *because the hotel does not allow pets.*

Correcting Relative Clause Sentence Fragments

Relative clause sentence fragments are those that begin with a relative pronoun and end, incorrectly, with a period:

Sentence fragment: **Which** I do not understand.
Sentence fragment: **Who** keeps students interested.

This type of fragment can be corrected one of two ways. First of all, you can rewrite the fragment to eliminate the relative pronoun and create an independent clause:

I do not understand the homework assignment.
Mrs. Washington keeps students interested.

Notice that you will usually have to add a subject or an object to those clauses that lack one.

The second way to correct a relative clause fragment is to attach it to the independent clause that completes its meaning. This independent clause is often the sentence that comes immediately before or after the fragment:

I have not done the homework assignment, *which I do not understand.*
Mrs. Washington is a great teacher *who keeps students interested.*

EXERCISE 9.7   **Correcting Sentence Fragments**

On the blanks provided, rewrite each of the following fragments in two different ways so that they are no longer sentence fragments. Add or delete words as necessary to make these fragments complete thoughts.

1. That I found.

   _____

   _____

2. Even though it was expensive.

   _____

   _____

3. Because she had no money.

   _____

   _____

4. Who does not know Roger.

_____

_____

5. Which was funny.

_____

_____

For information about avoiding other types of sentence fragments, see pages 45 and 75.

Fill in the blanks in the following statements.

1. A _____ is a group of words that contains both a subject and a verb and their modifiers and objects but must be attached to an independent clause to make sense.

2. A _____ consists of an independent clause and one or more dependent clauses.

3. _____ are words that indicate the subordinate relationship of a dependent clause.

4. A subordinating conjunction indicates the _____ between the dependent and independent clauses.

5. When a dependent clause that begins with a subordinating conjunction starts a sentence, the dependent clause is followed by a _____.

6. If the dependent clause _____ the independent clause, a comma is usually not necessary.

7. A _____ is a type of dependent clause that begins with a relative pronoun such as *that, which,* or *who.*

8. A _____ relative clause should be separated from the rest of the sentence with commas.

9. An _____ relative clause is not enclosed within commas.

10. The relative pronouns *that* and *which* refer to _____ while the relative pronouns *who* and *whom* refer to _____.

11. The word *that* begins _____ relative clauses while the word *which* begins _____ relative clauses.

12. The relative pronoun *who* is the _____ form, and the relative pronoun *whom* is the _____ form.

13. If a dependent clause or relative clause stands alone and ends with a period, it becomes a type of _____.

14. To correct a dependent clause sentence fragment that begins with a subordinating conjunction, you can remove the _____ or add an _____ that completes the dependent clause's meaning.

15. To correct a relative clause sentence fragment that begins with a relative pronoun, you can rewrite the fragment to eliminate the _____ or add an _____ that completes the fragment's meaning.

CHAPTER 9: TEST 1

A. In each of the following sentences, underline the dependent or relative clause and add missing commas, if necessary.

1. After we arrived the party started.

2. All was not lost even though Frank was worried.

3. When we get tired we will leave.

4. The woman whom they hired has a lot of experience.

5. Here is the belt that goes with the purse.

6. Unless you finish your dinner you are not getting any dessert.

7. Andrea writes the music while Maggie writes the lyrics.

8. Mrs. Anderson who worked in the cafeteria retired last year.

9. The new office building which will be five stories tall will block their view of the lake.

10. If you decide to make dinner let me know what we are having.

B. **In each of the following sentences, circle the correct relative pronoun.**

1. His sister, (who, whom) he misses, lives in Denver.

2. Dad's sister, (who, whom) will drop by later, always brings a cake.

3. Jogging, (which, that) is my favorite form of exercise, gives me a chance to think about my to-do list.

4. The form of exercise (that, which) I like the most is jogging.

5. The dog (that, which) Janis wants to get is called a West Highland terrier.

CHAPTER 9: TEST 2

On the blank next to each item, write *Fragment* if the item is a sentence fragment and *Complete* if the item is a complete sentence.

_____ 1. When she gets to work.

_____ 2. You will know it when you see it.

_____ 3. If you accept his invitation.

_____ 4. If he does not show up, I will be angry.

_____ 5. Who won her heart.

_____ 6. That I finished just in time.

_____ 7. Before the guests arrive.

_____ 8. The picture that she painted won an award.

_____ 9. Although he loves bacon.

_____ 10. He climbed the ladder even though she warned him against doing so.

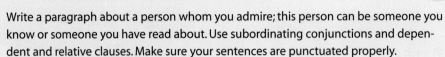

WRITING ASSIGNMENT

Write a paragraph about a person whom you admire; this person can be someone you know or someone you have read about. Use subordinating conjunctions and dependent and relative clauses. Make sure your sentences are punctuated properly.

WebWork

For more practice with complex sentences and correcting sentence fragments, go to the Guide to Grammar and Writing Web site and complete the quiz at **http://grammar.ccc.commnet.edu/grammar/quizzes/fragment_fixing.htm**.

Online Study Center   For additional information and practice with complex sentences, go to the Online Study Center that accompanies this book, at **http://www.college.hmco.com/pic/dolphinwriterone**.

Parallelism

GOALS FOR CHAPTER 10

▶ Define the term *parallelism*.

▶ Recognize and correct parallelism errors in simple, compound, and complex sentences.

Test Yourself

In each of the following sentences, underline the word, phrase, or clause that is preventing parallelism.

1. She is a painter, a sculptor, and draws well.

2. We petted, stroked, and bathing the dog.

3. The performers sing, dance, and do acting in their show.

4. The town members discussed the bill, voted on it, and the decision was to overrule it.

5. Her artwork is vivid, colorful, and has creativity.

6. My hobbies include to hike, reading, and watching television.

7. Jim drives to the train station, takes the train to Grand Central Station, and the subway is avoided.

8. By day, I am a mother; when nighttime arrives, I am a freelance reporter.

9. To dance and singing are two ways to explore your talents.

10. Two things we need to do are go shopping and getting some rest.

When a sentence contains either a pair or a series of elements, those elements must be **parallel.** That is, the elements must be in the same form or have the same structure. Parallelism gives sentences balance, which makes them easier to read and understand. Therefore, as you write, you will need to make sure that words, phrases, and clauses are all parallel.

Parallel Words

A pair or series of words in a sentence should have the same form or be the same part of speech:

Parallel nouns: **Friends, Romans, countrymen,** lend me your ears.
Parallel adjectives: Her singing was **loud, forceful,** and **awful.**
Parallel adverbs: He works **steadily** and **conscientiously.**

Can you find the parallelism error in the following sentence?

She enjoys cooking, dancing, and quilts.

This sentence contains a series of three direct objects. Although all three are nouns, the first two are gerunds, nouns that are formed by adding *–ing* to a verb. The third item in the series is not a gerund, so the sentence contains an error in parallelism. To correct it, we need to change the form of the third item in the series to a gerund:

She enjoys cooking, dancing, and quilting.

If the series takes the form of adverbs, make sure all of its elements are adverbs. If the series takes the form of adjectives, make sure all of its elements are adjectives, and so on. In addition, do not mix single-word elements with phrases:

She enjoys cooking, dancing, and **to quilt.**

In this series of direct objects, the first two are gerunds, but the last item is an infinitive phrase. Because all three elements in the series do not have the same form, the sentence contains a parallelism error.

Parallel Phrases

A pair or series of phrases must be parallel as well.

Parallel prepositional phrases:
She searched **in the closet, under the bed,** and **behind the refrigerator.**

Parallel infinitive phrases:
She is determined **to earn her diploma, to attend college,** and **to make a better life for herself.**

Parallel gerund phrases:
Falling in love, getting married, and **having children** are her current goals.

Can you find the parallelism errors in the following sentence?

To get out of debt, cut up your credit cards, paying cash for your purchases, and patient saving for more expensive items.

This sentence offers a list of things to do to get out of debt, but the three things are presented in three different forms:

cut up your credit cards (verb phrase)
paying cash for your purchases (gerund phrase)
patient saving for more expensive items (noun phrase)

Because of the parallelism errors, this sentence is difficult to comprehend. To correct it, rewrite the sentence so that all three phrases are in the same form:

To get out of debt, **cut** up your credit cards, **pay** cash for your purchases, and patiently **save** for more expensive items. (verb phrases)

To get out of debt, begin **cutting** up your credit cards, **paying** cash for your purchases, and patiently **saving** for more expensive items. (gerund phrases)

To get out of debt, you need **the courage** to cut up your credit cards, **the resolve** to pay cash for your purchases, and **the patience** to save for more expensive items. (noun phrases)

Also, avoid combining a series of phrases with a clause:

The week before the prom, he rented a limo, ordered a corsage, and the restaurant took his reservation.

In what should be a series of three verb phrases, the first two items are verb phrases, but the third item is in the form of an independent clause. To correct the parallelism error, revise the clause to be another verb phrase:

The week before the prom, he **rented** a limo, **ordered** a corsage, and **made** a dinner reservation.

The coordinating conjunctions—especially the words *and, or,* and *but*—will often signal the need for parallel construction of the phrases they join. Also, pay attention to parallelism when you write two words or phrases that are joined with pairs of conjunctions such as *either/or, neither/nor, not only/but also, but/and,* and *not/but:*

The gift was *not* **for her** *but* **for him.**

His responsibility was *not only* **to himself** *but also* **to his daughter.**

 **EXERCISE 10.1**   **Recognizing Parallelism Errors**

In each of the following sentences, underline the word or phrase that is preventing parallelism.

1. Jill is intelligent, creative, and has courage.

2. When I am sick, I like to read, sleep, and watching television.

3. Before we go out, take out the garbage, turn off the lights, and the door is locked.

4. If you want to become a better cook, watch cooking shows, take a cooking class, and interesting ingredients at the grocery store should be bought.

5. Buying a car, getting my master's degree, and to have financial security are three of my goals.

6. We went over the river, through the woods, and the field.

7. She feels great admiration for not only her grandfather and her grandmother.

8. The book was delivered not from Barnes and Noble, Amazon instead.

9. To adopt a healthy lifestyle, eat right, exercise, and sticking to a good sleep pattern.

10. Jim enjoys playing sports, volunteering, and sometimes he travels.

EXERCISE 10.2   **Correcting Parallelism Errors**

On your own paper, rewrite the sentences in Exercise 10.1 to eliminate parallelism errors.

> *Writing* REVIEW   **Writing Sentences That Are Parallel**
>
> Write ten sentences of your own that include parallel structures.

Parallel Clauses

Like words and phrases, clauses must be parallel. In pairs and series, both independent and dependent clauses should have the same structure.

Parallelism and Independent Clauses

When pairs or series of independent clauses express parallel ideas, they must be parallel in structure:

One brother is tall, and the other is short.

Notice how changing the structure of the second independent clause makes the relationship between the two clauses a little harder to understand:

One brother is tall, and "short" best describes the other one.

This sentence is not only more difficult to understand, but its lack of balance also causes it to sound cumbersome and awkward.

Now read two more compound sentences that lack parallelism and try to determine how the structure changes:

He broke up with his girlfriend, and the rejection was struggled with by her.

Does absence make the heart grow fonder, or out of sight out of mind?

In the first example, the first independent clause is in the active voice, and the second one is in the passive voice. Notice how much easier it is to understand this sentence when the second clause is revised to the active voice:

He broke up with his girlfriend, and **she struggled** with his rejection.

In the second example, the second clause is not in the question form of the first clause. To make the clauses parallel, we could write:

Does absence make the heart grow fonder, or **is** a person out of sight out of mind?

The coordinating conjunctions—especially the words *and, or,* and *but*—will often signal the need for parallel construction of the clauses they join. Also, pay attention to parallelism when you write two independent clauses that are joined with pairs of conjunctions such as *either/or, neither/nor,* or *not only/but also.*

Either **we will reach** the summit of the mountain, *or* **we will die** trying.

Not only **can he** prepare gourmet meals, *but* **he** *also* **can** repair a leaky faucet.

> **EXERCISE 10.3**   **Recognizing Parallelism Errors in Compound Sentences**

Identify each of the following compound sentences as parallel (*P*) or not parallel (*NP*). Write your answers on the blanks provided.

_____   **1.** Either she will go to medical school, or writing a novel will be her next pursuit.

___ 2. One brother is talkative, and "quiet" is how we think of the other one.

___ 3. Either we will go to the Dairy Queen, or we will go to Hoffman's Ice Cream Parlor.

___ 4. He ran into a tree, and damage was done to his car.

___ 5. She not only knows French; she knows Arabic.

___ 6. Jake wanted a scooter, so he began saving his money.

___ 7. Either we will watch the entire show, but we might have to go home in the middle of it.

___ 8. One of my sisters is a dancer, and the other is an artist.

___ 9. Are you an only child, or do you have siblings?

___ 10. Either we will stay here, or going to Marie's will be our plan.

EXERCISE 10.4 **Correcting Parallelism Errors in Compound Sentences**

On your own paper, rewrite the sentences you labeled *NP* in Exercise 10.3 to correct their parallelism errors.

Writing REVIEW   **Writing Parallel Compound Sentences**

Write ten parallel compound sentences of your own.

Parallelism and Dependent Clauses

In complex sentences, too, a pair or series of dependent clauses should be parallel in structure:

Parallel relative clauses:
I hope **that** you will come to my party and **that** you will bring me a gift.

Parallel dependent clauses:
When he was born and **where** he lives now are none of our business.

Parallel dependent clauses:
The murder occurred sometime **after** the caterer arrived but **before** he left.

Many errors in parallelism occur when writers unintentionally mix words, phrases, and/or clauses in pairs or series of elements. The following sentence, for example, is not parallel:

dependent clause   independent clause

He told her **that he loved her,** and **she should run away with him.**

In this sentence, the subject (*he*) says two things, so these two things should be expressed with parallel structure. But they are not: one is in the form of a dependent clause, and the other is in the form of an independent clause. To correct this error, we need only delete the comma after *her* and add the word *that* before the independent clause:

He told her **that** he loved her and **that** she should run away with him.

Can you spot the parallelism errors in the following sentences?

She is a talented golfer and who is also good at bowling.

He was angry about the change and that no one had notified him.

Because she lacked experience and displaying a negative attitude, she was not hired for the job.

The first sentence pairs a noun phrase (*a talented golfer*) with a relative clause (*who is also good at bowling*). To correct it, revise so that the sentence contains two noun phrases:

She is a talented **golfer** and a good **bowler.**

The second sentence pairs a prepositional phrase (*about the change*) with a relative clause (*that no one had notified him*). To correct it, revise the sentence so that it contains either two prepositional phrases or two relative clauses:

He was angry **about** the change and **about** the lack of notification. (prepositional phrases)

He was angry **that** the change had been made and **that** no one had notified him.

In the third sentence, a dependent clause (*Because she lacked experience*) is paired with a participial phrase (*displaying a negative attitude*). To correct this sentence, rewrite it to include either two dependent clauses or two participial phrases:

Because she lacked experience and **because** she displayed a negative attitude, she was not hired for the job. (dependent clauses)

Lacking experience and **displaying** a negative attitude, she was not hired for the job. (participial phrases)

In addition, you could also revise this sentence to include a compound object of a preposition:

> Because of her **lack of experience** and **negative attitude,** she was not hired for the job.

EXERCISE 10.5 **Recognizing Parallelism Errors in Dependent Clauses**

Identify each of the following complex sentences as parallel (*P*) or not parallel (*NP*). Write your answers on the blanks provided.

____   **1.** Because it was dark and failing to turn on the lights, I stubbed my toe.

____   **2.** She is an amazing mother and who is also a fantastic cook.

____   **3.** Frank was happy about winning the contest and that he was the only winner.

____   **4.** When Carla was a teenager and believing in true love, she eloped with her boyfriend.

____   **5.** Annie delighted in decorating the dining room and that it was the right color.

____   **6.** Because we have a close relationship and in addition to our living next door to each other, we see each other often.

____   **7.** She told me that she was ready to go and in two hours.

____   **8.** Because you like music, and because I do, too, we should go to the concert together.

____   **9.** After we eat but before we go to bed, we play checkers.

____   **10.** Because of the rain and that there was flooding in the region, our trip was canceled.

EXERCISE 10.6 **Correcting Parallelism Errors Relating to Dependent Clauses**

On your own paper, rewrite the sentences you labeled *NP* in Exercise 10.5 to correct their parallelism errors.

| _Writing_ REVIEW | **Writing Sentences with Parallel Dependent Clauses** |

Write ten sentences that include parallel dependent clauses.

CHAPTER 10 REVIEW

Fill in the blanks in the following statements.

1. When elements in a pair or series are _____, they have the same form or structure.

2. Parallelism gives sentences _____, which makes them easier to read and understand.

3. In sentences, pairs or series of _____, _____, and _____ must be parallel in form or structure.

4. _____, especially the words *and, or,* and *but,* often signal the need for the parallel form of words, phrases, or clauses.

5. When phrases or clauses are joined with _____ such as *either/or* or *not only/but also,* their form will need to be parallel.

CHAPTER 10: TEST 1

Identify each of the following sentences as either *P* for parallel or *NP* for not parallel. Write your answers on the blanks provided.

____ 1. The duties of the job include filing, typing, and the phone has to be answered.

____ 2. Neither Fred nor Amir thinks that the government should be involved in this decision.

____ 3. Frank is loving, kind, and possessing good humor.

____ 4. Marie is tall, thin, and has beauty.

____ 5. Not only did I forget to buy milk, but I also forgot to buy butter.

   —   6. Either we will both come to dinner, or we will both stay home.

   —   7. Wendy went shopping, stopped by my house, and her homework got finished.

   —   8. James is smart, artistic, and courageous.

   —   9. An unhealthy lifestyle includes not exercising, not eating right, and not getting enough sleep.

   —   10. When I am stressed out, I like to take a bath, watch some television, and not doing anything too taxing.

CHAPTER 10: TEST 2

In each of the following sentences, underline the word, phrase, or clause that is preventing parallelism.

1. On horseback, we rode through the river, over the mountain, and the woods.

2. Because of your cynical attitude and making unkind remarks, I do not like to chat with you.

3. She is a gifted musician and who is also good at singing.

4. He was dismayed at my response and that I did not support him.

5. Mary told me that she thought my hair was too long and I should get a nice haircut.

6. The jury found him guilty and that he had broken the law.

7. He insists that they failed to notice when he got there and the time he left.

8. She quit her job because she did not like it and after she won the lottery.

9. Neither the fans and the players knew what to do when the lights suddenly went out.

10. Sonja is a person who loves a challenge and well organized.

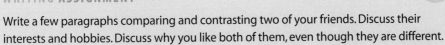

WRITING ASSIGNMENT

Write a few paragraphs comparing and contrasting two of your friends. Discuss their interests and hobbies. Discuss why you like both of them, even though they are different.

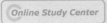

WebWork

For more practice with parallelism, go to the Guide to Grammar and Writing Web site at **http://grammar.ccc.commnet.edu/grammar/parallelism.htm** and complete the two quizzes on parallel structures.

Online Study Center For additional information and practice with parallelism in sentences, go to the Online Study Center that accompanies this book, at **http://www.college.hmco.com/pic/dolphinwriterone**.

Combining Sentences

▶ Combine sentences using compound elements, dependent and relative clauses, appositives, and prepositional and participial phrases.

Test Yourself

On the blank provided, write a sentence that combines the two sentences provided into one grammatically correct sentence.

1. I voted for a candidate. She has good ideas about protecting the environment.

   _____

   _____

2. Patrick ate his sandwich. He drank his juice.

   _____

3. The snow was falling. It was a beautiful day.

   _____

4. That television show is well written. It is my favorite.

   _____

5. Shaquille O'Neal is a center. He plays for the Los Angeles Lakers.

   _____

6. The dog was barking. She was making a lot of noise.

   _____

7. The car was in an accident. It was damaged.

   _____

8. Mario is an excellent cook. He is known for his meatballs.

_____

9. She saw a movie. Her favorite movie theater was showing it.

_____

10. Russell Crowe won an Academy Award. He is a great actor.

_____

To make the necessary connections for your readers, to reduce wordiness, and to increase the overall sophistication of your writing, you will want to vary the length of your sentences. In Chapter 8, which focused on the compound sentence, you learned to join two independent clauses together to more clearly indicate the relationship between the two ideas. In this chapter, you will learn how to combine two sentences. Combining sentences involves not simply linking but also *blending* them together. As you revise and edit your writing, experiment with the six different ways to turn one sentence into an element of another sentence.

Use a Compound Subject or a Compound Verb

One way to combine sentences is to create a compound subject or a compound verb to blend one sentence into another. For example, look at these two sets of short sentences:

Mr. Reynolds drives a Volvo. Mr. McMann drives one, too.

Jennifer made a deposit at the bank. Then she went to the car wash.

The first set of sentences can be combined by using a compound subject to blend the information in the second sentence into the first sentence:

subject   *subject*

Mr. Reynolds and **Mr. McMann** drive Volvos.

Note that the verb in the revised sentence must change to plural to match the compound subject.

The second set of sentences can be combined by using a compound verb to blend the information in the second sentence into the first sentence:

verb   *verb*

Jennifer **made** a deposit at the bank and then **went** to the car wash.

Note, too, that both of these revised sentences are less wordy.

> **EXERCISE 11.1** **Combining Sentences Using Compound Subjects or Compound Verbs**

On the blanks provided, combine each of the following pairs of sentences by using a compound subject or a compound verb.

1. Ken went to work. Jim went, too.

_____

2. Peggy gets up early. Jackie gets up early, too.

_____

3. Mary Lou went skating at Duck Pond. Then she did some ice fishing.

_____

4. Erin picked up her dry cleaning. Afterward, she had lunch.

_____

5. Pat enjoys hockey. Fred enjoys hockey as well.

_____

6. Mary Jo is a consultant for the company. Kellie is a consultant for the company, too.

_____

7. Abbie drove to the Jersey Shore. Then she went to Atlantic City.

_____

8. I went to the gym. Later I picked up my son.

_____

9. Alan installed the bookshelves. He sanded them.

_____

10. The nursery school is on this block. A Chinese restaurant is also on this block.

_____

Use a Dependent Clause

Another way to combine sentences is to turn one of the sentences into a dependent clause. For example, look at these sets of sentences:

She did not study. She failed the exam.

The carpenter had already cut the wood. He realized his mistake.

The first set of sentences can be combined by turning the first independent clause into a dependent clause and attaching it to the second independent clause:

     dependent clause   *independent clause*

Because she did not study, she failed the exam.

The second set of sentences can be combined by turning the second sentence into a dependent clause:

     independent clause   *dependent clause*

The carpenter had already cut the wood **before he realized his mistake.**

In both new sentences, the information in one of the original sentences becomes an adverb clause for the other original sentence. Notice how the relationship between the two original sentences becomes much clearer when they are combined.

The following list contains subordinating conjunctions that can be used to form dependent clauses.

after	unless
although	until
as	what
because	whatever
before	when
even if	whenever
even though	where
how	whereas
if	whether
in order that	whichever
since	while
though	whoever

Remember that when a dependent clause that begins with a subordinating conjunction starts a sentence, the dependent clause is followed by a comma. If the dependent clause *follows* the independent clause, you usually do not need a comma. For more information about dependent clauses, see Chapter 9.

EXERCISE 11.2   **Combining Sentences Using a Dependent Clause**

On the blanks provided, combine each of the following pairs of sentences by turning one of them into a dependent clause.

1. It was raining. We did not go to the outdoor concert.

   _____

2. I asked her about her trip. She told me all about it.

   _____

3. The show had already started. They let us in.

   _____

4. We did not answer the phone. We were eating.

   _____

5. Fred will go to the park. He will go when Julie arrives.

   _____

6. The motorcyclists moved to our building last summer. The neighborhood has become much noisier.

   _____

   _____

7. He searched the living room for the missing keys. She searched the desk drawers.

   _____

   _____

8. Jane had already begun mixing the cake flour. She realized she was out of butter.

   _____

   _____

9. There was a blizzard on Christmas. Rita did not go to her brother's house.

   _____

10. I will keep working here. I will stay until you hire my replacement.

_____

Use a Relative (*Who, Which,* or *That*) Clause

Sentences can also be combined by turning one of them into a relative (adjective) clause. Read the following two sets of sentences:

> Some people exercise regularly. These people are generally healthier.

> The film won an Academy Award. I liked it.

The first set of sentences can be combined by turning the first sentence into a relative clause and blending it into the second sentence:

> *relative clause*

> People **who exercise regularly** are generally healthier.

The second set of sentences can be combined by turning the second sentence into a relative clause:

> *relative clause*

> The film **that I liked** won an Academy Award.

Notice that the relationships are clearer when the sentences are combined.

Remember from Chapter 9 that a nonessential relative clause should be separated from the rest of the sentence with commas. An essential relative clause is *not* enclosed within commas.

 **EXERCISE 11.3**   **Combining Sentences Using a Relative Clause**

On the blanks provided, combine each of the following pairs of sentences by turning one of them into a relative clause.

1. Some cultures eat a high protein diet. These people generally live longer.

_____

2. That artist won an award. He is one of my favorites.

_____

3. The phone rang. We keep it in the kitchen.

_____

4. My green dress is my favorite. It is a designer original.

_____

5. Reynaldo showed up at the store. He was wearing a suit.

_____

6. The book won a Newbery award. Fred liked it.

_____

7. The house on the corner is for sale. It is one hundred years old.

_____

8. The zoo is in the Bronx. The zoo is very popular.

_____

9. People can develop heart disease. They are people under constant, prolonged stress.

_____

10. Mrs. Sanchez is a teacher. She is the teacher we admire most.

_____

Use an Appositive

Sentences can also be combined by turning one of them into an appositive. For example, read the following sentences:

> Renee delivered an interesting speech. She is the valedictorian.
> The coat was a gift from her parents. It was lime green.

The first set of sentences can be combined by turning the second one into an appositive and blending it into the first sentence:

> *appositive*
> Renee, **the valedictorian,** delivered an interesting speech.

The second set of sentences can be combined by turning the first one into an appositive:

appositive

The coat, **a gift from her parents,** was lime green.

EXERCISE 11.4   **Combining Sentences Using an Appositive**

On the blanks provided, combine each of the following pairs of sentences by turning one of them into an appositive.

1. The president of our company gave us raises. He is a very generous man.

_____

2. Lance Armstrong recovered from cancer. He is a great cyclist.

_____

3. Barbara is a soprano. She sang a beautiful song.

_____

4. The shoes are too tight. They are brown leather loafers.

_____

5. Janet prepared a wonderful meal. She is a gourmet chef.

_____

6. The vehicle is bucking and stalling. It is a minivan.

_____

7. The pastry is very flaky. It is an éclair.

_____

8. Mr. Wilson is our teacher. He received an award.

_____

9. The dog ran toward the woods. She is a Labrador retriever.

_____

10. My sister is a sales representative. She got a promotion at work.

_____

Use a Prepositional Phrase

Yet another way to combine sentences is to turn the information in one of them into a prepositional phrase. For example, read these sentences:

> The tree had the kite. The kite was stuck.
>
> She heard her favorite song. The radio was playing it.

The first set of sentences can be combined by turning the first sentence into a prepositional phrase and blending it into the second sentence:

> *prepositional phrase*
>
> The kite was stuck **in the tree.**

The second set of sentences can be combined by turning the second sentence into a prepositional phrase:

> *prepositional phrase*
>
> She heard her favorite song **on the radio.**

EXERCISE 11.5 **Combining Sentences Using a Prepositional Phrase**

On the blanks provided, combine each of the following pairs of sentences by turning one of them into a prepositional phrase.

1. The car was dead. Its location was the driveway.

   _____

2. I saw my favorite movie. The Cineplex was showing it.

   _____

3. He drove to New York City. It was raining.

   _____

4. She washed the dirty dishes. They filled the sink.

   _____

5. Patrick picked up the socks. The floor was where they were.

   _____

6. Maggie drove us to school. We used her car.

   _____

7. Donald burned the hamburgers. They were being grilled when it happened.

   _____

8. I found the batteries. Their location was the cabinet.

_____

9. John picked up the dishwasher. Home Depot is the place where he got it.

_____

10. Tom laid the tile. The foyer was where he put it.

_____

Use a Participial (–*ed* or –*ing*) Phrase

One last way to combine sentences is to turn one of the sentences into a participial phrase. For example, read the following sets of sentences:

He was a fugitive. He was wanted in three states.
She crouched down low. She remained hidden from sight.

The first set of sentences can be combined by turning the second sentence into a participial phrase and blending it with the first sentence:

participial phrase

He was a fugitive **wanted in three states.**

The second set of sentences can be combined by turning the first sentence into a participial phrase:

participial phrase

Crouching down low, she remained hidden from sight.

NOTE: When using this method, beware of creating dangling or misplaced modifiers. (For more information, see Chapter 5.)

 **EXERCISE 11.6**   **Combining Sentences Using a Participial Phrase**

On the blanks provided, combine each of the following pairs of sentences by turning one of them into a participial phrase.

1. They are job applicants. They are hoping to be hired soon.

_____

2. The dog hid in the grass. She waited for squirrels.

_____

3. He was a busy college student. He was taking a full course load.

_____

4. She drove too quickly. She caused an accident.

_____

5. Mary is a great writer. She is wanted for speaking engagements.

_____

6. Hernando tripped on the toy truck. The toy was lying on the step.

_____

7. Rose followed her heart. She rejected the billionaire's marriage proposal.

_____

8. Marlon is a broker. He is making deals in the millions of dollars.

_____

9. Alison is a writer. She is publishing her first novel in the spring.

_____

10. Fred is a race car driver. He is racing at the Indianapolis Speedway in May.

_____

Writing REVIEW   **Combining Sentences**

Find a paragraph that you wrote recently. Rewrite the paragraph, using some of the techniques described in this chapter to combine some of your shorter sentences.

CHAPTER 11 REVIEW

Fill in the blanks in the following statements.

1. Combining sentences involves not simply linking but also _____ them together.

2. There are six different ways to combine sentences; one way is to create a compound _____ or a compound _____.

3. Another way to combine sentences is to turn one of the sentences into a _____ clause that functions as an adverb.

4. Sentences can also be combined by turning one of them into a _____ (adjective) clause.

5. Sentences can be combined by turning one of them into an _____.

6. Yet another way to combine sentences is to turn the information in one of them into a _____ phrase that begins with words like *in, on, at,* or *under.*

7. One last way to combine sentences is to turn one of the sentences into a _____ (*–ed* or *–ing*) phrase.

CHAPTER 11: TEST 1

On the blanks provided, combine each of the following pairs of sentences by using a compound subject, compound verb, dependent clause, or relative clause.

1. George painted the living room. Then he went to Home Depot for more supplies.

   _____

2. The Mulligans went to Virginia on vacation. The Goldbergs went there, too.

   _____

3. I did my homework. Then I called my friend Hua.

   _____

4. Marisa has twins. Her sister has twins, too.

   _____

5. Mary is tired. She works too hard.

_____

6. The lifeguard reached her. She was about to sink beneath the water's surface.

_____

7. Someone else may volunteer. George will serve as club treasurer.

_____

8. A person will win. That person gets $100.

_____

9. That restaurant is always packed. It is the best in town.

_____

10. Dorothy really wanted to see the play. She donated her ticket to the charity auction.

_____

_____

CHAPTER 11: TEST 2

On the blanks provided, combine each of the following pairs of sentences by using an appositive, a prepositional phrase, or a participial phrase.

1. My son is in college. He is a biology major.

_____

2. Halloween is fun. It is a holiday children love.

_____

3. The furnace makes a lot of noise. It is an oil-burning unit.

_____

4. I went to Philadelphia. I took Route 95.

_____

5. Mary bought a rare book. A yard sale was the place where she found it.

_____

6. Alison is going to Florida. A private jet will be her transportation.

   _____

7. I stepped on a nail. Its location was the floor.

   _____

8. Nikki impulsively quit her job. She stormed out of the office.

   _____

9. The sun blinded him. He could not see his target.

   _____

10. Tom was a member of my graduating class. He was voted "Most Likely to Succeed."

   _____

WRITING ASSIGNMENT

Write about a major decision you made in the past. You could write about a choice to move somewhere new, change jobs, marry or divorce, or attend college. What factors did you have to consider as you made your decision? When you revise your paragraph, try to combine some of your shorter sentences by using the techniques discussed in this chapter.

WebWork

For more practice with combining sentences, go to the Guide to Grammar and Writing Web site at **http://grammar.ccc.commnet.edu/grammar/combining_skills.htm** and complete the three quizzes on sentence combining.

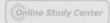 For additional information and practice with combining sentences, go to the Online Study Center that accompanies this book, at **http://www.college.hmco.com/pic/dolphinwriterone**.

12 CHAPTER

Punctuation

GOAL FOR CHAPTER 12

▶ Punctuate sentences correctly.

Test Yourself

In each of the following sentences, insert the necessary punctuation marks.

1. Who are you

2. I want you to sit down pay attention and raise your hand to speak

3. Do not talk to me like that

4. Because I like you so much I will let you borrow this special pen

5. She screamed to the thief Stop or I will call the police

6. The movie which contains a lot of violence is not appropriate for children

7. I went to Charlie's house but I forgot to ask him about the game

8. Do you know the way to San Jose

9. Jack said Please come to my house for lunch

10. How many pieces of jewelry are missing

Correct punctuation is important in sentences. The proper punctuation marks help readers read more easily, and these marks also prevent confusion and misreading. In this chapter, you will learn the rules for the major punctuation

172

marks: periods, question marks, exclamation points, commas, semicolons, colons, apostrophes, and quotation marks.

Periods, Question Marks, and Exclamation Points

Periods, question marks, and exclamation points are all types of end punctuation. That is, they indicate that a sentence has ended.

> I cannot find you.
> Where are you?
> There you are!

A period is the most common way to end a sentence. If a sentence does not ask a question or present something in an exclamatory way—such as the first sentence in the previous group—it ends with a period. The question mark ends a sentence that asks a question, such as *Where are you?* If a sentence is exclamatory in nature, such as the last sentence in the previous example, it ends with an exclamation point. You probably will not use exclamation points as frequently as you use periods and question marks in your writing, but if you want to emphasize the severity or excitement of a certain sentence, an exclamation point is appropriate.

A period is also used to indicate abbreviations, such as those for Doctor (*Dr.*), Registered Nurse (*R.N.*), or Mister (*Mr.*).

 **EXERCISE 12.1**   **Using End Punctuation Marks**

In each of the following sentences, supply the necessary end and abbreviation punctuation marks.

1. Where is Dr Logan

2. Take this man to the hospital

3. Do not forget to close the gate

4. Mr Michaels is my neighbor

5. Help I am drowning

6. Where do you want to go for lunch, Ms James

7. Did you buy a new car yesterday

8. Dee finished her homework

9. Is Jackie an RN or a hospital orderly

10. Do not forget to turn out the lights

Commas

Commas often seem to be tricky punctuation marks. However, there are actually only seven rules for comma usage. Memorize these seven rules; then, each time you wonder whether or not you should insert a comma, ask yourself if the situation is one of those described next.

Commas separate certain elements in sentences. Use commas to

■ Separate elements in a series of three or more words, phrases, or clauses:

I went to the store and bought apples, grapes, melons, and pears.
The dog ran across the street, down the sidewalk, and into the yard.

■ Connect two independent clauses that are joined by a coordinating conjunction (*and, but, for, nor, yet, or, so*):

I went to the store, **but** I forgot to buy fruit.

■ Separate introductory elements, including dependent clauses, from the independent clause:

Going to the store, I ran into an old friend.
Because she has an A average, she does not have to take the final exam.

■ Separate an element—such as an appositive, certain relative clauses, or the name of the person being spoken to—that could be removed from the sentence without changing its meaning:

This book, which is overly long, is difficult to read.
Mrs. Davis, my music teacher, is a brilliant pianist.
I wonder, Bob, if it is wise to proceed without getting approval.

■ Separate two or more coordinate adjectives:

We ate all of the ripe, delicious fruit.

■ Separate elements in direct quotations:

She said, "No."

- Separate phrases that indicate contrast:

  I told her to fetch me a fork, not a spoon.

 **EXERCISE 12.2** **Punctuating with Commas**

In each of the following sentences, add commas as necessary.

1. Because it is late I am going to bed.

2. He decided to buy pens pencils and paper.

3. We were going to leave but Jennie convinced us to stay.

4. This radio station which plays mostly hip-hop is fun to listen to.

5. Frank my plumber fixed the drain.

6. Is it wise to stay Fred?

7. Fred said "Yes it is wise to stay."

8. Jim advised us to run not walk to the sale at Best Buy.

9. Driving down the street Peg ran out of gas.

10. Do you need eggs juice or just milk?

Semicolons

There are only two uses of the semicolon in sentences:

- To link two independent clauses:

  You should go to school; I'm going to go to work.

  Make sure your car suits your lifestyle; otherwise, you will never feel comfortable in the driver's seat.

- To separate the items in a list in which one (or more) of the items contains a comma:

  In attendance at the meeting were Mr. Jones, president; Ms. Anderson, vice president; Mr. Lee, treasurer; and Mrs. Lopez, secretary.

EXERCISE 12.3 **Punctuating with Semicolons**

In each of the following sentences, add semicolons as necessary.

1. Jan stayed home we went without her.

2. We visited several cities on our trip, including Dallas, Texas New Orleans, Louisiana and Biloxi, Mississippi.

3. Most Valuable Player awards were given to Andy, the quarterback Tony, the linebacker and Craig, the wide receiver.

4. Do not forget to mail this letter it is very important.

5. The show starts at nine we do not want to be late.

Apostrophes

Apostrophes have only three uses.

- They form contractions:

  do not = don't
  have not = haven't
  there is = there's
  you are = you're

- They indicate possession:

  Mrs. Johnson's letters
  the girls' smiles
  my brother-in-law's house

- They are used to form plurals of single letters and numerals:

  She earned B's in all of her courses.

  When you are rolling dice, two 1's are called *snake eyes*, and two 6's are called *boxcars*.

EXERCISE 12.4 **Punctuating with Apostrophes**

In each of the following sentences, add apostrophes as necessary.

1. Dont go swimming in that pool.

2. Theres no time like the present.

3. Youre a wonderful person.

4. Marisas children are polite.

5. Penny got all A's in her courses.

6. Jims sister lives in Erie.

7. Shes going to college in the fall.

8. Its an amazing discovery.

9. The judges gave the gymnast 8s and 9s.

10. Were hoping that he wont forget.

Colons

Two of the main uses for colons are listed below.

- They introduce a list:

  Present at the meeting were the following people: the president, the vice president, the treasurer, the secretary, and three committee chairpersons.

- They introduce some direct quotations:

  Every time I would complain, my mother would say: "Count your blessings."

EXERCISE 12.5 **Punctuating with Colons**

In each of the following sentences, add colons as necessary.

1. The following members will attend our meeting Barbara, Christine, Andrea, and Maggie.

2. When you go to the store, pick up these items bread, milk, juice, and cereal.

3. My father always said "Save your money for a rainy day."

4. Do not forget to add these things to your list wash the car, make your bed, and prune the hedges.

5. To succeed, tell yourself "I can do it."

Quotation Marks

Quotation marks have three main uses in sentences. They are used to

- Indicate that you are using someone else's exact words:

  Jack Dugan said, "I do not agree with Mayor Elliott's position on the energy program."

- Indicate the use of a word in an unusual way or to indicate reservation:

  I do not agree with Mayor Elliott's position on the energy "program."

  Used in this way, the quotation marks indicate that the writer thinks that "program" is not the correct way to describe the energy situation.

- Indicate titles of poems, essays, short stories, song titles, and articles:

  The professor asked us to read William Faulkner's story "A Rose for Emily."

EXERCISE 12.6   **Punctuating with Quotation Marks**

In each of the following sentences, add quotation marks as necessary.

1. Barbara Cole said, Make a left at the light and then a right on Brook Street.

2. Have you read the article "The Roots of War"?

3. That is not what I would call "polite" behavior.

4. I did not enjoy reading the essay "Shooting an Elephant."

5. The announcer said, "Ladies and gentlemen, please take your seats."

Writing REVIEW   **Writing Sentences with Correct Punctuation**

Write ten sentences of your own and punctuate them correctly.

Fill in the blanks in the following statements.

1. Periods, question marks, and exclamation points are all types of _____ punctuation.

2. A _____ is the most common way to end a sentence.

3. The _____ ends a sentence that asks a question.

4. If a sentence is exclamatory in nature, it ends with an _____.

5. A period is also used to indicate _____ such as *Dr., R.N.,* and *Mr.*

6. Commas separate elements in a _____ of three or more words, phrases, or clauses.

7. Commas connect two _____ that are joined by a coordinating conjunction.

8. Commas separate _____ elements, including dependent clauses, from the independent clause.

9. Commas separate an element, such as an appositive or certain relative clauses, that could be removed from the sentence without changing its _____.

10. Commas separate two or more coordinate _____.

11. Commas separate elements in direct _____.

12. Commas separate phrases that indicate _____.

13. The two uses of the semicolon are to link two _____ or to separate the items in a _____ in which one (or more) of the items contains a comma.

14. Apostrophes have only three uses: they form _____, they indicate _____, or they are used to form _____ of special kinds of words.

15. Colons have just two main uses: they introduce a ___, or they introduce some _____.

16. Quotation marks have three main uses in sentences: they indicate that you are using someone else's _____; they indicate the use of a word in an _____ way or to indicate reservation; or they indicate _____ of poems, short stories, and articles.

In each of the following sentences, add the necessary punctuation marks. There may be more than one error in each sentence.

1. Please read the poem Stopping by Woods on a Snowy Evening.

2. I asked the person sitting next to me, What time is it?

3. Before you leave I must ask What were you thinking?

4. Francine screamed Get out of there!

5. Howard does not agree with you John,

6. Is Mark an MD or an RN.

7. There are several things you can do to make yourself more efficient buy a PalmPilot get a paper planner or just make lists.

8. Jane went to the service station but she forgot to ask about the air in her tires.

9. Glen reads books about cooking decorating and sports.

10. My teacher Mrs Davis likes to knit.

In each of the following sentences, add the necessary punctuation marks.

1. The rain came down the gutter into the driveway and under the door.

2. What do you think of this new dress

3. What time are we leaving for school Diane

4. I think you should invite these people to the party Jack Jamie Matt and Eileen

5. Did you read the poem The Flea?

6. Manny said Leave your shoes by the door please.

7. Youre in big trouble

8. I havent read the essay A Modest Proposal yet

9. Freda earned Bs in all of her math courses.

10. How much do you think that dog costs

WRITING ASSIGNMENT

Write a paragraph about an interesting discussion, debate, or argument you recently had with someone. Try to include some direct quotations. When you are finished, read over your paragraph and check your punctuation.

For more practice with punctuating sentences, go to the Guide to Grammar and Writing Web site at **http://grammar.ccc.commnet.edu/grammar/quizzes/punct_fillin.htm** and complete the quiz.

Online Study Center For additional information and practice with punctuation, go to the Online Study Center that accompanies this book, at **http://www.college.hmco.com/pic/dolphinwriterone**.

13 Capitalization

▶ Capitalize words in sentences correctly.

Test Yourself

In each of the following sentences, circle every word that should begin with a capital letter.

1. you should join a gym if you want to get in shape.

2. john and will went to cincinnati last week to see a show.

3. the university of miami is located in florida.

4. miami university, however, is located in ohio.

5. my mother has read *the adventures of huckleberry finn,* a novel by mark twain.

6. if you would like to join us on saturday, call me.

7. have you ever been to paris, france?

8. did you go to the martins' party last week?

9. the *challenger* was the space shuttle that exploded.

10. nasa is the government agency that oversees the space program.

It is important to use capital letters properly. To make sure you are capitalizing words correctly, memorize the rules in this chapter.

The Rules of Capitalization

- The first letter of the first word in every sentence is capitalized:

    *A*fter much thought, we settled on a vacation destination.

- Whenever the pronoun *I* is used in a sentence, it is capitalized, regardless of its placement:

    I wanted to go swimming, but *I* cannot swim.

- Proper nouns—those nouns that name specific people, places, and things—are capitalized, as are family relative titles:

    We went to *M*exico with *A*unt *R*ita, *U*ncle *E*d, and *J*immy.

- Proper adjectives—adjectives formed from proper nouns—are also capitalized:

    The *S*audi businessman traveled often for his work.

- Titles that precede names are capitalized, but those that are not followed by names are not capitalized:

    *P*resident Jimmy Carter, the thirty-ninth *p*resident, is a great humanitarian.

 **EXERCISE 13.1**   **Capitalizing Words**

In each of the following sentences, circle every word that should begin with a capital letter.

1. i think that your dog, spike, is vicious.

2. after her husband, president bill clinton, left office, senator hillary clinton began a successful political career.

3. i do not enjoy watching presidential debates.

4. when you eat sushi, it is acceptable to put the whole piece in your mouth.

5. at this time of year, cape cod is quite cold.

6. mary ann, marisa, and alison walk together every day.

7. we enjoy chinese food very much.

8. when frank visited italy, he met several family members.

9. i used to go to california three times a year for business.

10. our congressman often votes against tax cuts.

- Directions that are names of regions are capitalized; compass points (north, south, east, west) are not capitalized:

    The *M*idwest is a lovely part of the country to visit, as is eastern Kentucky.

- Capitalize the days of the week, the months of the year, and holidays:

    On *F*riday, *O*ctober 31, we will celebrate *H*alloween.

- Capitalize the names of countries, nationalities, and specific languages:

    Despite being *B*elgian and speaking *F*rench, Christian speaks fluent *E*nglish.

- Capitalize the major words in the titles of books, articles, or songs:

    The Catcher in the Rye is a wonderful novel.

- Capitalize the names of groups such as Jews, African Americans, and Hispanics:

    The Catholics in my town have two churches.

EXERCISE 13.2   **Capitalizing Words**

In each of the following sentences, circle every word that should begin with a capital letter.

1. morocco is a lovely vacation destination in north africa.
2. saturday, december 10, is liz's birthday.
3. what day of the week does new year's day fall on this year?
4. have you ever been to southwest florida?
5. the northeast is a beautiful part of the united states.
6. have you ever read wally lamb's wonderful novel, *she's come undone*?
7. simon is from the western part of lebanon, but his accent sounds french.
8. key west often gets hit with major hurricanes.
9. do you remember what the date of thanksgiving is this year?
10. jewish people celebrate yom kippur in the fall.

■ Capitalize names of organizations such as the Democratic Party, the National League, or the Association of Teachers:

> The *D*emocratic *P*arty is known for its fundraising efforts.

■ Capitalize the names of buildings and businesses such as Shea Stadium, Mount Sinai Hospital, or Bloomingdale's:

> The *W*aldorf *A*storia is a luxurious hotel.

■ Capitalize names of school courses such as Anatomy I and English 101:

> My *F*reshman *C*omposition course meets on Wednesdays at ten o'clock.

■ Capitalize historical periods, such as the Renaissance and the Ice Age, and the names of major conflicts such as the Civil War:

> *W*orld *W*ar I saw an increase in American casualties.

■ Acronyms—those letters that stand for a longer name—are capitalized:

> The National Rifle Association, or *NRA*, is a strong group in Washington.

EXERCISE 13.3   **Capitalizing Words**

In each of the following sentences, circle every word that should begin with a capital letter and every acronym that should consist of capital letters.

1. i take introduction to biology on thursdays.

2. ralph nader is the head of the green party, which is a political party.

3. the afl-cio is a labor organization.

4. have you ever been to the plaza hotel?

5. the holocaust occurred during world war II.

6. did you take algebra I last year?

7. the revolutionary war was a turbulent time in american history.

8. now is an organization devoted to women's rights.

9. south street seaport in new york is a tourist attraction.

10. dan went to yankee stadium to see the first game of the world series.

Writing REVIEW   **Writing Sentences with Correct Capitalization**

Write ten sentences of your own that include correctly capitalized proper nouns and proper adjectives.

Fill in the blanks in the following statements.

1. The first _____ of the first word in every sentence is capitalized.

2. Whenever the pronoun __ is used in a sentence, it is capitalized, regardless of its placement.

3. _____—those nouns that name specific people, places, and things— are capitalized, as are family relative _____.

4. _____—adjectives formed from proper nouns—are also capitalized.

5. _____ that precede names are capitalized, but those that are not followed by names are not capitalized.

6. Directions that are _____ are capitalized, but compass points (north, south, east, west) are not capitalized.

7. Capitalize the _____ of the week, the _____ of the year, and _____.

8. Capitalize the names of _____, nationalities, and specific _____.

9. Capitalize the major words in the _____ of books, articles, or songs.

10. Capitalize the names of _____ such as Jews, African Americans, and Hispanics.

11. Capitalize names of _____ such as the Democratic Party.

12. Capitalize the names of _____ and businesses.

13. Capitalize the names of _____ such as English 101.

14. _____ and names of major conflicts are capitalized.

15. _____—those letters that stand for a longer name—are capitalized.

In each of the following sentences, circle every word that should begin with a capital letter and every acronym that should consist of capital letters.

1. i do not like commuting to newark, new jersey.

2. *the merry wives of windsor* is one of william shakespeare's funniest comedies.

3. secretary of state rice is very knowledgeable about foreign affairs.

4. arab americans face discrimination on a daily basis.

5. many people enjoy working for big corporations like ibm.

6. would you like to get together on friday since thursday is thanksgiving?

7. armenia is a beautiful country.

8. aunt joan always gives her niece money for her birthday.

9. the empire state building was once the tallest building in the world.

10. the statue of liberty is located in new york harbor.

In each of the following sentences, circle every word that is *incorrectly* capitalized.

1. Ronald Reagan always acted very Presidential.

2. LAX is a very busy Airport in the City of Los Angeles.

3. The Civil War was a bloody War in American History.

4. The Puerto Rican Day Parade was held on a Beautiful Day in October last year.

5. The term *Senator* comes from Ancient Greece.

6. If you go Northeast of here, you will hit Boston.

7. The Hills of North Carolina are beautiful in the Fall.

8. Kathy's favorite Hobby is Antiquing.

9. Uncle Charlie is a retired Captain of the United States Army.

10. Any time you drive South, you will have to go on Route 95.

WRITING ASSIGNMENT

Write about an interesting trip you took. Where did you go? Who went with you? What did you see and do? Make sure to check your final draft for correct capitalization.

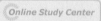

WebWork

For more practice in capitalizing words correctly, go to the Guide to Grammar and Writing Web site at **http://grammar.ccc.commnet.edu/grammar/capitals.htm**, review the information about capitalization, and then check your understanding by taking the quiz.

Online Study Center For additional information and practice with capitalization, go to the Online Study Center that accompanies this book, at **http://www.college.hmco.com/pic/dolphinwriterone**.

14

Spelling

GOALS FOR CHAPTER 14

▶ Identify misspelled words by applying some rules for spelling.

▶ Distinguish between commonly confused words.

Test Yourself

In the following sentences, circle every word that is misspelled.

1. When you go shoping, pick up some potatos and tomatos.

2. Their are some shelfs over there; put the books on them.

3. The babie crys a lot.

4. Sceince is my hardest subject.

5. How many pressents did you recieve?

6. I have some advise for you.

7. We were board by that movie.

8. My grandmother is loosing her site.

9. Wood you like some cake for desert?

10. Pore that milk into the pitcher.

The Importance of Correct Spelling

Before you submit anything you have written to someone else, you will need to check it carefully for spelling errors. Readers tend to judge writing that is marred

189

by misspellings as sloppy, careless, or indicative of a lack of knowledge. In order to avoid these kinds of judgments, make sure you have spelled every word in your paper correctly.

You can check spelling in three main ways:

1. **Look up words in a dictionary.** During the proofreading and editing stage of the writing process, comb your paper carefully for words that might be misspelled. If you have the slightest doubt that a word is correctly spelled, look it up.

2. **Use a computer spell-checker to help you locate misspelled words.** Word-processing programs such as Microsoft Word will identify possible misspellings for you and will even suggest the correct spellings. These programs are not foolproof, but they will help you find more errors so that you can remove them from your paper.

3. **Ask others to proofread your papers.** Ask people you know—relatives, friends, coworkers—who are known to be good spellers to read your draft and circle possible misspellings.

Some Spelling Rules

In addition to using one or more of the three methods for locating spelling errors, you can memorize a few rules that will help you improve your spelling.

Forming Plurals

Most words are made plural by adding an *-s* to the end of the word. For example, add an *-s* to *head* to make the plural *heads,* or add an *-s* to the word *hand* to make the plural *hands.* However, as with many of the rules you have learned so far in this handbook, there are exceptions to the rules. They are listed next:

Nouns that end with -s, -z, -x, -sh, and -ch
To form the plural of a noun that ends in *-s, -z, -x, -sh,* or *-ch,* add *-es:*

pass	pass*es*
buzz	buzz*es*
tax	tax*es*
crash	crash*es*
glitch	glitch*es*

Nouns that end in -o

In most cases, you will also add *-es* to nouns that end in *o:*

potato	potato*es*
tomato	tomato*es*

There are a few exceptions, such as the word *pianos.*

Words ending in -f or -fe

Words ending in *-f* or *-fe* are made plural in one of three ways. For some, you add *-s,* as with other plurals:

belief	belief*s*
chief	chief*s*

For words that end in *-ff* or *-ffe,* you add either *-s* or *-es:*

staff	staff*s*
giraffe	giraff*es*

Some words ending in *-f* or *-fe* are made plural with *-ves:*

shelf	shel*ves*
elf	el*ves*
wolf	wol*ves*
life	li*ves*

Words that are the same whether singular or plural

Some words are the same in both their singular and plural forms:

deer	sheep
elk	fish

 **EXERCISE 14.1**   **Spelling Plural Words**

For each of the following sentences, write on the blank provided the plural form of the highlighted word.

1. We realized that we did not have as many **pass** as we needed. _____

2. The computer that I bought has a lot of **glitch.** _____

3. Raul caught three **fish.** ____

4. At this company, we have a lot of **chief.** _____

5. The **staff** at each company are responsible for a variety of tasks. _____

Adding Suffixes to Words

-y words

Change the final -*y* to *i* and add -*es* to make words ending in -*y* plural or to change verb tense:

supply   supp*lies,* supp*lied*
cry   cr*ies,* cr*ied*
empty   emp*ties,* empt*ied*

-e words

When you add certain suffixes to many words that end in -*e,* you will drop that final -*e* before adding the suffix:

bike   bik*ing*
love   lov*able*
obese   obes*ity*

Doubling a final letter

Double the final letter if (1) it is a consonant, (2) its last two letters are a vowel followed by a consonant, (3) it is a one-syllable word or is accented on the last syllable, or (4) the suffix that you want to add starts with a vowel:

hop   hop*ped*   hop*ping*
rub   rub*bed*   rub*bing*
refer   refer*red*   refer*ring*

-ally and -ly words

A word becomes an adverb when -*ally* or -*ly* is added. If the word ends in -*ic,* add -*ally,* as in *frantically.* Otherwise, add -*ly* to the end of the word, as in *lovely.*

EXERCISE 14.2   **Spelling Words with Suffixes**

Add -*ing* or -*ed,* as appropriate, to the word in parentheses, and write the correct form of the word on the blank in each sentence.

1. We love to go _____. (*hike*)

2. We _____ to the finish line. (*race*)

3. When is the last time you went _____? (*shop*)

4. I _____ the spot to get it out. (*rub*)

5. Joe _____ hard to understand the math problem. (*try*)

Add *-ally* or *-ly* to the word in parentheses, and write the correct form of the word on the blank provided in each sentence.

6. He searched _____ for the lost dog. (*frantic*)

7. That company is _____ sound. (*financial*)

8. John _____ has any hair. (*bare*)

9. The snow _____ covered the sidewalk. (*partial*)

10. Mary solved the problem _____. (*logic*)

-ie and *-ei* Words

Usually, if we say the old rhyme "**I** before **E** except after **C** or when sounding like **A** as in *neighbor* and *weigh*," we can figure out how to spell *-ie* and *-ei* words. Again, there are exceptions to this rule.

> *-ie:* science, conscience, species, sufficient
>
> *-ei:* seize, either, weird, height, foreign, leisure, counterfeit, forfeit, neither, sleight

EXERCISE 14.3   **Spelling *-ie* and *-ei* Words**

In each of the following sentences, circle every word that is misspelled, and write above it the correct spelling. If there are no misspelled words, write *Correct*.

1. Your consceince should be your guide.

2. Do you have a sufficeint number of volunteers?

3. The television program was wierd.

4. Niether Jim nor Jane had an opinion.

5. What do you do with your leisure time?

6. Either we will go or we will stay.

7. When the team did not show up for the game, it had to forfiet.

8. That twenty-dollar bill is a counterfeit.

9. Have you taken any foriegn language courses?

10. The government seized all of the property.

Commonly Confused Words

Here are some commonly confused *homonyms* (words that sound alike), with their definitions. Study these words to learn the differences in their meanings:

accept	to agree to	*close*	to shut	*envelop*	to surround
except	excluding	*clothes*	apparel	*envelope*	cover; packet
adverse	negative	*coarse*	rough	*fair*	balanced
averse	reluctant	*course*	path; unit of study	*fare*	payment for services
advice	counsel				
advise	to give an opinion	*complement*	to balance; to go together	*farther*	beyond (distance)
affect	to influence			*further*	additional
effect	result	*compliment*	admiring comment	*faze*	to put off, disturb
allude	to refer to indirectly			*phase*	stage
elude	to evade	*conscience*	moral/ethical principles	*fiscal*	relating to money
allusion	indirect reference			*physical*	having to do with the body
illusion	false impression	*conscious*	aware		
assure	to state positively	*defuse*	to calm	*for*	in favor of; intended for
ensure	to make certain	*diffuse*	to spread		
insure	to cover or underwrite	*decent*	civilized or well mannered	*fore*	front
				four	a number
bare	naked	*descent*	act of going down	*formally*	officially
bear	large animal; to carry			*formerly*	previously
		dissent	to disagree with	*hear*	to perceive sound
bazaar	festival	*desert*	arid, sandy place	*here*	at this place; presently
bizarre	odd	*dessert*	a sweet served at the end of dinner		
bored	without interest			*hole*	gap
board	flat piece of wood; to climb on			*whole*	all together
		devise	to concoct	*incidence*	occurrence
		device	mechanism	*incident*	event
breath	mouthful of air			*instance*	example
breathe	to take breaths	*disburse*	to pay out		
		disperse	to scatter	*its*	possessive of *it*
by	near	*dual*	twofold	*it's*	contraction of *it is*
buy	to purchase	*duel*	contest between two combatants	*know*	to be aware of something
capitol	building in which a legislature meets				
				no	rejection
capital	assets; seat of government	*dye*	to change color	*liable*	accountable
		die	to expire	*libel*	written slander
cite	to refer to	*elicit*	to draw out	*later*	afterward
site	location	*illicit*	illegal	*latter*	concluding
sight	ability to see				

lead	to show the way; a metallic element	*pore*	small opening; to study	*than*	a conjunction used to indicate an unequal comparison or difference
led	showed the way	*pour*	to dispense		
lightening	lessening a load	*populace*	public		
lightning	electricity related to a storm event	*populous*	densely populated	*then*	subsequently
		pray	to meditate	*their*	belonging to them
lose	to misplace	*prey*	quarry or victim	*there*	in that place
loose	unfastened	*precede*	to come before	*they're*	contraction of *they are*
meat	animal protein	*proceed*	to go ahead		
meet	to convene or get together	*presence*	attendance	*threw*	tossed
		presents	gifts	*through*	during; from beginning to end
miner	someone who works underground in a mine	*principal*	head of a school		
		principle	belief	*to*	in the direction of
minor	of lesser importance	*quiet*	calm; without sound	*too*	also
				two	a number
passed	approved or accepted; gone by	*quite*	to a certain extent	*waist*	the midsection of the body
past	history; what went before	*rain*	precipitation	*waste*	garbage; to use up illogically
		reign	rule		
patience	endurance or fortitude	*rein*	strap to hold a horse	*weak*	without strength
				week	seven days
patients	people under the care of a doctor	*raise*	to lift up	*weather*	climate; to endure
		raze	to tear down	*whether*	a conjunction to indicate alternatives
peace	serenity	*right*	correct		
piece	a segment of something larger	*rite*	ritual	*which*	a pronoun indicating choice
		write	to put pen to paper	*witch*	a woman possessing magical powers
peak	climax; top of mountain	*root*	origin		
peek	to steal a look	*rout*	disorderly retreat; defeat	*who's*	contraction of *who is*
pique	to arouse interest or ire	*route*	direction	*whose*	the possessive form of *who*
personal	private	*road*	street	*wood*	a piece of lumber
personnel	group of employees	*rode*	traveled	*would*	past tense of the verb *will*
		sale	transaction		
plain	without adornment	*sail*	part of a boat	*yore*	of old
		scene	location	*your*	the possessive of *you*
plane	flat surface; aeronautical transportation	*seen*	noticed	*you're*	contraction of *you are*
		stationary	not moving		
		stationery	writing paper and envelopes		

EXERCISE 14.4   **Spelling Commonly Confused Words**

In each of the following sentences, circle the word that fits the context of the sentence.

1. (Your, You're) the best friend I have ever had.

2. Do you (accept, except) the deal?

3. The (rode, road) is not paved.

4. Mrs. Waters is the (principle, principal) of an elementary school.

5. Like him, I, (to, too, two), am hoping for a raise.

6. He (past, passed) the test.

7. I did not (hear, here) the announcement.

8. The library was very (quite, quiet).

9. (Their, There, They're) leaving at noon tomorrow.

10. She ate the (hole, whole) (piece, peace) of cake.

Abbreviations

In some respects, this might be called the era of abbreviations because writers are used to quick e-mails and instant messages with shorthand for common phrases such as "be right back" (brb). No doubt more and more written conversation abbreviations will show up all the time, but in writing paragraphs and essays for college, traditional rules for using abbreviations correctly continue to apply.

What to Abbreviate

Check this list to learn what you do need to abbreviate.

Abbreviate	*Examples*
Titles before and after people's names	Mr., Ms., Mrs., Dr., Jr., Sr., C.P.A., M.D., Ph.D., D.V.M.
Time and date words before and after a number	200 B.C.E., 554 C.E., A.D. 1776, 200 B.C., 5:00 A.M., 12:00 P.M.
Names of organizations, corporations, and countries	UK, USA, FBI, NAACP, NCAA, NSA, UNICEF

What Not to Abbreviate

Do Not Abbreviate	*Examples*
Titles before a person's last name	Professor Aguilar, Reverend Smith, Officer Jones, Sergeant Reyes
Days and months	Friday, Wednesday, August, January
Measurements	three pounds, one inch, six feet
States and countries (except when mailing)	Iowa, California, British Columbia, Canada, Nigeria, New Zealand
Courses	English (not Eng), Chemistry (not Chem)

Numbers

Here are some guidelines for when you need to spell out numbers:

When a number appears at the beginning of a sentence, spell it out:

Eight players showed up for the baseball game.

When a number can be expressed in one or two words, spell it:

eighteen children
two thousand years

Use a hyphen with numbers between twenty-one and ninety-nine:

She turned thirty-two the same day her great-great-grandmother would have turned two hundred.

NOTE: On the other hand, use numerals in your writing in the following situations:

When a number cannot be expressed as one or two words	672 redwoods left
Decimals, percents, fractions	5.2, 36 percent, $\frac{1}{2}$
Game scores	7–4
Precise sums of money used with a dollar sign	$2.19
Route or road number	Route 12, Interstate 95
Dates (days and years)	June 25, 1959
Chapters, pages, volumes	chapter 6, page 482, volume 32
Addresses	12 Beacon Street, 174 Elm Avenue

> *Writing* REVIEW   **Writing Sentences with Correct Spelling**
>
> Write ten sentences of your own that include some of the challenging spelling words discussed in this chapter.

CHAPTER 14 REVIEW

Fill in the blanks in the following statements.

1. You can check spelling in one of three ways: (1) look up words in a _____, (2) use a computer _____ to help you locate misspelled words, and (3) ask others to _____ your papers.

2. Most words are made plural by adding an __ to the end of the word.

3. However, to form the plural of a noun that ends in -s, -z, -x, -sh, or -ch, add ___.

4. To form the plural of a noun that ends in -o, add ___.

5. Words ending in -f or -fe are made plural in one of three ways; for many of them, such as *belief,* you add ___.

6. For words that end in -ff or -ffe (e.g., *staff* and *gaffe*), you add either ___ or ___.

7. Some words ending in -f or -fe, such as *shelf,* are made plural with ____.

8. Some words, such as *sheep* and *fish,* are the same in both their singular and _____ forms.

9. To add a suffix to a word that ends in -y, change the final -y to _ and add ___.

10. When you add certain suffixes to many words that end in -e, you will drop that final __ before adding the suffix.

11. Double the final letter if (1) it is a _____, (2) its last two letters are a _____ followed by a consonant, (3) it is a _____ word or the accent falls on the _____ syllable, or (4) the _____ that you want to add starts with a vowel.

12. To form an adverb, if the word ends in -ic, add ____. Otherwise, add __ to the end of the word.

13. The rule for *ie* and *ei* words is usually "*i* before *e* except after ___ or when sounding like *a* as in *neighbor* and *weigh*."

14. _____ are words that sound alike but are spelled differently and have different meanings.

CHAPTER 14: TEST 1

In each of the following sentences, circle every word that is misspelled, and write above it the correct spelling. If there are no misspelled words, write *Correct.*

1. Do you ride the stationery bike at the gym?

2. Some people refer to mistakes as gaffs.

3. I always refered to the dictionary when I was writing papers.

4. That bunny is always hoping around in my backyard.

5. Weather or not you go is up to you.

6. There going to love this show!

7. I do not want to leave either.

8. That dress looks lovly on you.

9. To what speceis does that animal belong?

10. Your taxes need to be paid by April 15.

CHAPTER 14: TEST 2

In each of the following sentences, circle the word that fits the context of the sentence.

1. Pablo is taller (then, than) Mitchell.

2. You have the (patients, patience) of a saint.

3. That doctor has a lot of (patients, patience) to take care of.

4. Did you see that (lightening, lightning) in the sky last night?

5. Frank was lucky that he (past, passed) that test.

6. Have you (seen, scene) that movie yet?

7. (Who's, Whose) making that noise?

8. Put the computer (there, their, they're).

9. Last (weak, week) I went to Canada on business.

10. This neighborhood is very (quite, quiet).

11. (Right, Rite, Write) the correct answer on the board.

12. Make sure you get a bill of (sail, sale) for your purchase.

13. The jury is ready to announce (its, it's) verdict.

14. We will just have to (weather, whether) this storm.

15. I told my boyfriend that we were (through, threw).

WRITING ASSIGNMENT

Identify one academic area that you would like to focus on in your educational journey. Write a paragraph about why this academic area is important to you. When you are finished, read through your writing and check to make sure all words are spelled correctly.

**Web**Work

For more practice in spelling words correctly, go to the Guide to Grammar and Writing Web site at **http://grammar.ccc.commnet.edu/grammar/spelling.htm**, review the information about spelling, and check your understanding by completing one or more of the quizzes.

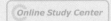*Online Study Center*   For additional information and practice with spelling, go to the Online Study Center that accompanies this book, at **http://www.college.hmco.com/pic/dolphinwriterone**.

Part II Review   Proofreading and Correcting Errors

In Part II, you practiced strengthening your sentences by learning to recognize and correct errors. In this review, you will proofread several passages and correct the errors you find. Cross out the errors, and write corrections above the lines.

Hint: Paragraph 1 includes one subject-verb agreement error, one apostrophe error, two sentences with comma errors, one sentence fragment, and one parallelism error.

1. Hip-hop is a style of popular music with two main elements, rapping and DJing. Rapping, which is also known as MCing, is the rapid, rhythmic delivery of a song's lyrics. Rhyme is a key ingredient of these lyrics. A hip-hop song often contains a long series of rhyming lines. Sometimes all lines in an entire song rhymes with each other. In fact, a songwriters ability to create raps with large sets of rhyming syllables is considered a sign of intelligence sophistication and achievement. The second main element of hip-hop music is the instrumental track, that accompanies the rapper. This track is created by a DJ, or disc jockey, who mixes audio sounds together in a process called DJing. Using a synthesizer, drum machine, turntable, and sampler machine that contains sound clips. The DJ first creates a strong beat and then adding in various other instrumental sounds.

Hint: Paragraph 2 includes one capitalization error, two sentences with comma errors, one run-on sentence, two usage errors, one past participle error, and one past tense verb error.

2. Cinco de Mayo, which is Spanish for the "Fifth of May," is a national celebration in Mexico. It commemorates Mexico's victory over french soldiers who were trying to seize Mexico City on May 5 1862. Emperor Napoleon III had sended his forces to Mexico in hopes of installing one of his relatives as

the country's new ruler. Because of the U.S. Civil War, American President Abraham Lincoln was unable to send ground troops to assist the Mexican government however, he did supply weapons and sent U.S. warships to block the French from entering the Mexican port of Veracruz. During the Battle of Puebla, General Ignacio Zaragoza leaded 4,500 Mexicans in crushing the invasion of 6,500 French soldiers and protecting Mexico's freedom. Today, Mexicans honor there heritage by celebrating this victory. Growing numbers of Mexican immigrants in the United States have contributed to the increasing popularity of this holiday in America. For example, the Cinco de Mayo celebration in Denver Colorado attracts 450,000 to 500,000 participants every year. In fact, Cinco de Mayo celebrations in the United States are often much larger then those in Mexico and include parades, music, piñatas, and a huge feast.

3. Each year, crashes involving 18-wheel tractor-trailer trucks kill approximately 5,000 people and injure more than 100,000. The Insurance Institute for Highway Safety reports that in accidents involving large trucks and other vehicles, 98 percent of the fatalities happen to the people, who are on the passenger vehicles. Huge trucks are necessary for transporting goods across America, however, they also increase the danger to motorists in more smaller, more lighter vehicles. Consequently, many state's are investigating ways to allow big trucks to get the job done while keeping other drivers safe some states are designating truck-only lanes on existing highways. Other states want to go further and create truck lanes that are physically separated with a barrier from lanes with passenger car traffic. If trucks stayed in lanes separated by concrete walls. They would no longer

collide with passenger vehicles. Other states are significantly reducing tolls in night to encourage truckers to drive during off-hours, when most passenger vehicles arent on the roads. Some people, though, want to take more drastic measures. They suggest for example setting specific hours during which trucks can and cant travel.

4. The National Aeronautic and Space Administration (NASA) wants to send astronauts back to the moon and eventually on to the planet Mars. Some people argue that space exploration is to dangerous and should be left to robots. However, there is many good reasons to send humans into space. First of all, sending astronauts to investigate the moon or another planet will help fill in gaps in scientists knowledge about those places. Collecting and bringing back samples of rocks and soil will give scientists more information about the universe and planet Earth, setting up a lunar base with telescopes will allow astronomers to get a better look at the far reaches of outer space. In addition, the space program and space exploration will inevitably produce technological advances that benefit society here on this planet. Because of the space program. Humans now have cell phones, better medical scanners and other equipments, global positioning satellites, and many other innovations that have improve people's lives. A space program can also help foster international cooperation and friendly relations. When nations work together to explore space they have a common goal that soothes tensions and brings them together. Finally, space travel satisfies the human need to explore the unknown. Everyone is born wanting to find out more about their environment, and sending astronauts into space fulfills that desire.

5. Curfews which generally prohibit anyone under eighteen from leaving home between 11:00 P.M. or midnight and 6:00 A.M. are intended to stop juvenile crime and mischief. In reality, though, they are doing more harm than good, they should be eliminated. First of all, curfews do not prevent crime. In fact, several surveys and studies of various American cities indicate that curfews have no affect on crime rates. Perhaps this is true because most juvenile crimes are not committed in the middle of the night the majority of youth crimes happen right after school, between 3:00 and 6:00 P.M. Not only are curfew laws ineffective, but they also create or exacerbate tension between teens and law enforcement agencies. These laws communicate to young people that adults believe them to be immature and untrustworthy, and some teenager rebel by engaging in mischief. In Detroit and New Orleans, for example, youth crime actually increased after curfews are instituted. Even worse, though, most curfew laws discriminate against minors. Juvenile crimes are committed by a tiny percentage of the teenage population. However, curfew laws restrict the movements of the innocent majority, preventing them from doing things like going for an early morning jog, being on time for a 6:00 A.M. sports practice, or participate in extracurricular activities that extend past 11:00 P.M. Consequently, judges from Washington, D.C., to Florida has been striking down these laws as unconstitutional.

Prewriting

▶ List the five steps of the writing process, and describe the major task of each one.

▶ Use freewriting, brainstorming, and clustering to generate ideas.

▶ Define the term *main idea,* and list the two components of a main idea.

The Writing Process

In Chapter 1 of this book, you learned that writing is complex because it requires a variety of different mental skills. Fortunately, though, these different kinds of thinking tasks do not have to occur at the same time. Instead, you can separate them into different steps or stages of a larger process. As a matter of fact, writing can be viewed as a series of five main steps, each of which focuses on a particular kind of thinking:

Step 1: Prewriting. Discover your topic and generate ideas about it.

Step 2: Organizing and Outlining. Use logic to determine the order in which you should present ideas, and create a plan for your paper.

Step 3: Writing. Using your outline as a guide, write the sentences and paragraphs that clearly state and develop your ideas.

Step 4: Revising. Reevaluate your paper's organization and development of ideas, and make the necessary improvements.

Step 5: Editing and Preparing the Final Draft. Correct grammatical and spelling errors, and generate a final copy that is ready to submit.

To make the writing process easier, faster, and more rewarding, always complete all of the five steps, and complete each one of them separately. As you work, return to previous steps as necessary. For example, if you realize during the revision step that you have not fully developed one of your points, return to the prewriting step to generate more ideas. If during the revision step you think of another great point that you left out, go back to the organization step to decide where to insert it. Then, go back to the writing step to compose the additional paragraphs.

The remainder of this chapter will focus on prewriting, the first step in the writing process. Then, Chapter 16 will cover organizing and outlining. Chapter 17 will show you how to make the paper's composition go more smoothly. Chapter 18 will focus on revising, and Chapter 19 will discuss the procedures to follow to edit and prepare the final draft.

Prewriting

In Chapter 1 of this book, you were reminded that everyone has important ideas, thoughts, feelings, and beliefs about the world we live in. In other words, everyone has something significant to say. You may not agree, of course, if you tend to experience "writer's block," the state of being unable to think of ideas whenever you sit down to write. It is indeed frustrating to be faced with a blank sheet of paper or a blank computer screen and be unable to think of anything to say. However, you can use techniques that will help you get started to begin coaxing those ideas out from where they are hiding. These techniques are known as **prewriting,** and this chapter will introduce you to three of them.

First, though, consider all of the benefits of prewriting. Prewriting is an important tool for writers because it has four uses:

1. **Prewriting can help you find a topic to write about.** On those occasions when your instructor allows you to write a paper about a topic of your own choice, prewriting can help you think of one.

2. **Prewriting can help you narrow a topic or find some interesting aspect of it.** A topic like "my goals for the future" or "my family" is much too big to cover in a paragraph or short paper. Prewriting helps you find one specific aspect of the broader topic. For example, prewriting might help you limit your topic to "my educational goals" or "my family's dinnertime rituals."

3. **Prewriting can help you remember or discover what you already know about a topic.** Not only can you prewrite to discover a topic, but you can also

prewrite to find out what you know about a topic. Prewriting can help you unlock this information from where it is stored in your mind.

4. **Prewriting can help you decide what you want to say about your topic.** Once you have decided on a specific topic and explored what you know about it, you can use prewriting techniques to help you find the idea or opinion you want to express about it. You can also use prewriting as a tool to help you begin to sort through your thoughts about the topic so that you can decide what you want to include in your paper.

As you can see, prewriting is a valuable step in the writing process. It breaks through writer's block, getting the ideas flowing and helping you find a starting point. As a result, it reduces the anxiety and frustration that you might have felt in the past as you began writing.

The next section of this chapter covers three effective prewriting techniques you can use to help yourself get started.

Freewriting

One very effective prewriting technique is **freewriting.** The goal of freewriting is to generate ideas by recording, as quickly as you can, the flow of thoughts going through your mind. Thus, you simply consider the topic and write down what you are thinking about that topic. At this stage, though, you do not censor or reject any thoughts, nor do you try to organize them. You do not bother to cross out or correct anything—that comes later. You also do not pause to think about where to place a comma or to determine exactly the right word. In fact, you do not pause at all; instead, you write nonstop, and if you run out of ideas, you continue writing something like "my mind is blank my mind is blank my mind is blank . . . " until another thought comes to mind. Then, you record that thought. Do not worry about neatness because freewriting is for your eyes only; it is a tool to get some ideas flowing, and readers do not see it.

When one student considered the topic "stress," she generated the following freewriting:

Stress

Stress is one topic I know a lot about. I've had enough of it. Theres stress at work trying to keep up with everything and deal with all of the personallity conflicts and stress at school so many asignments to do and tests make me nervous. I study all the time. I don't have any free time anymore. Financial stress too. Which has been the hardest to cope with. I never seem to have enough money for everything, I run *out of money a few days before I get my paycheck every two weeks. I worry about where I'll get the money to pay for next simester's tuition. So I try to work more hours at the grocery store and it's stressful dealing with difficult customers who are grouchy or difficult to please.*

You probably noticed as you read this freewriting that it contains errors like misspellings and missing punctuation. But that is fine because the point of freewriting is to explore thoughts without worrying about the mechanics of writing. By completing this freewriting about stress, this student touched on several different causes of her stress, and she is well on her way to writing a good paragraph about the topic.

Freewriting is also useful for finding a topic to write about and for narrowing a topic. If you are in search of a topic to write about, you can freewrite about "things that anger me" or "topics that interest me." Then, after you have generated several topic possibilities, pick one or two of the most promising and freewrite about each of them. Similarly, if you need to narrow a broad topic, freewrite about different aspects of it in order to find a more focused one that interests you. The student who generated the freewriting about stress, for example, may want to select one particular type of stress, such as financial stress, and freewrite again about that more specific topic.

When you freewrite, you may want to time yourself. For example, set a timer for ten minutes, and do not stop writing until the timer goes off. Doing so will encourage you to write longer than you might ordinarily write, helping you generate more ideas.

> ⭐ **EXERCISE 15.1**   **Using Freewriting to Generate Ideas**

Choose one of the topics from the following list and freewrite about that topic for at least ten minutes.

This weekend	A happy day
My hobby	Things that annoy me

EXERCISE 15.2   **Using a Photograph to Generate Ideas**

Look at the following photograph and use it to stimulate ideas for a five- to ten-minute freewriting.

© Getty Images

Brainstorming

Whereas freewriting involves recording ideas in the form of sentences, **brainstorming** involves writing down just the words and phrases that spring to mind when you think about a subject. You can write these words and phrases in rows and columns, or you can just write them all over the page. For example, one student was asked to brainstorm about the topic "college." His list follows:

financial
aid   learning   studying

                                   classes

major   professors
           COLLEGE

tuition   grades
                         tests

          degree

labs   classmates   lectures

Like freewriting, brainstorming is most effective when you decide to spend a certain minimum amount of time—such as ten minutes—generating all the ideas you can. Do not pause to evaluate the worth of an idea, and do not censor any ideas. Later, you will go back and reconsider the value of each idea, but while you brainstorm, you simply write them all down. Just focus on the topic and record everything that pops into your head as quickly as possible. Brainstorming is a tool for only you, the writer. Do not worry about spelling, organization, or neat penmanship, for no one else needs to see it.

Brainstorming can be useful for finding a subject to write about. For example, you could write down "things that make me angry" in the middle of a piece of paper and then fill up the page with your pet peeves. In addition, brainstorming is an effective tool for narrowing a subject. Write down your broad subject, and then record all of the specific aspects that occur to you. If you already have a topic, you can use brainstorming to generate ideas about it. For instance, you might write down "Reasons why students choose community colleges over universities" and then fill up the page with all of the reasons you can think of.

EXERCISE 15.3   **Using Brainstorming to Generate Ideas**

Select one of the following topics and brainstorm for at least ten minutes about that topic.

My goals   A popular celebrity
Fashion   A serious illness

Clustering

Clustering is like brainstorming in that you write down words or phrases that occur to you when you think about a topic. However, when you cluster, you loosely group ideas as chains of thought, recording them on the page in the order that they occur to you. Clustering is based on the idea that one thought leads to another. Therefore, if you were to create a cluster of ideas about the beach, you might begin by jotting down one particular train of thought:

BEACH
\ ocean
\ waves
\ swimming
\ body surfing

Then, you would add other thought chains:

kids playing in sand

seaweed   joggers

picking up shells   lifeguard

strolling   people

BEACH

sunshine ocean

tanning   waves

suntan lotion   swimming

sunscreen   body surfing

You exhaust one train of thought before beginning another one, continuing to add new clusters branching out from the main topic until you cannot think of any more ideas.

Clustering can be especially useful for generating descriptive details about a subject. You can guide yourself toward coming up with information related to each of the five different senses by focusing each train of thought on a particular kind of detail:

You would complete this cluster by creating a thought chain for each of the five senses.

 EXERCISE 15.4   **Using Clustering to Generate Ideas**

Select one of the following topics and create a cluster of ideas that contains at least six different branches.

My best friend   A childhood memory
One of my pets   My favorite vacation spot

WRITING FOR SUCCESS

Talking to Generate Ideas

In this chapter, you learned about three prewriting methods: freewriting, brainstorming, and clustering. All three are written methods of prewriting. However, you might also want to try a nonwritten form of idea generation: talking to others about your topic. As you prepare to sit down and write, it can be very helpful to discuss your ideas with fellow students, friends, or family members. Therefore, choose someone and start a conversation by saying, "What do you think about _____?" (Fill in the blank with your topic.)

When you talk about a topic with someone else, you may not only learn more about it but also discover what you think about it, and your thoughts will become clearer. If your thoughts are clearer, it will be easier for you to find the right words to express them when you begin to write.

Topic to Main Idea

At the beginning of this chapter, you learned that one use for prewriting is discovering what you want to say about a topic. After you decide on a topic and explore your ideas about that topic, the next step in the process is determining your **main idea,** the point that you want to make. In order to write a coherent paragraph or essay, you must begin with a very clear understanding of this main idea, so it is important to spend some time working on it until it expresses exactly what you want to communicate.

A main idea has two essential components. It includes, first of all, your topic. Usually your main idea statement will begin with this topic. Then, the main idea statement goes on to state the point you want to make about the topic. Here, for example, are some different main idea statements:

topic	*point*
Exercising	is essential to good health.
topic	*point*
A study group	can be an effective learning tool.
topic	*point*
New York City	is an enjoyable vacation destination.

Remember that a topic alone cannot be a main idea. The main idea includes both the topic and what you want to say about that topic:

Topic: Reality TV shows
Main Idea: Reality TV shows are becoming more mean-spirited.

Topic: Athletes' salaries
Main Idea: Athletes deserve their multimillion-dollar salaries.

Topic: Listening to music
Main Idea: Listening to music can help you relax and unwind.

EXERCISE 15.5 **Recognizing the Two Components of a Main Idea**

In each of the following main idea statements, circle the topic and underline the point.

1. Swimming is one of the best forms of exercise.

2. Many of today's popular video games are very violent.

3. The U.S. government should increase funding for AIDS research.

4. Sticking to a budget helps you meet your financial goals.

5. A high-speed Internet connection is better than a dial-up connection.

EXERCISE 15.6 **Writing Main Idea Statements**

Complete each of the following main idea statements by adding a point about each topic.

1. Friendship _____.

2. The Internet _____.

3. Dating _____.

4. Today's parents _____.

5. High school _____.

Prewriting to Main Idea: A Student Demonstration

For a demonstration of the writing process, you will follow the process that a student named John went through in order to write a paragraph for his English class. In this chapter, you will see how John began with prewriting, generated ideas, and decided on his main idea. Then, in Chapters 16 through 19, you will follow his progress as he completes each of the other four steps.

John's instructor assigned the class the task of writing a paragraph about the topic "Things I Cannot Live Without." Therefore, John decided to brainstorm about the topic first. He came up with the following ideas:

shelter

my car

food

freedom   THINGS I CANNOT
            LIVE WITHOUT   pets

computer

clothes   my cell phone

John looked over his brainstorming and decided that he was most interested in writing about his cell phone. However, he needed more ideas, so he decided to prewrite again, this time using freewriting to generate more ideas:

I don't know what people use to do before their were cell phones. Cell phones are nesessary. I mean, I use mine to keep in touch with my friends and make plans to get together. They keep your family members from worrying about you as much because they know they can call to check on you any time. There good to have in case of emergencys. They give you something to do while your stuck somewhere waiting, you can call someone to pass the time. Mine has a few video games on it. I can change the settings, too, so I can have different ring tones, and I can turn off the ringer. People that don't cut off their cell phones in places like libraries and movie theaters are rude. You have to think of others. I think they help you build relationships because they make it easier to stay in communication with people. They save time and money, and they make it easier to get help when your car breaks down.

Based on this freewriting, John realized that his cell phone is essential for several reasons. He wrote down this main idea:

My cell phone is one thing I cannot live without.

Then, he realized that he could write a more specific main idea statement:

My cell phone serves several necessary purposes in my life.

In Chapter 16, you will see how John organized and outlined his ideas for his paragraph.

⭐ **EXERCISE 15.7**   **Prewriting for a Paragraph**

In this chapter, you will begin writing a paragraph that you will work on in stages as you study the chapters on the writing process. To get started, choose a topic that seems interesting to you from the following list:

Someone I admire   An important decision
Something that is not fair   A day when I was very angry

Next, use at least two different prewriting methods to generate ideas about this topic. Finally, write a main idea statement that would be suitable for a paragraph.

As part of your work for Chapters 16 through 19, you will organize your ideas, write the paragraph, revise it, and then edit and prepare it for submission to your instructor.

Fill in the blanks in the following statements.

1. The five main steps of the writing process are _____, _____
   _____, _____, _____, and _____.

2. Techniques that help you discover ideas for writing are known as _____.

3. Prewriting helps writers find a _____ to write about, find a _____ or interesting aspect of a topic, discover _____ they already know, and
   decide what they want to say about a topic.

4. _____ involves recording, in sentence form, the flow of thoughts going
   through your mind.

5. _____ involves writing down words and phrases that spring to mind
   when you think about a subject.

6. _____ involves writing down words or phrases that are grouped together
   as trains of thought.

7. A _____ statement includes two components: a topic and the _____
   the writer wants to make about that topic.

WebWork

Go to the Guide to Grammar and Writing Web site at **http://grammar.ccc.commnet
.edu/grammar/composition/brainstorm_freewrite.htm** and read the information
about freewriting. Read the student freewriting and answer the questions that follow it.
Then, practice freewriting by reading the instructions to obtain the blank-text area.

Online Study Center   For additional information and practice with prewriting, go to the
Online Study Center that accompanies this book, at **http://www
.college.hmco.com/pic/dolphinwriterone**.

16 Organizing and Outlining

▶ Follow a three-step process to group and order relevant ideas.

▶ Complete informal outlines.

▶ Create an informal outline.

In Chapter 15, you learned how to use prewriting to generate ideas. The next step of the writing process is to organize those ideas and prepare an outline to follow as you write.

Organizing

When you prewrite, you want to free your creative mind to let the ideas flow without your worrying about the order they are in. Before you write, though, you must bring some organization to these thoughts. When you read something, you expect the author to have grouped ideas together, divided them into paragraphs, and linked thoughts together so that you can follow them. Likewise, the readers of your writing will expect you to have done the same. If you offer your readers a collection of disorderly, random thoughts, they are likely to become confused about what you are trying to say. They are also likely to miss important connections that you want them to make.

Determining the right order for ideas can be a challenging task because there are often several different ways to arrange your thoughts. To find the most effective pattern, you might have to think of several different possibilities before you can decide which one is best. It is important to devote some time and attention to examining all of the pieces and figuring out how to fit them together, for your organization (or lack of it) can make or break your paper. This chapter will show you some techniques that you can use to organize your ideas.

The first technique involves determining a framework. In Chapter 15, you learned that prewriting helps you discover your topic and what you want to say about that topic. Prewriting should include the creation of a main idea statement that will keep your writing focused on just one point. Next, you will need to determine the best framework for arranging your thoughts about your main idea statement. You begin to create this framework when you examine your main idea statement and your prewriting (your brainstorming, freewriting, cluster, or whatever you used) and go through a three-step process to decide what to include and how to order that information:

Step 1: Circle ideas and information that match your main idea statement, and ignore or cross out ideas that seem irrelevant.

Step 2: Group like ideas and information together.

Step 3: Decide on the best way to put these groups of ideas in order.

Step One: Circle Relevant Ideas

In Step One of the organization process, you look at the ideas you collected during prewriting with your main idea statement in mind. You evaluate each thought or piece of information, asking yourself if it relates to or supports the point in your main idea statement. Then, you circle, highlight, or otherwise mark these relevant ideas. At the same time, you either ignore or cross out the ideas and information that do not relate to the point in your main idea. Do not erase these ideas; you might decide later that one or two really are useful, so you should not eliminate them for good. But develop a system for marking the ideas that will be useful. For example, recall the freewriting about stress in Chapter 15. After completing this freewriting, the student came up with the following main idea statement:

I have a lot of stress in my life.

When she looked over her freewriting for ideas that matched this point, she circled some key words and phrases:

Stress is one topic I know a lot about. I've had enough of it. Theres
stress (at work) trying to keep up with everything and deal with all of

the ⟨personallity conflicts⟩ and stress ⟨at school⟩ so many ⟨asignments⟩
to do and ⟨tests⟩ make me nervous. I study all the time. I don't have any
free time anymore. ⟨Financial stress⟩ too. Which has been the hardest
to cope with. I never seem to have enough money for everything,
I ⟨run out of money⟩ a few days before I get my paycheck every two
weeks. I worry about where I'll get the money to pay for next simester's
⟨tuition⟩. So I try to work more hours at the grocery store and it's
stressful ⟨dealing with difficult customers⟩ who are grouchy or difficult
to please.

These words and phrases that are circled all seem to be examples of stress-
causing things in the writer's life.

Another student, who was assigned to write about a favorite vacation spot,
chose to brainstorm about the beach. He generated this main idea statement:

The beach is the perfect vacation spot for the whole family.

Then, he went back over his brainstorming, circling ideas that seemed related
and crossing out ideas that seemed unrelated. Notice that some of the ideas are
neither circled nor crossed out, for he was not yet sure whether they would be
useful.

⟨swimming⟩   getting a tan   ⟨relaxing⟩

sun   ⟨exercise⟩   casual

⟨collect shells⟩   ⟨pool⟩   ⟨building sandcastles⟩

⟨restaurants⟩   ⟨arcades⟩   ⟨body surfing⟩

~~crowds~~   ~~sand~~   lifeguards

~~seagulls~~   ~~sharks~~   ⟨romantic sunsets⟩

As you complete this first step of the organizing process, you will need to
honestly evaluate the quantity of your ideas. Did you generate enough ideas in
your prewriting, or did you come up with only a few? If the number of ideas
you have generated seems skimpy, go back to the prewriting stage, perhaps selecting another technique, and try to think of more.

 **EXERCISE 16.1**   **Evaluating the Relevancy of Ideas**

Examine the main idea statement and the brainstorming provided next. In the prewriting, circle words or phrases that match the main idea statement. Either ignore or cross out words and phrases that do not relate to the main idea statement.

Main idea statement: Community colleges offer students several benefits.

small classes	close to home	classes
grades	degree	bookstore
cafeteria	work while in school	computer lab
diverse student body	affordable tuition	helpful instructors
studying	financial aid	

Step Two: Group Like Things Together

After you have identified relevant ideas in Step One, you are ready to go on to Step Two, which involves grouping like things together. Before you see how to do this with prewriting, consider how you would go about doing it with common household items. Let us say you are going to organize the items in your desk drawers by putting like things together in the same place. You have the following items:

paper clips	paper	stapler
envelopes	pencils	erasers
scissors	notepads	computer disks
printer ink cartridges	pencil sharpener	tape
rubber bands	pens	address labels

If you mix all of these items up, it might be more difficult to locate something when you need to find it. Therefore, you will want to group them together logically in separate drawers. How would you go about doing it? Actually, you could group the items together in different ways. For example, you could organize them by function and put all of the things that are associated with writing (such as the paper, pencils, erasers, and pencil sharpener) in one drawer, the computer supplies (ink cartridges and computer disks) in another, and fasteners that bind items together (such as the paper clips, rubber bands, and tape) in yet another. Another way to group them would be to put all of the paper products (paper, envelopes, notepads) in one place, all of the tools (pencil sharpener, stapler, and scissors) in another, and all of the writing implements (pencils and pens) in yet another. There are actually a number of possible logical groupings.

For another example, think of how you would organize your personal collection of DVDs. At the video store, they are usually arranged first by genre (comedy, drama, horror, science fiction, and so on) and then alphabetically by title within each genre. You could certainly organize your own collection that way. Then, when you were in the mood to watch a comedy, it would be easier to find just what you were looking for quickly. Or if you have some favorite actors and actresses, you might want to group your DVDs according to the films' stars. You would put all of your Eddie Murphy films in one place, all of your Julia Roberts movies in another, and so on. Of course, you could also arrange your whole collection simply by alphabetizing the films' titles.

As you can see, things can often be grouped in a number of different ways. Such will be the case when you look at the ideas you have generated for writing. Sometimes the right grouping will be immediately apparent to you. At other times you may have to experiment with different ways to group thoughts together.

Now, we will apply this same procedure to ideas generated in a prewriting exercise. When you were circling key words and phrases in Step 1, you probably circled some things that actually go together or say the same thing in different words. For example, look back at the student's freewriting about stress on pages 219–220. Which of the circled phrases seem to belong together? Several of the phrases relate to stress at work:

> at work
> personallity conflicts
> dealing with difficult customers

Other circled words and phrases in the freewriting relate to stress at school:

> at school
> asignments
> tests
> tuition

Finally, another set of words and phrases relates to financial stress:

> Financial stress
> run out of money
> tuition

Organizational Skills and Your Career

When you are searching for a new job and reading advertisements for available positions, notice how often employers ask for candidates with "good organizational skills." Almost every job you can name, from grocery store bagger to attorney, will require you to organize things or ideas. Companies want to hire people who are good at organizing because they know that organization aids efficiency and smooth operations.

Practicing with organizing ideas for your paragraphs can be an effective way to exercise and strengthen the organizational skills that you will need for career success. Consider the organization step of the writing process as a tool for improving your logical thinking.

As you sort these items into groups, you can see that for this writer, stress is produced by three specific things: work, school, and financial struggles.

Of course, this is not the only way to group these thoughts. You could, for instance, group them according to human and nonhuman sources of stress. Therefore, one category might include personality conflicts and dealing with customers, while another might include tests and financial difficulties. There may be other possibilities as well.

Now, look back at the brainstorming about the beach on page 220. How would you group those ideas together? Here is one possibility:

Appeal to adults	*Appeal to children*
relaxing	swimming
exercise	pool
collect shells	building sandcastles
restaurants	arcades
romantic sunsets	body surfing

EXERCISE 16.2   **Sorting Items into Groups**

Group the items in each of the following sets according to how they are alike. On the blank provided, write down any item that does not belong with the others.

1. rose   math   daisy   English   science   toad

Group 1: _____

Group 2: _____

Item that does not belong: _____

2. blue   lunch   red   rag   yellow   breakfast

Group 1: _____

Group 2: _____

Item that does not belong: _____

3. ant   cousin   baseball   soccer   fly   mosquito

Group 1: _____

Group 2: _____

Item that does not belong: _____

4. pilot   engineer   teacher   conductor   flight attendant   airplane mechanic

Group 1: _____

Group 2: _____

Item that does not belong: _____

5. wolf   rabbit   giraffe   snake   lion   dolphin

Group 1: _____

Group 2: _____

Item that does not belong: _____

EXERCISE 16.3   Sorting Items into Different Groups

In the space provided, group each of the following sets of items in at least two different ways.

1. cows   dogs   horses   chickens   parakeets

2. coat   shorts   T-shirt   long underwear   sandals

3. firefighter   pro basketball player
    police officer   construction worker
    doctor   racecar driver

EXERCISE 16.4   **Grouping Ideas from a Prewriting**

Go back to Exercise 16.1 and examine the items that you circled. How would you group the relevant items in this brainstorm? List your groups in the space provided:

Step Three: Put the Groups in Order

After you have determined possible groupings for relevant items, Step Three involves determining the order in which you should present these groups to your reader. Sometimes the groups will naturally organize themselves. When you tell a story, for instance, or write a set of directions to explain how to do something, you will give your readers the events or the steps chronologically, in the order in which they occur.

For those topics that do not naturally order themselves, you will have to use logic, letting the relationships among the groups suggest the best arrangement. Two common ways to arrange groups are by order of importance and by causes and effects.

When you use size, you put the groups in order from largest to smallest or from smallest to largest. For example, look back at the groups of different kinds of stress on page 222. If this student decides to include all three types in her paragraph, she might want to order them according to *how much* stress each one causes. In that case, she might conclude that she should discuss work as the *least* stressful, then school as a little *more* stressful, and finally, financial struggles as the *most* stressful of the three. Thus, she might write her groups in this order:

1. Work stress (least stressful)
2. School stress (more stressful)
3. Financial stress (most stressful)

However, this same student might also use causes and effects to arrange the same three groups. In that case, she might decide that she should discuss financial stress first, for it caused her decision to go to college. Then, she might explain how college not only is stressful on its own but also causes her stress at work by interfering with her sleep and relaxation. As a result, college adds to her workplace stress, for she does not deal as well with difficult customers and personality conflicts on the job. She would list the groups in this order:

Financial stress
↓
School stress
↓
Work stress

Chapters 20, 21, and 24 of this book present more detailed information about three common types of order for arranging ideas: time order, space order, and order of importance.

 **EXERCISE 16.5**   **Deciding on the Best Order for Groups of Ideas**

Decide on the best order for the following three groups of ideas. On the blanks provided, number them in order from 1 to 3 to indicate which one should be discussed first (1), which one second (2), and which one third (3). Then, write a brief explanation of why you chose that particular order.

1. **Main idea:** Working as a cook in a fast-food restaurant was the worst job I have ever had.

_____ Low pay

_____ Tiring work (standing on feet all day, boring job)

_____ Supervisor was always in a bad mood

Explanation of order: _____

_____

_____

2. **Main idea:** Keeping a dog as a pet is not for everyone.

_____ Cost of food, veterinarian bills, collar, toys, and so on

_____ Time required to train the dog, walk it, and play with it

_____ Inconvenience when you want to travel

Explanation of order: _____

_____

_____

3. **Main idea:** My grandmother is the person I admire most.

_____ Her actions (volunteers for charities, never too busy to help others)

_____ Her values (honesty, generosity, compassion)

_____ Her personality (optimistic, lively, energetic)

Explanation of order: _____

_____

_____

EXERCISE 16.6   **Determining the Right Order for Ideas**

In what order would you place the groups you created in Exercise 16.4? In the following space, write each of your groups in order, numbered 1, 2, 3, and so on.

_____

_____

_____

_____

_____

Outlining

During or after your completion of the three steps of the organization process, you should create an outline of your ideas. **Outlines** come in different forms, but they all list the ideas or information you will present in the order in which you will present them. The best outlines also indicate how ideas are related to one another. Regardless of their form, they all provide the writer with a guide to follow as he or she writes.

It is important to create an outline of your ideas before you write. An outline will help you keep the overall big picture in mind as you concentrate on the smaller details. It will also prevent you from

- straying from your main point and including information or ideas that are irrelevant

- rambling or jumping from thought to thought in a manner that confuses the reader

- mixing different kinds of information together

- discussing an idea in the wrong place

Many students try to skip the outlining stage because they assume that they must create a formal outline, the kind with Roman numerals. However, this format is not necessary. When you are creating an outline to use only as a tool to follow as you write, then you are free to use a less formal method. Informal types of outlines can take the form of brief lists of ideas in the order in which you want to discuss them. For example, the following sketch is an informal outline:

Main idea: Learning a foreign language offers several benefits.

1. Helps improve overall academic performance
   – Thinking skills improve
   – College entrance exam statistics

2. Good skill for job market
   – Asset for many different careers

3. Helps kids understand other cultures, leading to tolerance and world peace

An informal outline can also take the form of branching. This form looks a lot like the clustering prewriting technique. It starts with a topic and then has "branches" of subtopics and details radiating from that central topic. Here is an example of branching:

Main idea: Fast food may be bad for our health, but it is definitely here to stay.

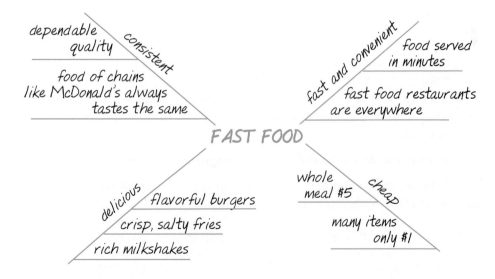

EXERCISE 16.7   **Completing an Informal Outline**

Complete the following informal outline by filling in the blanks.

Main idea: The mall is my favorite place to shop.

1. _____

   – Can buy anything from video games to slippers
   – Several large department stores plus one hundred specialty stores
   – Many different restaurants

2. _____

   – Cool in summer, warm in winter
   – Great place to go on rainy days

3. Special displays and events

   – _____

   – _____

   – _____

4. _____

Organizing and Outlining: A Student Demonstration

In Chapter 15, you saw the prewriting generated by John, a student who was assigned to write about something he could not live without. John's main idea statement was

My cell phone serves several necessary purposes in my life.

Next, John needed to complete the three-step organizing process. First, he circled relevant ideas in his freewriting:

I don't know what people use to do before their were cell phones. Cell phones are nesessary. I mean, I use mine to keep in touch with my friends and make plans to get together. They keep your family members from worrying about you as much because they know they can call to check on you any time. There good to have in case of emergencys. They give you something to do while your stuck some-where waiting, you can call someone to pass the time. Mine has a few video games on it. I can change the settings, too, so I can have different ring tones, and I can turn off the ringer. People who don't cut off their cell phones in places like libraries and movie theaters are rude. You have to think of others. I think they help you build relationships because they make it easier to stay in communication with people. They save time and money, and they make it easier to get help when your car breaks down.

Note that John ignored ideas that did not match his main idea statement. Then, he moved on to Step 2 of the organizing process and grouped similar ideas together:

Relationships with others
keep in touch with my friends
make plans
family
they can call to check on you
build relationships
stay in communication

Gives you something to do
call someone to pass the time
video games

Emergencys
get help when your car breaks down
save time and money?

Notice that John was not sure if the "save time and money" idea belongs, so he put a question mark next to it.

In Step 3, John saw that he would have to use logic to find the right order for the groups. He decided to use order of importance because some of the purposes were more important than others.

Finally, he created a brief, informal outline to guide him as he wrote his paragraph:

Main idea: My cell phone serves several necessary purposes in my life.
    1. Stay in touch with friends and family (most important)
    2. In case of emergencys
    3. Use to pass the time (least important)

In Chapter 17, you will see how John completed the next step, composing his paragraph.

EXERCISE 16.8   **Preparing an Outline for Your Paragraph**

In Chapter 15, you generated some ideas about one of the following topics: someone I admire, an important decision, something that is not fair, a day when I was very angry. Then, you wrote a main idea statement. Reread this main idea statement, and examine the prewriting you generated. Follow the three-step organization procedure. First, circle all of the words and phrases that seem relevant to your main idea. Next, group like ideas and information together. Third, decide on the best order for those groups.

Finally, create either a formal or an informal outline of your ideas. You will use this outline again in Chapter 17 when you actually write your paragraph.

CHAPTER 16 REVIEW

Fill in the blanks in the following statements.

1. You begin to create a framework for your ideas when you examine your _____ and your _____ and go through a three-step process to organize your ideas.

2. Step 1 of the organization process involves circling ideas and information that are _____ to your main idea statement and ignoring or crossing out ideas that seem _____.

3. Step 2 of the organization process involves _____ like ideas and information together.

4. Step 3 of the organization process involves deciding on the best way to put your groups of ideas in _____.

5. The ideas for some topics, such as stories or directions, naturally organize themselves with _____ order; for other groups you will have to use logic, letting the _____ among the groups suggest the best arrangement.

6. Two common ways to order groups are by _____ and by _____.

7. An _____ lists the ideas or information you will present in the order in which you will present them; it should also indicate how ideas are _____ to one another.

8. Creating an outline will prevent you from digressing from your main point and including information or ideas that are _____ .

9. Creating an outline will also prevent you from _____ from thought to thought in a confusing manner, from mixing different kinds of information together, and from discussing an idea in the wrong place.

10. An _____ outline can take the form of a brief list or branching.

WebWork

For more information and examples of informal outlines, go to the Hunter College Reading/Writing Center at **http://rwc.hunter.cuny.edu/reading-writing/on-line/informal.html**.

Online Study Center For more information and practice with organizing and outlining, go to the Online Study Center that accompanies this book, at **http://www.college.hmco.com/pic/dolphinwriterone**.

17 Writing a Paragraph

GOALS FOR CHAPTER 17

▶ Revise ineffective topic sentences.

▶ Write effective topic sentences.

▶ Write a paragraph that includes layers of development and transitions.

In Chapter 15 you learned some prewriting techniques for generating ideas, including a main idea, and in Chapter 16 you practiced organizing and outlining ideas. This chapter focuses on the third step of the writing process, composing a draft of a paragraph.

The Paragraph and Its Purpose

A **paragraph** can be defined as a group of sentences that all support or develop one particular idea about a topic. Paragraphs vary in length from just a few sentences to many sentences. A paragraph can stand alone, or it can be combined with other paragraphs to form a longer piece of writing, such as an essay.

The following diagram shows the form of a paragraph. The first sentence of a paragraph is indented five spaces from the left margin. The remaining sentences follow each other with only two spaces between them, and blank space follows the last word of the last sentence.

Indent
5 spaces
_____
_____
_____
_____
_____
_____
_____
_____

The purpose of a paragraph, particularly in a longer piece of writing, is to group related sentences together so that readers can clearly understand the writer's ideas. Imagine if the books or articles that you have read contained no paragraphs and presented thoughts and information in no particular order, leaving you to try to make sense of it all. Reading such a book or article would be a confusing and unpleasant task. Just as you expect writers to have grouped their sentences into related units of thought, the readers of your writing will expect you to have done the same with your own ideas.

A paragraph has two main parts: a topic sentence and a body. The topic sentence states the paragraph's main idea, and the remaining sentences—the body—develop that idea with more information and explanation.

The Topic Sentence

In Chapter 15, you generated main idea statements as part of your prewriting practice. This main idea statement becomes the **topic sentence,** the sentence in the paragraph that states the main idea. Therefore, just like the main idea statement that you generate in prewriting, the topic sentence has two parts: it states the topic of the paragraph, and it also states the writer's point about that topic. Notice how each of the following topic sentences contains both a topic and an idea about that topic:

    topic   *point*

Procrastination   is my worst habit.

    topic   *point*

The motorcycle   was a work of art.

    topic   *point*

Police officers   deserve higher salaries.

Remember that the term *topic sentence* might seem a little misleading, for the topic sentence does more than state the sentence's topic. It also states an *idea* about that topic.

 **EXERCISE 17.1**   **Identifying the Parts of Topic Sentences**

In each of the following topic sentences, circle the topic and underline the point the writer makes about that topic.

1. Good communication is an essential ingredient of a happy marriage.

2. *Cold Mountain* is an excellent novel.

3. The Red Cross helps people in a number of important ways.

4. All high school students should be required to perform community service.

5. Although they look alike, the twins have very different personalities.

In a well-written paragraph, the topic sentence will be apparent. It will be the most general statement in the paragraph, and all of the other sentences will clearly develop the point that it makes. Topic sentences are often the first sentence of the paragraph, but they do not have to be. They can appear anywhere in the paragraph: at the beginning, in the middle, or at the end. Read the following paragraph, and see if you can underline the sentence that expresses the main idea.

> Americans haven't given up on marriage as a cherished ideal. Indeed, most continue to prize and value it as an important life goal, and the vast majority (an estimated 85 percent) will marry at least once in a lifetime. Almost all couples enter marriage with a strong determination for a lifelong, loving partnership, and this desire may even be increasing among the young. Since the 1980s, the percentage of high school seniors who say that having a good marriage is extremely important to them as a life goal has gone up, though only slightly.*

Did you underline the first sentence? That is the sentence in the paragraph that states the paragraph's main idea. Then, the rest of the paragraph goes on to offer information that explains this statement.

EXERCISE 17.2 **Recognizing Topic Sentences in Paragraphs**

Underline the topic sentence in each of the following paragraphs.

1. I never considered taking public transportation to work. But then my car broke down and I had to take the bus. I quickly discovered that the bus is an excellent way to commute. Riding the bus is less expensive than driving my car because the bus fare is actually cheaper than the cost of gas and parking. Also, the bus drops me off a lot closer to work than I got when I parked my car in the parking lot. But best of all, I am not as irritable when I get home because I did not have to drive in heavy traffic. I can sit back, relax, and let someone else do it for me!

*Excerpted from David Popenoe and Barbara Defoe Whitehead, "The State of Our Unions," *USA Today* (Magazine), July 1, 2002.

2. The next time you reach for your cell phone, thank NASA (the National Aeronautics and Space Administration). If your doctor recommends an MRI, thank NASA. The space agency deserves another moment of gratitude when you pop in a DVD and settle back for a good movie, or when you reach for a composite golf club, hoping to out-drive your buddies. And think of NASA when a smoke detector blares to save your life. NASA often is seen as driven by starry-eyed scientists looking to grab funds away from better use on Earth. But NASA has contributed to the technological advancement of everyday life on Earth as much as—and maybe more than—anything else.*

3. For two reasons, many vehicle owners are "upside down" when it comes to their vehicle's value, owing more than it is worth. This is a growing phenomenon, first of all, because of five-, six-, and even seven-year car loans. These longer loans make payments smaller, but the car is losing value faster than the owner is paying off the balance owed on it. The second reason for the problem is large discounts on new cars. The more car dealers take off the price of a new car, the less they give for used trade-ins. Thus, many car owners cannot get enough for a traded-in vehicle to pay off the loan on it.†

When you write topic sentences for paragraphs of your own, remember that an effective topic sentence has three essential characteristics: it is a complete sentence that includes both a topic and a point, it is neither too broad nor too narrow, and it takes into account not just the topic but also the paragraph's audience and purpose.

First of all, a topic sentence must contain both of its required parts: a topic and some point about that topic. A topic in the form of a sentence fragment is not a topic sentence:

Incomplete:	Tattoos and body piercings
Complete topic sentence:	Tattoos and body piercings are very fashionable right now.
Incomplete:	Missy Elliott
Complete topic sentence:	Missy Elliott is one of rap music's most talented performers.
Incomplete:	My relationship with my ex-boyfriend
Complete topic sentence:	My relationship with my ex-boyfriend went through three stages.

*Adapted from David J. Eicher, "Despite Far-reaching Goals, NASA Benefits Earth Most," *USA Today*, January 22, 2004, p. 15A.
†Adapted from David Kiley, "Lack of Trade-in Value Burns Car Buyers," *USA Today*, July 7, 2003, p. 1A.

If you try to begin writing with only a topic in mind, then you will probably not produce a coherent and well-developed paragraph. When you are unsure about exactly what you mean to say, then your paragraph will probably ramble aimlessly. Make sure that before you begin to write, you have a complete topic sentence that includes both your topic and your point.

In addition to being complete, a topic sentence must also be appropriately specific. If an idea is too broad or too vague, it will not keep you properly focused as you write. For example, look at the following examples:

Too broad: There are a lot of problems at this school.
Too vague: Something should be done about bad drivers.

Neither of these statements expresses one clear idea, so each would probably lead to rambling when it came time to write. To improve these two statements, rewrite them to narrow the topic and/or the idea:

Expanding the parking lot should be one of this school's main projects for improvement.

Driver education programs need to be improved.

On the other hand, though, you do not want to make your topic sentence so specific or limited that you cannot develop it at all:

Too specific: My hourly wage is only $6.00.

Because this sentence states a fact, there is not much more you can say about it. To improve it, broaden the topic and the idea:

I deserve a raise in pay.

Be aware that your topic sentence may not be perfect on your first try. You may have to work on it, experimenting with the wording and rewriting it, even after you have begun writing, until it says exactly what you want to express.

EXERCISE 17.3   **Revising Ineffective Topic Sentences**

On the blanks provided, rewrite each of the following topic sentences that is either incomplete, too broad, too vague, or too specific. If the main idea seems complete and appropriately specific, write *OK* on the blank.

1. My first babysitting job.

_____

2. Pets are fun.

_____

3. It snowed three feet last night.

_____

4. Something should be done about rude people with cell phones.

_____

_____

5. Yoga exercises benefit the body in many different ways.

_____

So far, you have learned that effective topic sentences are complete and appropriately specific. A good topic sentence also takes into account the paragraph's audience and purpose. When you are composing your topic sentence, you will want to consider not only *what* you want to say but also *why* and *to whom* you want to say it. Therefore, in addition to the topic, there are two other factors—audience and purpose—that will affect how you express your topic sentence.

The first of these factors is your audience, or readers. *Who* is going to read your writing? *What* does this person need to know or want to know about the topic? Your topic sentence should take into account this audience's needs and desires.

The second factor is your purpose. Do you want to entertain your readers? Do you want to inform them about your topic so that they can learn something new? Or do you want to persuade them to believe what you believe about the topic? Your topic sentence should clearly reflect this purpose.

For example, take the topic sentence "Several people I have known have been seriously injured on trampolines." The writer intends to explain to someone who is interested in jumping on trampolines how they have harmed people. But notice how the purpose of this next statement differs from the first:

You should not jump on a trampoline without a safety net.

Although the audience might be the same, the phrase *you should* indicates that the writer's purpose is persuasive.

> ## EXERCISE 17.4   Topic, Audience, and Purpose in Topic Sentences

A. Answer the question that follows each topic sentence by circling the letter of the correct response.

There are three steps in performing CPR on a heart attack victim.

1. The writer's purpose is to

   a. entertain readers with a story about CPR.
   b. inform readers about how to perform CPR.
   c. persuade readers to learn CPR.

You must see the new film that stars talented actor Johnny Depp.

2. The writer's purpose is to

   a. entertain the reader by telling a story about Johnny Depp.
   b. inform readers about Johnny Depp's new film.
   c. persuade readers to see Johnny Depp's new film.

Bungee-jumping is the craziest thing that I have ever done.

3. The writer's purpose is to

   a. entertain the reader with a description of a bungee-jumping experience.
   b. inform readers about how bungee-jumping works.
   c. persuade readers not to bungee-jump.

I decided to go to college for three reasons.

4. The writer's purpose is to

   a. entertain readers with an amusing story about college life.
   b. inform the reader about the reasons behind her decision to attend college.
   c. persuade readers that they should attend college.

You should shop online rather than at the mall.

5. The writer's purpose is to

   a. entertain the reader with a story about an online shopping experience.
   b. inform the reader about the differences between shopping online and shopping in a mall.
   c. persuade readers to begin shopping online.

B. Use prewriting techniques to generate ideas, and then write a topic sentence for each of the following topic/audience/purpose sets.

Topic: The college you attend
Audience: One of your relatives
Purpose: To inform

1. Topic sentence: _____

Topic: The college you attend
Audience: A high school student who is trying to decide where to attend college
Purpose: To persuade

2. Topic sentence: _____

Topic: An embarrassing moment
Audience: Your friends
Purpose: To entertain

3. Topic sentence: _____

Topic: Something you recently learned to do at work or at school
Audience: Someone who needs to learn to do this
Purpose: To inform

4. Topic sentence: _____

Topic: Making driving while talking on a cell phone illegal
Audience: People who want to learn more about the issue
Purpose: To inform

5. Topic sentence: _____

The Body

The **body** of the paragraph includes all of the sentences that support, explain, or prove the idea expressed in the topic sentence. These sentences provide all of the evidence that the reader will need in order to accept the main idea as true, and this evidence can take a variety of different forms, including

facts
statistics and other data
examples
stories
reasons
comparisons
descriptive details

In the following paragraph, the topic sentence is highlighted. Read the paragraph and try to decide which of the different kinds of evidence in the previous list is given to support the topic sentence.

> Soccer may not yet be a prominent professional sport in the United States. **However, soccer has become very popular among the nation's youth.** According to ESPN, in the 1990s, the number of kids age 6 to 17 who play on soccer

teams doubled. Now, two million young people are playing soccer. At the same time, participation in most other sports has declined. My son, for example, recently decided to concentrate on soccer instead of baseball because he thought soccer was faster paced, more action-oriented, and more physically challenging.*

This paragraph supports the topic sentence (in bold print) with facts, a comparison with other sports in general and baseball in particular, and an example of someone (the writer's son) who enjoys playing soccer.

The next sections of this chapter will cover some techniques for writing the body of a paragraph.

A Step-by-Step Guide to Composing a Paragraph

After you have generated ideas through prewriting and then organized them and created an outline, you are ready to write your paragraph.

Step One: Transform Your Main Idea into a Topic Sentence

As mentioned earlier, a topic sentence does not have to be the first sentence of a paragraph, but as you work on strengthening your writing skills, it is usually best to begin your paragraph with this statement because it will help you stay focused as you write the rest of the paragraph. Therefore, look first at the main idea statement that you generated during the prewriting stage of your process. Evaluate it to make sure it is complete (containing a topic and an idea about that topic), appropriately specific, and suited to your purpose and audience, and rewrite it if necessary. Once it contains all of these characteristics, write it down as the first sentence of your paragraph.

Look, for example, at one student's main idea statement. Lee generated prewriting on the topic "An Interesting Person I Know" and came up with the following: *My interesting cousin, Jorge.* But then he realized that this statement was not a complete sentence, so he revised it to read: *My cousin Jorge is one of the most interesting people I know.*

Another student, Cindy, generated prewriting on the same topic and decided on this main idea: *My friend Sharona is an interesting person.* When she evaluated it to see whether or not it would be a good topic sentence, though, she decided that it was too vague. She revised it to read: *My friend Sharona is a very creative person.*

---

*Adapted from Robert Lipsyte, "Soccer Lacks Attention? That's Fine with Me," *USA Today*, November 17, 2003, p. 13A.

As you can see, main idea statements and topic sentences may not come out perfect the first time. If yours seems to be lacking something, do not proceed with writing the rest of the paragraph until you have figured out what is missing and have corrected the problem. If you are not sure of exactly what you are trying to communicate to your readers, then you will be in greater danger of rambling or failing to adequately develop what you want to say.

 **EXERCISE 17.5** **Writing a Topic Sentence**

In Chapter 15, you wrote a main idea statement about one of the following topics: someone I admire, an important decision, something that is not fair, a day when I was very angry. Turn this main idea statement into a topic sentence, and write that topic sentence on the following blanks:

_____

_____

Next, evaluate this topic sentence.

Is it complete? Yes _____ No _____

Is it appropriately specific? Yes _____ No _____

Is it suited to the audience and purpose? Yes _____ No _____

If you checked *No* in response to any of these questions, revise your topic sentence and write that revised version on the following blanks:

_____

_____

Step Two: Reevaluate Your Outline and Consider the Modes of Development

Once you have written down your topic sentence, the next step involves reevaluating your outline to make sure that it still matches the idea you have expressed in the topic sentence. Make sure that this outline still includes the right kinds of supporting ideas, and decide if they are still listed in the right order. Make any necessary adjustments to your outline before you begin.

Look, for example, at Cindy's revised topic sentence and existing outline:

My friend Sharona is a very creative person.

— She makes her own clothes, which are fun and colorful.
— She was born and raised in Morocco.
— She is a talented painter.
— She sets interesting goals for herself, like backpacking across Australia one day.
— She writes poetry that has been published.

The topic sentence and outline no longer seem to match because the revised topic sentence focuses more specifically on Sharona's creativity, so Cindy made a few changes to her outline:

My friend Sharona is a very creative person.

— She makes her own clothes, which are fun and colorful.
— She is a talented painter.
— She writes poetry that has been published.

Notice that Cindy omitted the information that did not match, and then her outline was more appropriate for the topic sentence she planned to develop.

As part of this step, you will want to consider the **modes of development,** which are patterns that often organize the evidence provided in the body of a paragraph. Chapters 20 through 24 of this text provide explanations and illustrations of each of these different modes. The list that follows provides a brief description of each one.

- **Time order.** Tell a story from your own or someone else's experience, providing details about people, places, and things so that readers can picture them in their minds. Alternately, describe the steps in a process or procedure. (See Chapter 20.)

- **Space order.** Describe a person, place, or thing by explaining how its details are arranged in space. (See Chapter 21.)

- **Give examples.** Illustrate a general idea by providing specific examples. (See Chapter 22.)

- **Comparison/Contrast.** Examine how two things are alike and/or different. (See Chapter 23.)

■ **Order of importance.** Present reasons or other information in order of priority to argue that readers should change their minds or behaviors. (See Chapter 24.)

As you continue working your way through this book and learning more about each mode of development, you will begin to see how you can use the different modes to organize your ideas in paragraphs. You might even want to read ahead in this text if you see a particular mode that seems appropriate for a paragraph you need to write right now.

 **EXERCISE 17.6**   **Evaluating Outlines**

In each of the following outlines, circle the point that does not match the topic sentence.

1. Topic sentence: The town I live in is struggling economically.

   A. Many people have lost their jobs.
   B. Several businesses have closed.
   C. Traffic is a serious problem during rush hour.

2. Topic sentence: My aunt's wedding reception was the most memorable one I have ever attended.

   1. The bride and groom arrived in a helicopter.
   2. All of the guests were served a piece of wedding cake.
   3. The bride performed with the band, playing drums in her wedding gown.

3. Topic sentence: Fall is my favorite season of the year.

   – beautiful sunsets
   – colorful leaves
   – crisp, cool air
   – football games
   – Thanksgiving holiday

EXERCISE 17.7   **Evaluating Your Outline**

Compare the topic sentence you wrote in Exercise 17.5 with the outline you created for Exercise 16.8. Make adjustments to the outline so that it matches the topic sentence, and write your new outline in the space provided.

_____

_____

_____

_____

_____

_____

_____

_____

Step Three: Using Your Outline as a Guide, Compose with Layers of Development and Transitional Expressions

After you have made the final adjustments to your outline, you are ready to begin writing the sentences of your paragraph's body. Using your outline as a guide, write about the first group of ideas you have listed. Then, write about the second group, and so on.

As you write, think of using layers of development to explain each of your ideas. A **layer of development** provides more specific information about a general idea in the sentence that came before it. Therefore, a layer of development anticipates and answers questions that pop into readers' heads as they read. For example, let us say you write the sentence "Reruns of the classic sitcom _I Love Lucy_ are still funny." The word _funny_ is a relatively general one that could mean many different things. As your readers read this sentence, they will probably immediately think, _What do you mean by "funny"?_ or _How is the show funny?_ Instead of going on to another new idea, you need to add some information—a layer of development—to answer these questions. In other words, you need to explain what you mean. Thus, you might add this sentence:

For example, in every show, Lucille Ball performs wacky stunts.

This sentence helps the reader better understand what *funny* means. However, you should ask yourself, *Will readers have any questions about this sentence?* They will probably ask, for instance, *What do you mean by "wacky stunts"?* or *What are some of these wacky stunts?* You might add another layer of development to answer these questions:

> In one episode she tries to please her husband by decorating their small apartment like Cuba, complete with palm trees, chickens, and a mule.

By adding these two sentences, you have made it very clear to readers how the show is funny.

Every time you write a sentence, ask yourself this question: *Is there some idea here that I should explain more by giving another fact, detail, or example?* There is no rule about how many layers of development should be included in a paragraph. The number of layers you include will always depend on the idea or information in each different sentence you write. But if you get into the habit of wondering if you just wrote something that might need further development, then you will be less likely to leave readers guessing what you really mean, and your ideas will be clear.

EXERCISE 17.8   **Adding Layers of Development**

For each of the following pairs of sentences, circle the letter of the one that needs to be explained with a more specific fact, detail, or example.

1. a. My brother is overweight.
   b. My brother weighs over 250 pounds.

2. a. The storm caused two million dollars' worth of property damage.
   b. The storm was very destructive.

3. a. My dog can sit, fetch, roll over, and speak on command.
   b. My dog can perform many tricks.

4. a. The health club offers something for everyone.
   b. Exercise options include swimming, aerobics, weight training, and racquetball.

5. a. Drunk driving can be very dangerous.
   b. In 2002, 17,419 people were killed in crashes involving alcohol.

WRITING FOR SUCCESS

Offering Evidence for Ideas

When you write, pretend that you are a lawyer arguing a case in a courtroom. Just like a lawyer, you must make your main point very clear, so work on your topic sentence until it says exactly what you mean to say.

Then, like a lawyer, present your case in the body of your paragraph. Include plenty of evidence, for just as a lawyer cannot win a case unless he or she has enough proof to back up the argument, you cannot convince your readers to accept your main idea unless you present plenty of evidence to support that idea.

To help your readers see how the sentences are related to each other, add transitions. **Transitions** are words and phrases whose function is to show the relationships between thoughts and ideas. The word *transition* comes from the Latin word *trans*, which means "across." Transitions bridge the gaps across sentences and paragraphs and reveal how they are related. The following box gives some common types of transitions with a few examples of each type.

Transitions that signal addition

also	in addition	too	first, second, third
furthermore	finally	and	another

Transitions that show time order

now	then	today	next
soon	later	finally	previously
eventually	meanwhile		

Transitions that indicate causes or consequences

so	therefore	as a result	consequently
hence	because	thus	for this reason

Transitions that signal examples

for example	for instance	in one case	as an illustration
to illustrate			

Transitions that signal comparisons

also	too	likewise	similarly
however	but	yet	on the other hand
in contrast			

EXERCISE 17.9   **Adding Transition Words and Phrases**

Add appropriate transitions in the blanks in the following passage.

People gain knowledge in three major ways: by seeing things, by hearing things, and by touching things or completing activities. _____,
Cause or consequence
the three major learning styles have been described as visual, auditory, and kinesthetic. Everyone uses all three styles. _____, many
Comparison
people have a dominant style that helps them learn best.

Visual learners are people who learn most effectively when they see what they are learning. _____, they need information to be pre-
Cause or consequence
sented in visual form. _____, they need to
Example
be able to see the teacher's face, books, displays, and demonstrations, and they can absorb information by reading about it. They memorize and recall information by visualizing it in their minds. _____, they tend to be
Cause or consequence
good spellers.

_____ type of learner is the auditory
Addition
learner, who gains knowledge best by hearing it. These people like verbal instruction in the form of lectures, discussions, and even songs. _____,
Cause or consequence
they often learn better by reading aloud. They frequently talk, hum, or whistle to themselves.

_____, there are the kinesthetic learners,
Addition
who process information by touching things or

by exploring the world around them. They prefer

doing things. _____, they enjoy taking
Example
things apart or putting them together, put-

ting on performances, and creating art. These

people find it difficult to sit still for long peri-

ods of time. _____, they usually fidget
Addition
when they are bored. The other two kinds of

learners remember what they see or hear.

Kinesthetic learners, _____, remem-
Comparison
ber what they do.*

Writing a Paragraph: A Student Demonstration

In Chapter 16 you saw how John organized his ideas from his prewriting about
his cell phone. Here are his main idea and informal outline again:

Main idea: My cell phone serves several necessary purposes in my life.

1. Stay in touch with friends and family (most important)
2. In case of emergencys
3. Use to pass the time (least important)

Next, he began composing his paragraph. He started by examining his main idea
statement and then decided that he could revise it to be clearer about his topic
and his point about that topic. His revised main idea became this topic sentence:

My cell phone serves three essential purposes in my life.

Next, John evaluated his outline. He decided that it still included the ideas that
he wanted to discuss, in the order in which he wanted to discuss them. There-

*Adapted from Linda Young and Deborah Greenwood, "How Understanding Your Child's Learning
Style Can Lead to Academic Success," *Parents' Source*, January 20, 2002, **www.parentssource.com/
1.02.article.html**.

fore, he began composing his paragraph, consciously adding layers of development and transitions to help his readers follow his ideas from one sentence to the next. Here is his first draft:

> My cell phone serves three essential purposes in my life. It helps me stay in touch with my family and friends. We make plans to get together, we check on each other. It's good for emergencys. Like once when my car broke down. I call my brother on my cell phone and he comes to get me. I can always count on my brother to help me out when I'm in trouble. I use my cell phone for something to do to pass the time. Calling people helps the time go by faster when your waiting.

John's paragraph is just a first draft, so it is not perfect. However, it is a good start. In Chapter 18, you will see how he revised and improved it.

EXERCISE 17.10   **Writing Your Paragraph**

Following the revised outline in Exercise 17.7, write your paragraph, adding layers of development and transitions.

EXERCISE 17.11   **Writing About a Photograph**

Study the following photograph and generate ideas for a paragraph. Then, organize those ideas and write your paragraph.

© AP/Wide World Photos

CHAPTER 17 REVIEW

Fill in the blanks in the following statements.

1. A _____ is a group of sentences that all support or develop one particular idea about a topic.

2. The purpose of a paragraph is to group related _____ together so that readers can clearly understand the writer's ideas.

3. The _____ is the sentence in the paragraph that states the paragraph's main idea.

4. A topic sentence has two parts: it states the paragraph's _____, and it also states the writer's _____ about that topic.

5. An effective topic sentence has three essential characteristics: it is a _____ sentence, it is neither too _____ nor too _____, and it takes into account not just the topic but also the paragraph's _____ and _____.

6. The _____ of the paragraph includes all of the sentences that support, explain, or prove the idea expressed in the topic sentence.

7. The body of a paragraph provides _____, such as facts, statistics, examples, and reasons, which helps the reader accept the main idea as true.

8. _____, such as narration, description, and classification, are patterns that often organize the evidence provided in the body of a paragraph.

9. A _____ provides more specific information about a general idea in the sentence that came before it.

10. _____ are words and phrases whose function is to show the relationship between thoughts and ideas.

WebWork

Go to the Paragraph Punch Web site at **www.paragraphpunch.com**. This Web site provides questions that you answer as you are guided step-by-step through the actual process of composing a paragraph. Follow the directions to create your own paragraph, and then print that paragraph.

Online Study Center   For more information and practice with writing a paragraph, go to the Online Study Center that accompanies this book, at **http://www.college.hmco.com/pic/dolphinwriterone**.

18

Revising

GOALS FOR CHAPTER 18

▶ Explain the difference between revising and editing.

▶ Name the three characteristics that should be evaluated as part of the revision process.

▶ Identify areas for revision in paragraphs.

▶ Use a peer review sheet to identify needed revisions for a paragraph.

In Chapter 17, you practiced the third step in the writing process, composing a draft. However, even after a paragraph is written, you are still not quite finished. The fourth step of the process is revising.

Revising Versus Editing

Take a moment and think about the word *revision*. Notice that it includes the prefix *re-*, meaning "back or again," and the root word *vision*. Thus, *revision* literally means "to look at again." Once you have written your paragraph, you need to look at it again to make sure you have successfully explained your main idea for your readers.

Revising and editing, which is the fifth step of the writing process, are not the same things. When you revise a paragraph, you are looking for and then correcting paragraph-level problems. In other words, you are evaluating and improving, if necessary, the way your whole paragraph is organized or developed. Editing, which will be discussed in Chapter 19, involves examining the paragraph at the sentence and word levels and correcting errors in sentence construction, grammar, word choice, and spelling. It is best to accomplish revision and editing as two separate, distinct steps, for each process involves looking at different aspects of the paragraph.

To revise a paragraph, you will need to evaluate it for the three C's: completeness, cohesiveness, and coherence.

Revising for Completeness

In Chapter 17, you learned about including layers of development as you wrote your first draft. A layer of development provides more specific information about a general idea in the sentence that came before it. It anticipates and answers readers' questions about more general statements, so it increases their understanding.

When you are examining a paragraph to make sure it is *complete*, or adequately developed, you evaluate the paragraph's layers of development. Does it provide enough information and explanation of general ideas? Should you add more facts or examples to develop your ideas? To determine whether or not you have provided enough development, consider using the following techniques:

Use different colors of highlighter markers to identify the layers in your paragraph. Use one color, such as yellow, to highlight the topic sentence, which is the most general sentence in the paragraph. Use another color, such as pink, to highlight the second sentence, which should develop the first sentence. If the third sentence develops the second sentence, use yet another color to highlight it. If the third sentence develops the first sentence, highlight it with the same color you used for the second sentence. Follow this same procedure for all of the other sentences in the paragraph. Then, after you have highlighted every sentence, see how colorful your paragraph is. In general, paragraphs that contain more colors are probably developing the main idea with sufficient details. A paragraph that is highlighted with only two colors, however, may need the addition of more specific information and examples.

Use the highlighting technique to determine the sentence in the following paragraph that needs more development:

> I decided to become a nurse for several reasons. First of all, I wanted a career that would give me opportunities to help people. When you are a nurse, you help people every day by soothing their pain, calming their fears, and helping to heal their wounds and their diseases. Secondly, I chose nursing because it pays well. Nurses can make about $20 to $25 per hour, which will provide me with the means to support my family. Nursing is also fast-paced, exciting work, which is the third reason I chose the profession.

Did you identify the sixth sentence as the one that needs more development? Following this sentence should be at least one layer of development that gives at least one example of how nursing is fast-paced and exciting.

> **Count the sentences in your paragraphs.** There is no magic minimum or maximum number of sentences for a paragraph. The number of sentences a paragraph contains will depend on the main idea and supporting information. However, if a paragraph contains only three or four sentences, it may be incomplete because it is not adequately developed. Get in the habit of scrutinizing short paragraphs, in particular, to make sure that they include enough layers of development.

> **Scan your drafts for the phrase** *for example.* This phrase often begins sentences that really help readers grasp your ideas. If you never begin sentences this way, you may not be including the specific information your reader needs in order to understand your thoughts on a topic.

 **EXERCISE 18.1** **Identifying Sentences That Need Development**

Underline the one sentence in each of the following paragraphs that is *not* adequately developed with more specific information or examples.

1. The Internet has become an important tool for college students. The Internet provides students with another way to communicate with their fellow students and professors. For example, they can e-mail questions to professors or ask their classmates for information about upcoming assignments. In addition, the Internet has become a valuable research tool. When students need information about a topic for a paper or a class project, they can often find what they need by searching for it online. Finally, the Internet is useful for acquiring needed supplies.

2. Playing on organized sports teams is good for children. First of all, children benefit physically. The running, jumping, and other exercises in most team sports help keep kids active and fit and help prevent them from becoming overweight. Also, playing on a team helps children's mental development. Sports can help children develop character, too. When children play on teams, they learn about playing fairly, adhering to the rules, and losing gracefully, which are all good skills for life in general.

3. Everyone can do more to conserve our limited natural resources. For one thing, we can all stop wasting so much clean water. In addition, we can conserve more trees. We can avoid wasting paper, for example, by writing

on both sides before throwing a sheet away. Also, we can use rags rather than paper towels to mop up spills. Finally, we can do more to conserve fuel like oil and gas. We can set the thermostats lower in our homes to use less fuel to heat them, and we can decide to drive more fuel-efficient cars to avoid wasting gas.

EXERCISE 18.2   **Adding Layers of Development**

Each of the following paragraphs lacks adequate layers of development. On the blanks provided, add sentences that further explain or illustrate the idea in the preceding sentence.

1. I am grateful for my best friend.

   He/she and I share an interest in many things.

   _____

   _____.

   He/she and I also have fun together.

   _____

   _____.

   He/she has helped me through some difficult times in my life, too.

   _____

   _____.

2. I really enjoy playing the game of _____.

   This game is very entertaining.

   _____

   _____.

   It is also challenging.

   _____

   _____.

   I am good at this game.

   _____

   _____.

3. Americans have always liked to display status symbols.

The vehicles that we drive are one of our biggest status symbols.

_____

_____.

Certain clothes function as status symbols, too.

_____

_____.

Particular accessories that people carry around are yet another kind of status symbol.

_____

_____.

Revising for Cohesiveness

If a paragraph is *cohesive*, all of its sentences "stick together" to support one main idea. In other words, a cohesive paragraph has unity because it focuses on just one point.

After you decide if your paragraph includes enough layers of development, the next step is to make sure that every sentence in your paragraph relates to the idea in your topic sentence. When you are writing, it is easy to get sidetracked and to go off on tangents when new thoughts come to mind. Evaluating a paragraph for cohesiveness is a process of looking for any sentence that does not directly relate to the main idea.

Can you find the sentence in the following paragraph that does not relate to the main idea? Read the paragraph, and then underline the sentence that prevents cohesiveness.

I love living in a big city. In a large metropolitan area, there are more job opportunities than in small towns or rural areas. Also, when you live in a big city, you never lack for things to do. On any day of the week, I can find an interesting leisure activity. I can choose from sports events, cultural activities like concerts or art shows, or gatherings like club meetings and classes. In my spare time, I also like to read and solve crossword puzzles. Plus, I can get just about anything I need or want in the city. Any kind of food I could possibly want is available in the city.

Did you underline the sixth sentence in this paragraph? Because it is about the writer's interests rather than the benefits of city life, it disrupts the unity in this paragraph.

To determine whether or not you have included any sentence that prevents cohesiveness, try these two techniques:

Count the sentences in your paragraph. When you evaluate a paragraph for completeness, you learn to become aware of especially brief paragraphs. When you evaluate for cohesiveness, pay particular attention to especially long paragraphs. A relatively long paragraph might be trying to develop too many different ideas, so it may not be cohesive. It may need to be divided up into smaller, more unified units.

Read the sentences of your paragraph backwards, beginning with the last sentence. After you read each sentence, reread the topic sentence. Decide if each individual sentence truly relates to the main idea.

EXERCISE 18.3   **Recognizing Sentences That Prevent Cohesiveness**

In each of the following paragraphs, underline the sentence that does not directly relate to the main idea.

1. The dentist's office was very child-friendly. In the waiting room there were several video games and a TV tuned to a cartoon station. Children's books, along with blocks, dolls, and other toys, were scattered around the room. Back in the treatment rooms, too, were stuffed animals, coloring books and crayons, and hand-held video game players to help calm and distract children. The staff members were very caring and patient, and they soothed kids' fears by talking to them in language they would understand. Dental technology has definitely gotten much more sophisticated in the last twenty years.

2. At Worldwide Airlines, safety always comes first. Worldwide hires and thoroughly trains only the best certified mechanics. When you fly Worldwide, you know the airplane in which you are flying meets all of the federal government's and the manufacturer's maintenance requirements. It will have undergone at least one comprehensive inspection in the past week. We are committed to customer service, too, so everyone from the reservation agent to the flight attendant will be friendly and helpful. You also have the comfort of knowing that your pilot is among the most experienced and completely trained pilots in the entire airline industry. Many Worldwide pilots have well over 15,000 hours of flight time, and all of our pilots continue their training at frequent and regular intervals each year.

3. In many ways, I behave differently with my family members than I do with friends, acquaintances, and coworkers. With my family, I am much more outgoing and outspoken. When I am out in the world, I tend to be more shy and reserved, and I often keep my opinions to myself. When I am at home with my parents and sisters, though, I feel free to speak my mind on any subject. I am also more silly when I am with my family. I am usually pretty serious when I am out in public, but when I am home, I am comfortable with cutting up and joking around. My family members like to laugh, so we tend to watch comedies more than any other kind of TV program. I am also more emotional at home. If I am angry or sad or really happy, I let those feelings out when I am with family members, but I often keep them to myself when I am at work or school.

Revising for Coherence

In addition to being complete and cohesive, a paragraph needs to be coherent. If a paragraph is *coherent,* it makes sense because it offers a clear progression of thought. In other words, readers can easily follow the writer's ideas from sentence to sentence.

Evaluating a paragraph's coherence involves examining its overall organization and its transitions as well as repetition of key words and ideas.

Organization and Transitions

The ideas in paragraphs are often presented in certain types of order that are familiar to readers. For example, paragraphs that relate a series of events or explain the steps in a process are organized with **time order.** In other words, the events or steps are presented in chronological order, or in the order in which they happened. In addition, transition words and phrases—words like *first, next, then, finally, later, afterward,* and *eventually*—help readers more easily see how the ideas or information is related.

To recognize how readers use both time order and transitions to make sense of information, number the following four sentences in the order in which they should appear:

_____ Finally, make changes or rearrange things if you are still having a hard time keeping the area neat.

_____ Second, you will need to pull out everything and decide what you want to keep, throw out, or give away.

_____ To organize something like a closet, the first step is to set aside a block of time and gather the containers you will need.

_____ Evaluate those things that you decide to keep, group them together according to similar function, and assign a place for each group.*

You should have numbered these four sentences 4, 2, 1, 3. If you did, you used the time order of these statements, along with transition words or phrases such as *Finally, Second,* and *the first step* to figure out the order in which they should be arranged. For more discussion of time order, see Chapter 20.

A second common type of order in paragraphs is **order of importance.** Using this order, a series of ideas or reasons may be presented with the most important item either given first or saved until last. Transition words and phrases—such as *first, second, third, last, in addition, plus, most important,* and *for one thing*—help readers understand when a new item is being presented. See if you can use order and transitions to help you put these next four sentences in the order in which they should appear:

_____ Fifteen percent would relax in the mountains or at a lake, and 14 percent would head for a major city such as Chicago.

_____ The second-largest group of people (26 percent) said that they would like to go on a cruise.

_____ When asked where they would like to vacation this year, the majority of people—32 percent—said they would love to go to a beach or island.

_____ The smallest groups would prefer to drive cross-country (9 percent) or just stay home (4 percent).†

Did you number these sentences 3, 2, 1, 4? Order of importance, as well as transitions, help you determine how these four sentences should be arranged. For more discussion of order of importance, see Chapter 24.

Another kind of order is **space order,** which is used in descriptions of people, places, or things. This order can take the form of front-to-back, left-to-right, top-to-bottom, inside-to-outside, or whatever other pattern best suits the topic. It usually includes transition words and phrases—such as *in front of, beside, above, below, next to,* and *on the left*—that help the reader mentally

*Adapted from Pamela S. Kramer, "Order in the House," *Woman's Day,* February 11, 2003, p. 22.
†Adapted from a survey in *Woman's Day,* June 17, 2003, p. 26.

picture how the descriptive details are related to one another. Use spatial order and transitions to arrange this next group of sentences:

_____ When visitors first step through the library's front door, they see the circulation desk on their left and the shelves containing the reference collection on their right.

_____ At the very back of the library are the racks containing current issues of magazines, newspapers, and journals.

_____ The shelves of fiction books begin where the nonfiction collection ends.

_____ Just past the reference collection are long rows of tall shelves that contain the nonfiction collection.

These four sentences should appear in this order: 1, 4, 3, 2. These sentences should appear in front-to-back order, which is indicated by the transitions. For more discussion of space order, see Chapter 21.

In Chapter 16, you practiced determining the best order for ideas during the organizing and outlining step of the writing process. After the paragraph is written, however, you should again evaluate whether or not your choice of order is effective. Do your ideas lead logically from one to another? Is the progression of thought easy to follow from sentence to sentence? Have you included transitions that help the reader understand how ideas are related to one another? These are the characteristics of a coherent paragraph.

 **EXERCISE 18.4** **Evaluating the Coherence of Paragraphs**

In each of the following paragraphs, underline the sentence that is out of order and prevents the paragraph from being coherent.

1. The seating in the theater was divided into three sections. Closest to the stage, on the main floor, was the front orchestra section. This section of seats was directly behind the pit where members of the orchestra sat. Farthest from the stage was the balcony section, a section of seats elevated above the main floor and reached by climbing a flight of stairs. Directly behind the front orchestra section on the main level was the rear orchestra section of seats.

2. The Internet can help you decide on a name for your new baby. First, check out the possibilities by visiting new Web sites such as www.justbabynames .com. Some of them allow you to search for names with certain meanings, like "blessing," for example. Then go to the Social Security Administration's

Web site at www.ssa.gov/OACT/babynames to find out if any of the names on your list are popular baby names in your area. Next, make a list of your favorite five or ten names. If you do not want your child to be confused with three other classmates who all have the same name, then cross those particular names off your list. Finally, cross off any names that are overly trendy and will be dated by the time your child starts school. Also, cross off names that might be cute for a baby but will look silly one day on a business card.*

3. You should consider completing your first two years of coursework at a community college. One good thing about going to a community college is convenience. Chances are good that the college will be within easy commuting distance of your home, so you will not have to move to be closer to campus. The best thing, though, about attending community college is the lower cost because community college tuition is hundreds or even thousands of dollars less than university tuition. Another important benefit of a community college education is the smaller size of many classes. Students are usually able to get more individual attention from instructors and also find it easier to participate in class.

Repetition of Key Words and Ideas

Another feature of coherent paragraphs is the repetition of key words and ideas, which link the sentences of the paragraph together. Repeating the words that name the topic, along with synonyms and pronouns that either rename or refer to the topic, causes the whole paragraph to "stick together." In the following paragraph, for example, note the highlighted words and phrases:

> Regular **exercise** will benefit you in a number of different ways. First and foremost, **working out** at least three times per week will improve your health. **Exercising** strengthens the cardiovascular system, and **it** helps prevent obesity, along with diseases from diabetes to cancer. As you tone and strengthen your muscles through **physical activity,** you will also feel better about the way you look. In addition, vigorous **workouts** are a great stress-reliever.

These repetitions and substitutions help to give the paragraph coherence.

*Adapted from Alisa Bauman, "How to Name a Baby," *Better Homes and Gardens*, April 2004, p. 298.

EXERCISE 18.5   **Recognizing the Repetition of Key Words and Ideas**

In the following paragraph, circle all repetitions of the highlighted topic, along with all of the synonyms and pronouns that either rename or refer to the topic.

According to a new study from the University of Minnesota, about a third of children ages eight to thirteen drink **soft drinks** every day. Eighty-five percent of them usually drink regular, not diet, soft drinks. This data troubles nutrition experts for three reasons. First of all, as children drink more carbonated sugary beverages, they consume less milk. Therefore, they may not be getting adequate calcium during their bone-forming years. Second, the sugar in soda could be contributing to dental problems. Children do not brush their teeth after downing cans of pop, so tooth decay is the result. Third, these drinks provide children with calories but no nutritional value. Thus, they are contributing to the rise in obesity among young people.*

*Adapted from Bev Bennett, "Mom and Pop, Listen Up: Drink Soda? So Will Kids," *Charlotte Observer,* August 29, 2004, p. 2A.

WRITING FOR SUCCESS

The Importance of Feedback

Getting feedback from others is useful as a short-term tool for the revision of a particular writing assignment. However, this feedback can also be a valuable tool for long-term learning. After you have gotten into the habit of asking others to comment on your papers, you may begin to notice that you tend to make the same mistakes over and over again. You may, for example, notice that people who read your papers almost always mention that you could improve the organization of your ideas.

Or they may indicate repeatedly that you need to work on writing clear topic sentences. You can use this information to identify general areas that you need to work on. Then, you can pay special attention to these areas the next time you write.

In Chapter 1, you learned about the importance of resisting the urge to label yourself a "bad writer." Instead, see every paper you write as a chance to improve your writing skills through increasing your knowledge and practicing.

The Importance of Getting Feedback

Often, it is difficult to evaluate your own writing. You are so intimately connected with your creation that it can be challenging to see its flaws and figure out how to make it better. Therefore, as you learned in Chapter 1, you should ask others—including your teacher, classmates, family members, or friends—to read your draft and provide you with feedback about your paragraph's strengths and weaknesses. Get in the habit of allowing enough time to ask one or more people to offer their comments and suggestions. Then, carefully consider the feedback you receive. Make the effort to understand it, and decide how you can use it to improve your writing skills in the future.

You can ask for feedback from others in two ways. The first way is informal. Simply ask people to read your draft and tell you what they like and what confuses them. The second way is a little more formal, for it involves using some type of peer review sheet to guide your readers' feedback. These sheets ask reviewers to examine specific aspects of a paragraph and comment on each one. On the next page is an example of a peer review sheet that focuses on the specific qualities of an effective paragraph covered in this chapter:

Sample Peer Review Sheet #1

Writer: _____

Reviewer: _____

Topic of paragraph: _____

	Yes	No

1. Does the paragraph contain a topic sentence that clearly states one main idea?   _____ _____

   Suggestions for improvement:

2. Does every sentence in the paragraph support the main idea?   _____ _____

   Suggestions for improvement:

3. Does the paragraph seem complete or adequately developed?   _____ _____

   Suggestions for improvement:

4. Is the paragraph organized effectively?   _____ _____

   Suggestions for improvement:

5. Has the author included transitions to help readers follow the progression of thought from one sentence to the next?   _____ _____

   Suggestions for improvement:

6. Does the paragraph repeat key words and ideas?   _____ _____

   Suggestions for improvement:

   Additional suggestions for improvement:

This sheet guides reviewers to evaluate the paragraph's topic sentence as well as its completeness, cohesiveness, and coherence.

You may have noticed that this peer review sheet does not ask for information about the paragraph's errors in grammar and spelling. Those sentence- and word-level issues will be addressed in the next chapter.

Revising a Paragraph: A Student Demonstration

In Chapter 17, you saw the first draft of John's paragraph about the importance of his cell phone. Here is his draft again:

> My cell phone serves three essential purposes in my life. It helps me stay in touch with my family and friends. We make plans to get together, we check on each other. It's good for emergencys. Like once when my car broke down. I call my brother on my cell phone and he comes to get me. I can always count on my brother to help me out when I'm in trouble. I use my cell phone for something to do to pass the time. Calling people helps the time go by faster when your waiting.

After John wrote this paragraph, he knew he needed to evaluate it for the three C's. In addition, he asked one of his classmates to read his paragraph and complete a peer review sheet. Here is his classmate's feedback:

Sample Peer Review Sheet #1

Writer: *John*

Reviewer: *Rita*

Topic of paragraph: *Cell phone*

	Yes	No
1. Does the paragraph contain a topic sentence that clearly states one main idea?	√	

Suggestions for improvement:

The topic sentence is very clear.

	Yes	No
2. Does every sentence in the paragraph support the main idea?		√

Suggestions for improvement:

I think that the 7th sentence—the one about your brother helping you whenever you're in trouble—may not go with your topic sentence.

	Yes	No
3. Does the paragraph seem complete or adequately developed?		√

Suggestions for improvement:

Adding a few more examples would help.

	Yes	No
4. Is the paragraph organized effectively?		√

Suggestions for improvement:

Should you use order of importance to arrange the details?

	Yes	No
5. Has the author included transitions to help readers follow the progression of thought from one sentence to the next?		√

Suggestions for improvement:

You might consider adding transitions like "first," "second," "third," or "more important" and "most important."

	Yes	No
6. Does the paragraph repeat key words and ideas?	√	

Suggestions for improvement:

Additional comments and suggestions for improvement:

I see some grammar errors that you'll need to fix when you edit. But your paragraph has a clear main idea and supporting points. Some reorganization and a little more development could improve it even more.

John considered Rita's suggestions and revised his draft with her feedback in mind. In particular, he used order of importance to reorganize his points, deleted the sentence that did not belong, and added transitions and more development. His revision follows:

> My cell phone serves three essential purposes in my life. Most impor-
> tant, it's good for emergencys. Like once when my car broke down.
> I call my brother on my cell phone and he comes to get me. I have also
> used it before to call for help, when I saw a car acident and had to call
> 911. The second most important use is it helps me stay in touch with
> my family and friends. We make plans to get together, we check on
> each other. For example, no matter where I am, I can call my girlfriend
> to make sure she gets home safe. Last, I use my cell phone for some-
> thing to do to pass the time. Calling people helps the time go by
> faster when your waiting. I can use my phone to surf the net too.

In the next chapter, you will see how John got help with editing his paragraph and producing a final draft.

EXERCISE 18.6   **Revising Your Paragraph**

Ask one of your classmates to read the paragraph you wrote about someone you ad-mire, an important decision, something that is not fair, or a day when you were very angry. Then, ask that classmate to complete the following peer review sheet.

Sample Peer Review Sheet #1

Writer: _____

Reviewer: _____

Topic of paragraph: _____

	Yes	No

1. Does the paragraph contain a topic sentence that clearly states one main idea? _____ _____

   Suggestions for improvement:

2. Does every sentence in the paragraph support the main idea? _____ _____

   Suggestions for improvement:

3. Does the paragraph seem complete or adequately developed? _____ _____

   Suggestions for improvement:

4. Is the paragraph organized effectively? _____ _____

   Suggestions for improvement:

5. Has the author included transitions to help readers follow the progression of thought from one sentence to the next? _____ _____

   Suggestions for improvement:

6. Does the paragraph repeat key words and ideas? _____ _____

   Suggestions for improvement:

   Additional suggestions for improvement:

Use the feedback on this sheet to decide what revisions to make to your paragraph. Also, evaluate your paragraph yourself for the three C's: completeness, coherence, and cohesiveness. Finally, rewrite your paragraph, making any necessary changes.

CHAPTER 18 REVIEW

Fill in the blanks in the following statements.

1. The word _____ literally means "to look at again."

2. When you _____ a paragraph, you are looking for and then correcting paragraph-level problems; in other words, you are evaluating and improving, if necessary, the way your whole paragraph is organized or developed.

3. To revise a paragraph, you will need to evaluate it for the three C's: _____, _____, and _____.

4. When you are examining a paragraph to make sure it is _____, or adequately developed, you evaluate the paragraph's layers of development.

5. If a paragraph is _____, all of its sentences "stick together" to support one main idea.

6. Evaluating a paragraph for cohesiveness is a process of looking for any sentence that does not directly relate to the _____.

7. If a paragraph is _____, it makes sense because it offers a clear progression of thought; in other words, readers can easily follow the writer's ideas from sentence to sentence.

8. Paragraphs that relate a series of events or explain the steps in a process are organized with ____ order.

9. Using order of _____, a series of ideas or reasons may be presented with the most important item either given first or saved until last.

10. _____ order, which is used in descriptions of people, places, or things, can take the form of front-to-back, left-to-right, top-to-bottom, or another pattern that suits the topic.

11. Coherent paragraphs include the repetition of _____, which link the sentences of the paragraph together.

12. Because it can be challenging to see the flaws in your own writing, it is often beneficial to ask others to read your draft and to provide you with _____ about your paragraph's strengths and weaknesses.

13. A _____ asks reviewers to examine specific aspects of a paragraph and to comment on each one.

WebWork

An online writing lab (OWL), which is also known as an online writing center, is a Web site on the Internet that often offers students online resources to help them improve their writing. These resources usually include tutorials and practice exercises. The following are links to several popular OWLs. Visit a few of these sites, and jot down a list of their resources that seem especially useful to you.

Purdue University's Online Writing Lab
http://owl.english.purdue.edu

St. Cloud State University's The Write Place
http://leo.stcloudstate.edu/index.html

Colorado State University's Online Writing Center
http://writing.colostate.edu

Capital Community College's Guide to Grammar and Writing
http://grammar.ccc.commnet.edu/grammar

Online Study Center For more information and practice with revising paragraphs, go to the Online Study Center that accompanies this book, at **http://www.college.hmco.com/pic/dolphinwriterone**.

19 Proofreading, Editing, and Preparing a Final Draft

GOALS FOR CHAPTER 19

▶ Proofread and edit sentences for style, sentence errors, grammatical and mechanical errors, and spelling errors.

▶ Use a Peer Review Sheet to identify errors that need editing.

▶ Prepare a final draft of a paragraph according to certain guidelines.

The fifth and final step of the writing process involves editing and preparing a final draft. When you reviewed your writing during the revision step, you were searching for large-scale errors, such as problems with the overall organization or development of your idea. To edit your writing, you **proofread,** or search for errors at the sentence and word levels. In other words, you comb through the paper carefully, searching for grammatical and spelling errors and making adjustments to sentences to improve your overall style. **Editing** means making the necessary corrections. After locating and fixing errors, you prepare your final draft for submission.

This chapter briefly covers the kinds of errors you will need to find and correct as part of the editing stage of the writing process. For more information about how to recognize and eliminate errors of this type, see Chapters 3–14.

Editing to Improve Style

The **style** of writing refers to the words the writer has chosen and the way that sentences are constructed. There are many different kinds of writing styles, and you will surely develop your own style as you continue to improve your overall writing skills. Right now, however, you should concentrate on choosing words and constructing sentences so that your writing will be interesting, clear, and easy to read. You can do that by paying attention, especially during proofreading, to the length and type of your sentences as well as to the words you have selected.

Sentence Length

Writing that is composed mostly of very short sentences usually sounds dull and monotonous to readers. If readers are bored by your sentences, they will have a more difficult time concentrating on your meaning. Plus, short sentences may not be making important connections, so readers may not fully understand your ideas. The following paragraph contains too many short sentences:

> Fall is my favorite season of the year. I like the weather. The cooler temperatures feel great after a long, hot summer. I love the changing colors of the leaves. The colors are beautiful. I enjoy football games. They are fun. They are exciting, too. I also like the Thanksgiving holiday. It is one of my favorites. My family gets together. We eat a big turkey dinner.

As this example shows, too many short sentences make the whole paragraph sound unsophisticated. But notice how the paragraph becomes clearer, easier to read, and less childish when the length of sentences is varied:

> Fall is my favorite season of the year. I like the weather because the cooler temperatures feel great after a long, hot summer. I love the beautiful changing colors of the leaves. I enjoy football games, which are fun and exciting. I also like the Thanksgiving holiday, one of my favorites. My family gets together and eats a big turkey dinner.

Now the paragraph includes a mix of shorter and longer sentences, which not only are more pleasurable to read but also sound much more sophisticated.

Techniques for Combining Sentences

If you have a tendency to write too many short sentences, try to combine some of them using the following techniques:

1. Join two sentences with a coordinating conjunction—*and, or, but, nor, for, yet,* or *so.*

Two short sentences:	He is trying to lose weight.
	He is on a diet.
Combined sentence:	He is trying to lose weight, so he is on a diet.

2. Turn one sentence into a dependent clause and attach it to an independent clause:

Two short sentences:	Her car broke down.
	She was late for work.
Combined sentence:	Because her car broke down, she was late for work.

3. Embed the information of one sentence into another sentence:

Two short sentences:	Tom is a good friend of mine.
	He was promoted to vice president.
Combined sentence:	Tom, a good friend of mine, was promoted to vice president.
Three short sentences:	Xavier walked home.
	It was cold.
	Rain was falling.
Combined sentence:	Xavier walked home in a cold rain.

For more on combining sentences, see Chapter 11.

EXERCISE 19.1   **Combining Sentences**

On the blank provided, combine each group of sentences to write one new sentence. Try to use each of the three techniques for combining sentences at least once.

1. The wild rabbits are damaging my garden.
   I need to build a fence around it.

   _____

2. She loves animals.
   She is not a pet owner.

   _____

3. Hawaii became America's fiftieth state in 1959.
   It is about 2400 miles west of San Francisco.

   _____

   _____

4. Deena brushes her teeth twice a day.
   She also flosses regularly.
   She never gets cavities.

   _____

   _____

5. I will buy the gift.
   I will wrap it.
   I will do these things tomorrow.

   _____

Word Choice

The individual words you choose affect your style, so you should make sure that they are appropriate in a number of respects. In particular, you should evaluate the appropriateness of your words' level of formality, specificity, emotion, and originality. To determine whether a word is appropriate or not, you must consider your readers and decide if the word is suitable for those readers.

First of all, evaluate your choices of words for their **level of formality.** Although each pair of words in the following chart are synonyms, notice that the words in the two columns vary in their level of formality.

Formal	*Informal*
man	dude
relax	chill out
husband	hubbie
stolen	hot
kiss	smooch
tired	pooped
impoverished	broke

Many writing situations, including academic papers and work-related documents, call for a relatively high level of formality. It is unlikely that the words labeled *Informal* in the previous chart would be appropriate in such documents, for readers expect a more elevated style. In contrast, more personal kinds of writing, such as e-mail messages and letters to family members and friends, can be much more informal. They are likely to include slang terms and conversational words like those that are labeled *Informal* in the chart.

EXERCISE 19.2 **Identifying Inappropriately Informal Words**

The following passage was submitted to a political science professor for an academic assignment that asked students to summarize a magazine article. Circle all of the words and phrases that are inappropriately informal.

I read an article called "Youth Turnout Has Declined" by Peter Levine and Mark Hugo Lopez. These dudes say that eighteen-to-twenty-one-year-olds were first allowed to vote in 1972. But it's weird that since then, the participation of young people in political elections has decreased. It ain't easy to calculate the actual totals because you can't know the age of people who cast ballots. The people who figure this stuff out have to rely on polls and surveys. Still, though, it's clear that young people have been blowing off voting. In 1972, 55 percent of eighteen-to-twenty-four-year-olds were down with voting in the election. By the year 2000, though, it was only 42 percent.*

You will also need to evaluate whether your words are **specific** enough. Specific words help readers form clear images in their minds so that they can grasp your meaning more easily. Using general or more vague terms makes it harder for readers to understand your ideas. Notice how the following revised sentences become clearer with the substitution of more specific terms.

Too general: He was dressed very formally for the occasion.
More specific: He wore a black tuxedo to the prom.

Words and phrases like *occasion* and *dressed very formally* do not provide the reader with much information. The revised sentence, however, substitutes more specific terms that provide readers with a lot more detail and help them form a clear mental image.

Which words in the following sentence are too vague and general? Circle them as you read the sentence.

The place was nice and in a good location.

Did you circle the words *place*, *nice*, and *good location*? These are the words and phrases that provide little information. If this sentence were rewritten to read "The cozy, candlelit restaurant overlooked the river," it would be much clearer for the reader.

*Adapted from the Center for Information and Research on Civic Learning and Engagement, **www.civicyouth.org**.

EXERCISE 19.3 **Identifying Vague Words**

Rewrite each of the following sentences on the blank provided to replace vague, general words and phrases with more specific words and phrases.

1. She was very upset.

_____

2. The bully was mean.

_____

3. The animal looked very menacing.

_____

4. The weather was really nice.

_____

5. The teenagers left a mess.

_____

_____

The next aspect of diction to examine is the **emotion** in the words you have chosen. Some words, like *cat,* are relatively neutral. That is, they carry no particular emotional suggestion. But compare it with the word *kitty,* which indicates affection for that animal. Notice in the following chart how some synonyms reveal more than others about the feelings of the person who chose to use the word:

Neutral	*Emotional*
overweight	fat
disabled	crippled
inexpensive	cheap
police officer	cop
inform	tattle
mother	mom

When you are evaluating your word choices, think about the emotions they reveal. While it is fine to feel strongly—either positively or negatively—about the subject you are writing about, you must also think about your reader, especially when your topic is a controversial one. You do not want to offend, insult, or annoy readers because if you do, they will reject your ideas. Therefore, make sure that your words are not inappropriately emotional.

For example, the following sentence contains an emotional word choice:

A gang of teenagers was hanging out in the mall.

The word *gang* may offend or insult some readers because of the negative, judgmental emotions attached to the word. Revising the sentence to include a less emotional word choice, like *group,* might be a good idea.

EXERCISE 19.4   **Identifying Inappropriately Emotional Words**

On the blank provided, rewrite each of the following sentences so that it expresses the same idea with more neutral language.

1. She was addicted to watching television reality shows.

_____

2. The manager demanded a staff meeting.

_____

3. My Aunt Jane is a spinster.

_____

4. The senator has got one foot in the grave.

_____

5. She stubbornly said no.

_____

Eliminating Wordiness

When you are examining the diction of your writing, one last problem to look for is **wordiness,** or unnecessary words. Clear writing always expresses an idea in as few words as possible. Wordy writing just makes it more difficult for readers to understand your thoughts, for the extra words slow them down and get in the way. Notice how the following wordy sentences express ideas that become clearer when the unnecessary words are eliminated:

Wordy: He asked for her hand in holy matrimony due to the fact that he feels great affection for her as an individual.

Revised: He proposed to her because he loves her.

Wordy: During the same time that she failed to arrive back at her home at the appointed hour, her father began to experience feelings of nervous anxiety and worry.

Revised: When she was late coming home, her father began to worry.

Always ask yourself, *Can I find a way to say this in fewer words?* Notice how in the first example, the word *because* substitutes for *due to the fact that,* the word *proposed* substitutes for *asked for her hand in holy matrimony,* and the word *loves* substitutes for *feels great affection for.* The phrase *as an individual* was unnecessary, so it was deleted. In the second example, *when* replaces *during the same time that,* *was late* replaces *failed to arrive back at her home at the appointed hour,* and the word *worry* replaces *experience feelings of nervous anxiety and worry.*

It is quite natural to be wordy when you are writing your first draft and trying to find the right words for expressing your ideas. However, you should get in the habit of examining your drafts in the editing stage and eliminating the words that are not contributing anything. When you are examining your writing for wordiness, look for the following common expressions, which add unnecessary words:

Instead of . . .	Use . . .
due to the fact that	because
in order to	to
for the purpose of	to
in the near future	soon
in the event that	if
at this point in time	now
at the present time	now
at that point in time	then
in today's world	today
this day and age	today
has the ability	can
during the same time that	when
until such time as	until
in spite of the fact that	although
are of the opinion that	think
green in color	green
small in size	small
short in length	short
the reason why is that	because
given the fact that	because
put forth an effort	try
a number of	some

Also, look for redundant expressions, which contain words that simply re-peat each other. Here are a few common redundant expressions:

Instead of . . .	*Use . . .*
close proximity	proximity
each and every	each
he is a man who	he
my personal feeling	my feeling
first and foremost	first
is located in	is in
past history	past (or history)

Finally, get in the habit of examining the especially long sentences that you write. Ask yourself if you can pare these sentences down so that they say the same thing in fewer words.

EXERCISE 19.5   **Eliminating Wordiness**

On the blank provided, rewrite each of the following sentences to eliminate unnec-essary words.

1. In the outdoors, frozen precipitation in the form of snowflakes began falling from the sky.

   _____

2. In spite of the fact that the team put forth an effort, it still failed to be victorious.

   _____

3. We are of the opinion that people who are attending school to learn should not behave dishonestly while they are completing assessments of their indi-vidual knowledge.

   _____

4. In times that are in the past, I did not ever participate in any physical activity, but at the present time, I go to a workout facility on a regular basis.

   _____

5. In the event that a fire begins to burn, call the emergency services at the phone number 911 with no delay in your response.

   _____

Editing Errors in Grammar and Mechanics

In addition to locating and correcting major sentence errors—like fragments, comma splices, dangling modifiers, and faulty parallelism—you will need to scan your writing for the many other kinds of grammatical and mechanical errors, including subject-verb agreement errors, errors in verb tense, and capitalization and punctuation errors. Part II of this text provided review and practice in recognizing and eliminating these problems.

Of course, it can be difficult to identify these errors in your own writing. One good technique for locating errors is to have others read your drafts and point them out. Consider adding questions about possible word- and sentence-level errors to the Peer Review Sheet you give your reviewers to fill out. Doing so will encourage them to look for very specific kinds of errors that may be reducing the effectiveness of your writing. You could add a page like the one that follows, for example, to your Peer Review Sheet.

Peer Review Sheet (page 2)

	Yes	No
1. Does the writer include a mixture of sentence lengths?	____	____
Suggestions for improvement:		
2. Is the word choice appropriately formal, specific, and emotional?	____	____
Suggestions for improvement:		
3. Is the writing free of wordiness?	____	____
Suggestions for improvement:		
4. Is the writing free of major sentence errors such as sentence fragments, comma splices, run-on sentences, dangling or misplaced modifiers, and faulty parallelism?	____	____
Suggestions for improvement:		
5. Is the writing free of other grammatical and mechanical errors?	____	____
Suggestions for improvement:		

If you use a Peer Review Sheet, ask your reviewers to identify the specific locations of possible errors in your draft. Then, make sure you correct all of those errors before or during your preparation of your final draft.

Another way to find errors is to learn to recognize them yourself. Increase your knowledge of grammar and mechanics so that you will stop making the same mistakes over and over again. Go over Chapters 3–14 of this text to review, and complete the exercises provided to make sure you understand how to correct the various kinds of errors. Also, pay special attention to your instructors' comments. If an instructor identifies subject-verb agreement errors in a paper you have written, go to the corresponding chapter and find out what subject-verb agreement errors are and how to correct them.

Correcting errors in your writing is very important because submitting a final draft that is marred with errors will undermine your credibility as a writer. When a paper contains errors, readers often question the writer's intelligence and overall writing ability, or they assume that the writer did not care enough about the document to ensure that it was error free.

Editing Spelling Errors

Your final draft should always be free of spelling errors. There are three ways to identify and correct errors in spelling:

1. **Use a computer spell-checker.** If you have an electronic version of your draft, use the spell-check feature of your word-processing program to locate errors. Most of these spell-checkers will suggest possible alternative spellings for each error identified. Note, however, that these spell-checkers are not foolproof. They may actually ignore words that are incorrectly spelled, so use the next two methods in addition to this one.

2. **Ask someone to proofread your draft for spelling errors.** Ask someone you know who is a good speller to circle possible errors in spelling in your draft.

3. **Whenever you have the slightest doubt that a word is spelled correctly, look it up in a dictionary.** Always check the spellings of words you question in a book or online version of a dictionary. You can find several different online dictionaries at **www.onelook.com.**

WRITING FOR SUCCESS

The Harmful Effects of Errors

You learned in this chapter that documents filled with errors lead readers to believe that the writer may not be credible, intelligent, or caring. Do errors have any other effects on readers? In fact, they do. Errors can actually inhibit readers' comprehension of your ideas. Every time a reader encounters an error, he or she must stop, back up, and mentally correct the mistake. If a reader has to do this over and over again, he or she will have to read more slowly, in fits and starts, a process that can interfere with comprehension. In addition, he or she may become increasingly frustrated.

Even worse, though, errors can cause actual misunderstanding of your thoughts.

Consider, for example, the effect of a misplaced comma. There is an old joke about a panda who is sitting in a café. The animal eats a sandwich, fires a gun into the air, and then begins walking toward the door. A shocked waiter asks the animal what it is doing. The panda pulls out a badly punctuated book about wildlife and shows him this entry: "Panda: Large black and white bear-like mammal, native to China. Eats, shoots and leaves." The humor, of course, depends on your understanding of two meanings of the word *shoots* as well as your recognition that there should be no comma after the word *eats*. Placing one there changes the entire meaning of the sentence.

 **EXERCISE 19.6**   **Proofreading a Passage for Grammar and Spelling Errors**

Edit the following passage to correct grammar and spelling errors. Cross out the errors and add corrections directly to the text of the passage.

> For centuries, people have wondered how we can
>
> create hapiness. Psychologist Mihaly Csikszent-
>
> mihalyi has call highly enjoyable periods of time
>
> flow states. Flow is characterized by total
>
> absorbtion in what one is doing, an altered
>
> sense of time (which seems to pass more quick
>
> than usual), and a loss of concern about oneself.
>
> When do you suppose a typical working
>
> american experiences the most flow? If you

guessed on the weekends or on vacations. You will be surprised by what Csikszentmihalyi found. Typical working adults reports experiencing flow on their jobs three times more often than during free time.

Therefore, if you want to create a positive experience of your life engage in work that makes use of your talents and your inborn desires. For the next couple of decade at least, you will probly spend many of your waking hours at work. You do not have to settle for just a paycheck, some people do what they love. Why shouldn't you.*

Preparing the Final Draft

After you have edited your paragraph for style and errors, you are ready to prepare your final draft for submission. You will, of course, need to follow your instructor's guidelines for final drafts. Regardless of your paragraph's final format, however, it should always be neat, clean, and professional looking. It should be typed or handwritten, as your instructor requires, and its appearance should reflect the fact that you have invested time and effort in your paragraph.

In general, both typed and handwritten final drafts usually have one-inch margins at the top, bottom, and left and right sides of the paper. This means that the first sentence begins an inch from the top edge of the paper, and the last line on the page stops an inch away from the bottom edge of the paper. Each line be-

*Source: Downing, Skip, *On Course*, 4th Edition. Copyright © 2005 by Houghton Mifflin Company. Reprinted with permission.

gins one inch from the left edge of the paper and reaches all the way to one inch from the right edge of the paper. Every new paragraph is indented five spaces. Many instructors require assignments to be double-spaced, which means that a handwritten paragraph should skip every other line on the page. At the top of the first page, put your name and any other information the instructor wants you to include (such as course name or number and date).

Your name

1-inch top margin

Title

Indent 5 spaces

1-inch left margin

1-inch right margin

1-inch bottom margin

After you prepare your final draft, you should go over it one more time to look for **typographical errors,** which are accidental mistakes that occur during the typing or printing of a document. If you find such an error, you should always neatly correct it either by carefully striking through the error and writing in the correction with a black pen or by covering the error with correction fluid and then writing the correction.

Editing a Paragraph: A Student Demonstration

In Chapter 18, you saw how John revised his paragraph about his cell phone. Here is his revised draft again:

> My cell phone serves three essential purposes in my life. Most important, it's good for emergencys. Like once when my car broke down. I call my brother on my cell phone and he comes to get me. I have also used it before to call for help, when I saw a car acident and had to call 911. The second most important use is it helps me stay in touch with my family and friends. We make plans to get together, we check on each other. For example, no matter where I am, I can call my girlfriend to make sure she gets home safe. Last, I use my cell phone for something to do to pass the time. Calling people helps the time go by faster when your waiting. I can use my phone to surf the Net too.

Next, he needed to look over his draft for word- and sentence-level errors. Thus, he asked his peer reviewer, Rita, to help him find grammatical and mechanical errors and to help him polish his style. Rita completed the following addition to the first Peer Review Sheet:

Peer Review Sheet (page 2)

	Yes	No
1. Does the writer include a mixture of sentence lengths?		√

Suggestions for improvement:

I think you could combine a few of these sentences.

| **2.** Is the word choice appropriately formal, specific, and emotional? | √ | |

Suggestions for improvement:

Should "Net" be spelled out as "Internet"?

| **3.** Is the writing free of wordiness? | √ | |

Suggestions for improvement:

Mostly yes, but the sixth sentence seems a little wordy.

| **4.** Is the writing free of major sentence errors such as sentence fragments, comma splices, run-on sentences, dangling or misplaced modifiers, and faulty parallelism? | | √ |

Suggestions for improvement:

I think the third sentence is a fragment. The seventh sentence is a comma splice.

| **5.** Is the writing free of other grammatical and mechanical errors? | | √ |

Suggestions for improvement:

You misspelled "emergencies," "accident," and "you're" (in the second-to-last sentence). The verb tense shifts in the fourth sentence. I think there are a few comma errors. "Safe" should be the adverb form, "safely."

After receiving Rita's feedback, John found the errors she mentioned and edited his paragraph to eliminate these mistakes. Then, he typed his final draft according to his teacher's guidelines. Here, finally, is the draft he submitted:

My Cell Phone

by John Jackson

My cell phone serves three essential purposes in my life. Most important, it's good for emergencies, like the time when my car broke down. I called my brother on my cell phone, and he came to get me. I have also used it before to call for help. Once, for example, I saw a car accident and had to call 911. The second most important use is for communication with family and friends. We make plans to get together, and we check on each other. For example, no matter where I am, I can call my girlfriend to make sure she gets home safely. Last, I use my cell phone for something to do to pass the time because calling people helps the time go by faster when you're waiting. I can use my phone to surf the Internet, too.

Because John completed all five steps in the writing process to create this paragraph, it is clearly developed, well organized, and easily read and understood.

EXERCISE 19.7   **Editing Your Paragraph**

For your paragraph on either your favorite sport, your goals, an embarrassing moment, or artistic expression, ask a classmate to complete the following Peer Review Sheet to help you identify errors that need correction.

Peer Review Sheet (page 2)

	Yes	No
1. Does the writer include a mixture of sentence lengths?	____	____

Suggestions for improvement:

| 2. Is the word choice appropriately formal, specific, and emotional? | ____ | ____ |

Suggestions for improvement:

| 3. Is the writing free of wordiness? | ____ | ____ |

Suggestions for improvement:

| 4. Is the writing free of major sentence errors such as sentence fragments, comma splices, run-on sentences, dangling or misplaced modifiers, and faulty parallelism? | ____ | ____ |

Suggestions for improvement:

| 5. Is the writing free of other grammatical and mechanical errors? | ____ | ____ |

Suggestions for improvement:

Use the feedback on this sheet to edit your paragraph, and then prepare your final draft according to the following guidelines:

1. Type the paragraph with double spacing, or write it neatly by hand, skipping every other line on your paper.
2. All margins should be one inch.
3. Include your name and a title for your paragraph somewhere at the top of the page.

Fill in the blanks in the following statements.

1. To edit your writing, you _____, or search for errors at the sentence and word levels.

2. *Editing* means making the necessary _____.

3. The _____ of writing refers to the words the writer has chosen and the way that sentences are constructed.

4. Writing that is composed mostly of very short sentences usually sounds _____ _____ to readers; short sentences also may not be making important _____, so readers may not fully understand the ideas.

5. To combine sentences, join them with a _____ (*and, or, but, nor, for, yet,* or *so*), turn one sentence into a _____ and attach it to an independent clause, or embed the information of one sentence into another sentence.

6. The individual words you choose must be appropriately _____, _____, and emotional.

7. Writing that suffers from _____ includes unnecessary words.

8. In addition to proofreading your drafts for sentence variety, appropriate language, and wordiness, you need to find and eliminate major errors in _____.

9. Two ways to locate errors in your drafts involve asking peer reviewers to fill out a _____ and learning to recognize errors yourself.

10. Correcting errors in your writing is very important because submitting a final draft marred with errors will undermine your _____ as a writer.

11. Three ways to identify and correct spelling errors are (1) use a _____ _____, (2) ask someone to proofread your draft for spelling errors, and (3) look up possible misspellings in a _____.

12. Regardless of a paper's final format, it should always be ____, ____, and

_____.

13. _____ are accidental mistakes that occur during the typing or
printing of a document.

WebWork

One useful tool for learning about grammar is the Guide to Grammar and Writing Web
site at **http://grammar.ccc.commnet.edu/grammar/index.htm**. This Internet site not
only explains grammatical concepts but also includes computer-graded quizzes that
give you instant feedback, so you know immediately whether or not you have
understood the information.

What particular error (commas, subject-verb agreement, run-ons, sentence
fragments, and so on) do you need to learn more about? Go to the Guide to Grammar
and Writing Web site and find the tutorial about that particular error. Then, complete
at least one of the quizzes provided at the end of the lesson.

Online Study Center For more information and practice with proofreading, editing, and
preparing a final draft, go to the Online Study Center that accompanies
this book, at **http://www.college.hmco.com/pic/dolphinwriterone**.

20 Time Order: Narration and Process

GOALS FOR CHAPTER 20

▶ Define the terms *time order, narrative,* and *process.*

▶ Describe the steps in writing a narrative paragraph.

▶ Write a narrative paragraph.

▶ Describe the steps in writing a process paragraph.

▶ Write a process paragraph.

In Chapter 17 of this book, you practiced developing the main idea of a paragraph or essay with various kinds of information and examples. In the next five chapters (Chapters 20–24), you will look more closely at different patterns that will help you organize your development of your topic sentence or thesis. You will begin in this chapter with the time order pattern.

In **time order** paragraphs, the details are arranged according to their chronological relationships. In other words, time order paragraphs present details in the order in which they happened or should happen. Two types of time order paragraphs are narrative and process. A **narrative** paragraph tells a story or recounts a sequence of events. Here is an example of a narrative paragraph that arranges details according to the time order pattern:

> During the summer between my sophomore and junior years in college, I used all of my savings to visit Hawaii. While there, I met a beautiful young woman, and we spent twelve blissful[1] days together. I promised to return to Hawaii during Christmas break. Back in college, though, six thousand miles away, I had

1. **blissful:** very happy

no idea how, in just three months, I could raise enough money to return. I spent weeks inventing and rejecting one scheme after another. Then, one day, I happened upon a possible solution. Maybe the editors of *Sports Illustrated* would buy an article about the sport I played, lightweight football. Every evening for weeks, I worked on an article. Finally, I dropped it in the mail and crossed my fingers. Then one day my phone rang, and I learned that my article had been accepted. I spent Christmas on the beach at Waikiki, with my girlfriend on the blanket beside me.*

The second type of time order paragraph is process. A **process** paragraph explains how something is done or could be done. Its details are organized in steps or stages, in the order in which they occur or should occur. Here is an example of a process paragraph:

Most bears will sprint away at the first sight of man. But if, on a side hike, you come across a bear that stands his ground, don't panic and run, for this may excite the bear and invite pursuit. Slowly put down any food or candy you might be carrying and retreat, keeping downhill from the bear and glancing around for escape routes and nearby trees to climb. If the bear advances in a threatening manner, either scoot up a tree or lie still on the ground, with knees drawn up and hands protecting the back of your head. In either case, stay put until you are certain the bear has gone.†

Writing a Narrative Paragraph

You probably use **narration,** or storytelling, fairly often. You tell stories about the things that happen to you, to your friends, and your family members, and you also tell stories that you have heard about other people's experiences. As a writer, you will need to be able to tell a good story in order to develop some point or idea. Sometimes the story will be something that happened to you. At other times, you will tell a story that happened to someone else. In either case, though, you will need to incorporate some features that are common to all effective narratives. These essential features are discussed in the following sections of this chapter.

---

*Adapted from Skip Downing, *On Course,* 4th ed. Copyright © 2005 by Houghton Mifflin Company. Reprinted with permission.
†From William McGinnis, "Bear Attack," in Mary Lou Conlin, *Patterns Plus,* 7th ed. (Boston: Houghton Mifflin, 2002), p. 179.

Determining a Main Idea and Writing a Topic Sentence

The first step in writing an effective narrative paragraph involves deciding on the point you want to make about the events you will relate. As you look at the details you generated during the prewriting stage, ask yourself *why* you want to tell the story. Is there some moral or lesson to be gained from hearing the story? Does the story illustrate some truth about your life or the lives of everyone? Do you want to help readers learn something, or do you want to entertain them? These questions will help you decide on the one main idea you would like your readers to know or to accept. Then, write a topic sentence that states this main idea.

For an example, look at a brainstorming sample generated by a student who was assigned to write about a memorable childhood experience. She thought of the time her first boyfriend broke up with her:

- Jerry—my very first boyfriend
- met in 6th grade
- he was tall, handsome, sweet, kind
- gave me a leather bracelet stamped with his name
- I adored him
- he had 5 brothers and sisters
- his parents were nice
- we left elementary school and went to junior high school for 7th grade
- I still adored him
- he began hanging out with older friends
- older girls became interested in him
- I began to hear rumors that he was going to break up with me
- our friends would make jokes about him dumping me
- I got anxious and upset
- he said he wanted to talk to me during lunch
- I can still remember trudging to the cafeteria that day
- I was devastated
- All he said was "you know, right?"
- I couldn't speak, just nodded my head
- so upset I could hardly breathe
- I was crushed

After completing this brainstorming, the student decided that she wanted to entertain readers with her story about her first romantic breakup. She wrote this topic sentence:

My very first romantic breakup is still one of my most painful.

As you complete this step in the process, remember what you learned in Chapter 17 about topic sentences. A topic sentence does not always have to be the first sentence of a paragraph. It may be more appropriate to save it for last or to put it in the middle of the paragraph.

 **EXERCISE 20.1** **Writing Topic Sentences for Narratives**

For each of the following topics, use some prewriting techniques to generate ideas on your own paper, and then write a topic sentence you could use for a narrative paragraph.

1. A dangerous thing I did

   Topic sentence: _____

2. An emergency

   Topic sentence: _____

3. A day I was very happy

   Topic sentence: _____

4. My first date

   Topic sentence: _____

5. A memorable trip I took

   Topic sentence: _____

Organizing Details and Using Transitions

The next step in writing a narrative paragraph is reviewing your prewriting to make sure that you have included all of the major, important events. If anything important is missing, jot it down. Narratives organize themselves naturally because the events are almost always presented in chronological, or time, order. Chances are good that when you were generating ideas, you wrote the details in chronological order as you were remembering them. Preparing the outline, then, is usually just a matter of making sure that the important events are listed in order, from beginning to end.

EXERCISE 20.2   **Organizing Events in Narratives**

On your own paper, prewrite to generate ideas, and then complete each of the following topic sentences by filling in the blank. Then, on the other blanks provided, prepare an informal outline by listing the major events of the story in the order in which they occurred.

1. I had never been so angry as when I _____.

   _____

   _____

   _____

   _____

   _____

2. _____ was a very frightening experience for me.

   _____

   _____

   _____

   _____

   _____

3. I was proud of my problem-solving skills when I _____.

   _____

   _____

   _____

   _____

   _____

To help the reader understand the time frame of the events, writers include transition words and phrases. The following list includes common time-related transitions:

first, second, third	next	as
before	soon	when
now	in the beginning	until
then	once	later

after	today	eventually
while	previously	last
finally	often	meanwhile
over time	during	
in the end	in, on, or by (followed by a date)	

In addition, writers include information about the passage of time, usually in short phrases like *in a few hours* or *two weeks went by* or with specific dates. Notice how the writer of the following paragraph uses both time-related transitions and information about how much time has passed to help you follow the events in the story.

By the time I was a teenager, Abuelo's[1] advancing age was making him vulnerable to merciless thugs[2]—the bad guys. **The first time that this happened,** Abuelo was helping out at a nephew's bodega.[3] A young man, a child in Abuelo's eyes, came in and pointed a gun at Abuelo. He indignantly[4] smacked it away from his face. **Then,** he handed over the money. He was angry, but still in control. **A few years later,** he was pushed into a hidden vestibule,[5] and another child demanded money from him. Frightened by the anger, rage, and fear in this child's eyes, he felt defeated for the first time in his life. **For days afterward,** he sat sullenly,[6] overcome by the burden of his advancing years. He was no longer the one in control.*

EXERCISE 20.3   Recognizing Narrative Transitions

Circle all of the transitions and time-related information in the following paragraph.

> The famous Leaning Tower of Pisa has been tilting for over eight hundred years, and recent improvements should allow it to continue tilting for another three hundred more. On August 9, 1173, construction began on this well-known Italian

1. **Abuelo:** Spanish for "grandfather"
2. **thugs:** violent young criminals
3. **bodega:** a small Hispanic shop
4. **indignantly:** with anger at something unjust or wrong
5. **vestibule:** entrance area
6. **sullenly:** in a bad mood

*Adapted from Lilliam Diaz-Imbelli, "El Viejo," in *Horizons: A Reader of Experiences* (Boston: Houghton Mifflin, 2004), p. 60.

bell tower. Almost immediately, it began leaning
because it was being erected on the soft silt[1] of
a buried riverbed. Between 1178 and 1360, work
stopped and started two more times as work-
ers tried to continue the project and figure out
how to compensate for the tilt. Over the next six
centuries, the tower's lean continued to increase, although tourists were still allowed to
visit. Then, in 1990, Italy's prime minister feared
the tower would collapse and closed it to the
public. From 1999 to 2001, engineers excavated[2]
the soil from beneath the tower. Now, the tower
still leans out about fifteen feet beyond its
base, but it should remain stable for several
more centuries.*

EXERCISE 20.4   **Writing a Narrative Paragraph That Includes Transitions**

Choose one of the topic sentences and outlines that you prepared in Exercise 20.2.
Write the paragraph, including transitions that indicate the time frame of the events.

Using Vivid Language

Using vivid and interesting language is important in all types of writing. However, it is especially important in narrative writing, where your goal is to enable

1. **silt:** mud or clay deposited by a river   2. **excavated:** dug out
    or lake

*Adapted from Richard Covington, "The Leaning Tower Straightens Up," *Smithsonian*, June 2001,
pp. 41–47.

readers to picture people and events in their minds. There are three kinds of vivid language that will help you re-create experiences in words.

Specific Words

You will create more vivid mental images for your reader if you choose specific words over more general ones. For example, the word *food* is a relatively general term that includes many different kinds of food. Therefore, to help your reader picture the scene more clearly, substitute a more specific word or words, such as *ripe peach* or *ham-and-cheese sandwich*. Instead of writing *flower*, write *daisy*. Instead of writing *dog*, write *beagle*, and so on. The more precise your word choice, the sharper the picture becomes in the mind's eye of your readers.

Factual and Sensory Details

Like specific words, factual and sensory details will create more vivid mental images for your reader. **Factual details** offer information such as names, quantities, dates, and dimensions (height, length, width, weight). Thus, in describing your own or someone else's actions, you might want to specify when and where these actions took place, as well as how long they lasted. **Sensory details** provide information about what something looks, smells, tastes, sounds, or feels like. When you write narratives, include information about the sights, sounds, and other sensations of the scenes you are re-creating in words.

Action-oriented Verbs

In narratives especially, you will want to use action-packed verbs to describe the events and the participants' behaviors. Therefore, instead of writing *Joe moved down the hallway*, write *Joe shuffled down the hallway*, a description that provides more of a mental picture of *how* he moved. Also, choose verbs that offer the most precise explanation of what happened. For example, instead of writing that *Hannah was amused*, you might want to say that *Hannah laughed so hard that tears rolled down her cheeks*. The more specific the verb, the easier it is for the reader to picture what happened.

 **EXERCISE 20.5**   **Writing with Vivid Language**

Rewrite each of the following sentences to substitute more specific words, add factual and sensory details, and use more action-oriented verbs.

1. The storm was bad.

2. She performed well.

_____

3. The animal did an interesting trick.

_____

4. The people left the burning building.

_____

5. It was a very noisy place.

_____

In Summary: Steps in Writing Narrative Paragraphs

1. Prewrite to generate ideas and determine a main idea.
2. Create an outline of the major events in chronological order.
3. As you write, include time-related transitions and information. Also, use vivid language, including specific words, factual and sensory details, and action-oriented verbs.

Writing a Process Paragraph

Some topic sentences need to be developed with an explanation of how something is done or should be done. When you develop an idea with process, you explain the steps in a procedure using chronological order.

Determining a Main Idea and Writing a Topic Sentence

The topic sentence of a process paragraph will identify the process you are explaining and will state the goal or end result of this process:

Anyone can learn how to use an Internet search engine.

The topic sentence may also identify the number of steps in the process. Thus, for example, a paragraph about how to resolve a conflict might begin with this topic sentence:

To successfully resolve a conflict, follow four important steps.

 **EXERCISE 20.6**   **Writing Topic Sentences for Process Paragraphs**

For each of the following topics, use some prewriting techniques to generate ideas on your own paper, and then write a topic sentence you could use for a process paragraph.

1. Meeting someone new

   Topic sentence: _____

2. Doing a specific household chore correctly

   Topic sentence: _____

3. A great recipe

   Topic sentence: _____

4. How something works

   Topic sentence: _____

5. How to do something sports-related (swing a golf club, dribble a basketball, and so on)

   Topic sentence: _____

Organizing Details and Using Transitions

Most process paragraphs, like narrative paragraphs, organize themselves naturally. The writer breaks the process down into a series of clear steps and then presents those steps chronologically, in the order in which they occur.

EXERCISE 20.7   **Organizing Details in Process Paragraphs**

On your own paper, prewrite to generate ideas, and then complete each of the following topic sentences by filling in the blank. Then, on the other blanks provided, prepare an informal outline by listing the major steps in chronological order.

1. If you want to _____, follow these steps.

   _____

   _____

   _____

   _____

   _____

2. _____ is a process that occurs in _____ stages.

_____

_____

_____

_____

_____

3. To create your own _____, you should _____.

_____

_____

_____

_____

As you write, show how the steps in the process are separated from and related to one another by including transitions. In a process that presents the steps chronologically, transitions will help the reader follow their order in time. The following list includes common process transitions:

first, second, third	next	as
before	soon	when
now	in the beginning	until
then	once	later
after	often	meanwhile
while	finally	last
in the end	afterward	

EXERCISE 20.8   **Recognizing Process Transitions**

Circle all of the time order transitions in the following paragraph.

If you feel like giving up when you encounter a very long or hard assignment, you probably have a low tolerance for unpleasant tasks. However, you can change your attitude so that you can concentrate and get these tasks done. First, remind yourself that the sooner you start, the sooner you will finish. Next, remind yourself that your attitude toward studying may be causing you to lose concentration and

may be keeping you from doing your work as well as you can. Third, make long or difficult assignments easier to handle by breaking them into smaller segments that you can complete in one sitting. Then reward yourself for doing the work.*

EXERCISE 20.9   **Writing a Process Paragraph That Includes Transitions**

Choose one of the topic sentences and outlines you prepared in Exercise 20.7. Write the paragraph, including transitions that indicate the order of the details.

Developing a Process Paragraph

Have you ever tried to put something together by following poorly written instructions? The process was probably time-consuming and frustrating. Therefore, to help the reader easily re-create or comprehend the procedure you are explaining, you must anticipate all of your readers' questions and make sure you provide the answers to those questions.

To make sure that you are providing all of these answers, always give definitions of terms that you use. Explain to the reader how to accomplish minor steps, such as "remove the bolts" or "filet the fish." Be very specific. If you tell readers to sit, specify whether they should sit in a chair or on the floor. If you tell readers to attach two things, specify whether that attachment should occur with glue, nails, screws, or something else.

After you have written your paragraph, make sure that you have not overlooked any essential details and information, especially for minor actions or events. If possible, have someone actually follow your directions as you read them aloud. Pay attention to any questions that person asks you, for you may need to add the answers to your paragraph.

In Summary: Steps in Writing Process Paragraphs

1. **Write a topic sentence or thesis that mentions the process and the end result.**
2. **Organize the steps in the process.** Create an outline that lists these steps in chronological order or another kind of order, as appropriate.

*Adapted from Carol C. Kanar, *The Confident Student*, 5th ed. (Boston: Houghton Mifflin, 2004), p. 258.

WRITING FOR SUCCESS

Time Order in Work-Related Writing

Mastering the use of time order for organizing ideas will strengthen much of your on-the-job writing. The following is a list of work-related documents that are typically organized chronologically, with time order:

- **Résumés.** You will organize some parts of your résumé, such as the work experience section, with time order.
- **Instructions or explanations of procedures.** Directions for completing tasks are organized using time order.

- **Incident reports.** Reports about something that happened, such as an accident or a work interruption, are usually organized with time order.
- **Progress reports.** Details in reports about an ongoing project are usually arranged chronologically.
- **Lab reports.** Reports about laboratory experiments are often organized with time order.
- **Summaries of meetings or other activities.** Summaries of events or discussions are often arranged chronologically.

3. **Develop each step with all of the essential information.** Make sure that you define terms, explain the use of materials, and describe each step as appropriate for your intended readers. Use transitions that help readers understand how the steps are related.

CHAPTER 20 REVIEW

Fill in the blanks in the following statements.

1. A narrative is a _____ about your own or others' experiences.

2. The first step in writing an effective narrative paragraph involves deciding on the _____ you want to make about the events.

3. Narratives organize themselves naturally because the events are almost always presented in _____ order.

4. Preparing an outline for a narrative is usually just a matter of listing the important _____ in the order in which they occurred.

5. To help the reader understand the time frame of the events, writers include _____ words and phrases, such as *in the beginning*, *after*, *next*, and *meanwhile*.

6. _____ language helps readers picture people and events in their minds.

7. Three kinds of vivid language are _____ words, _____ and _____ details, and _____ .

8. _____ offer information such as names, quantities, dates, and dimensions.

9. _____ provide information about what something looks, smells, tastes, sounds, or feels like.

10. _____ is an explanation of how something is done or should be done.

11. The topic sentence of a process paragraph will identify the process you are explaining and state the _____ of this process.

12. Most process paragraphs break the process down into a series of steps and then present those steps _____, in the order in which they occur.

13. As you write, show how the steps in the process are separated from and related to one another by including _____ .

14. Common process _____ include *first, second, third, then, next, finally,* and *meanwhile.*

15. To help the reader easily re-create or comprehend the procedure that you are explaining, anticipate all of your readers' _____ and make sure that you provide answers.

Topic Ideas for Time Order Paragraphs

Exercises 20.1 and 20.6 include topic ideas you may want to develop into time order paragraphs. Here are some additional ideas:

- A natural disaster
- My favorite family story
- A painful moment
- A special occasion
- A time when you felt successful
- An educational experience
- Something unusual you have done
- A great story from history

- A valuable lesson
- How to build a good fire
- How to repair something
- How to housetrain a pet
- How to save time or money
- Getting out of debt
- How bad habits develop
- How to correct a problem
- Tell the story shown in the following series of photographs:

All photos on pages 306–308 © AP/Wide World Photos

WebWork

For more information about writing interesting narratives, go to **http://leo.stcloudstate .edu/acadwrite/narrative.html**.

    To find out more about writing clear instructions, visit **http://leo.stcloudstate.edu/ acadwrite/process.html**.

Online Study Center   For more information and practice using time order, go to the Online Study Center that accompanies this book, at **http://www .college.hmco.com/pic/dolphinwriterone**.

Space Order: Description

▶ Define the terms *space order* and *description*.

▶ Describe the steps in writing a descriptive paragraph.

▶ Write a descriptive paragraph.

In **space order** paragraphs, the details are arranged according to their arrangement in space. Space order paragraphs present details so that the reader can form a mental picture of the person, place, or thing being described. A **descriptive** paragraph, then, provides details about what something or someone looks like, sounds like, smells like, and so on. The following paragraph, which presents details using space order, is descriptive:

> Just as a light snow begins to fall, I cross the boundary of the Indian reservation; somehow it seems as though I have stepped into another world. In the deep woods of the white-and-black winter night, a faint trail leads to the village. I go into the woods. As I cross a frozen lake, I begin to hear the drums. Soft in the night the drums beat. It is like the pulse beat of the world. The white line of the lake ends a black forest, and above the trees the blue winds are dancing. I come to the outlying houses of the village. Simple box houses, etched black in the night. From one or two windows soft lamplight falls on the snow. I walk along the trail to the lodge, watching the northern lights forming in the heavens. The lights are white waving ribbons that seem to pulsate[1] with the rhythm of the drums. Clean snow creaks beneath my feet, and a soft wind sighs through the trees, singing to me. Everything seems to say, "Be happy! You are home now— you are free."*

1. **pulsate:** expand and contract

*Adapted from Tom Whitecloud, "Blue Winds Dancing," in *Horizons: A Reader of Experiences* (Boston: Houghton Mifflin, 2004), pp. 50–51.

309

Writing a Descriptive Paragraph

Sometimes you will need to develop a topic sentence by describing someone or something. When you describe, you provide factual and sensory details that help readers form a mental image of your subject. To write an effective description, you will need to include the essential features that are illustrated in the next sections.

Prewriting

Although you can use any of the prewriting methods described in Chapter 15 of this text to generate ideas for description, clustering is especially useful. Re-creating a person, place, or thing in words for your readers will require that you provide details related to all five senses, so you might want to add a group of details for each sense to your cluster. For example, if you were going to describe the student lounge on a college campus, your cluster might look like this:

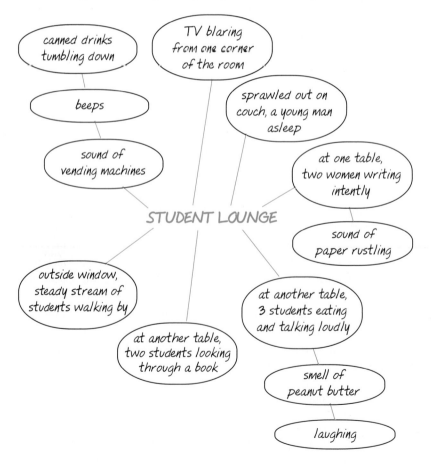

Determining a Main Idea and Writing a Topic Sentence

The first step in writing an effective descriptive paragraph involves deciding on the point that you want to make about the subject you are describing. This point offers a **dominant impression,** an essential quality that you want to convey about your subject. Sometimes you will know before you begin writing what your dominant impression will be. For example, if you are assigned to write about a place that is beautiful to you, then "beautiful" is your dominant impression, and you would select a subject—perhaps a rose garden or the beach at sunset—that fits this impression.

However, if you are assigned to write about a place like the student lounge, then you may not know what your dominant impression is until you generate some details. Look back, for example, at the cluster on page 310. When you consider these details, what one impression do most of them convey to you? Would you say that this room seems to be bustling? Noisy? Dull? Unfriendly? Each of the details might support at least one of these characterizations. But if you were to write a topic sentence for a paragraph about this lounge, you would need to select one particular impression on which to focus. You might write the following topic sentence:

The student lounge is a very noisy place.

This topic sentence clearly indicates the dominant impression that you will convey in your description. As you complete this step in the process, remember what you learned in Chapter 17 about topic sentences. A topic sentence does not always have to be the first sentence of a paragraph. It may be more appropriate to save it for last or to put it in the middle of the paragraph.

 **EXERCISE 21.1** **Writing Topic Sentences for Descriptive Paragraphs**

For each of the following topics, use some prewriting techniques to generate ideas on your own paper, and then write a topic sentence that you could use for a descriptive paragraph.

1. A beautiful scene from nature

   Topic sentence: _____

2. My favorite store

   Topic sentence: _____

3. A special person

   Topic sentence: _____

4. My favorite article of clothing

   Topic sentence: _____

5. My favorite meal

   Topic sentence: _____

Selecting the Right Details for a Description

The next step toward writing an interesting descriptive paragraph is selecting the right details to include. You cannot include every detail about your subject because your paragraph would be too long and too tedious to read, and your point would get lost in irrelevant information. Therefore, you will have to examine your prewriting and decide which pieces of information will convey your dominant impression. Circle every detail that supports the idea in your topic sentence, and ignore the other details.

For some practice in selecting details, think back to the previous example about describing the student lounge. On the blank next to each of the following details, write an *N* if the detail suggests "noisy," *A* if the detail suggests "annoying or rude," and *S* if the detail suggests "studious." Some details might warrant more than one label.

_____ TV blaring a morning talk show from one corner of the room

_____ sprawled out on a couch, a young man asleep

_____ at one table, two women writing intently

_____ at another table, three students eating and talking too loudly

_____ at another table, two students discussing the information in a book

_____ sounds of vending machines

Did you label the details in this list *N/A, A, S, N/A, N/S, N*? This is how you would go about deciding which details match your dominant impression.

EXERCISE 21.2   **Selecting Details for Descriptive Paragraphs**

Choose one of the topic sentences you wrote for Exercise 21.1, and on your own paper, list the details that you would definitely need to include if you developed that statement in a descriptive paragraph.

Organizing Details and Using Transitions

Once you have circled all of the appropriate details in your prewriting, you next need to decide how to organize these details. Descriptions require some type of spatial organization. In other words, they orient the specific details for the reader by explaining how those details relate to one another in space. Some common spatial patterns for arranging details are

front to back (or vice versa)
left to right (or vice versa)
top to bottom (or vice versa)
inside to outside (or vice versa)
near to far (or vice versa)

Descriptive details can also be arranged using a narrative pattern. For example, if you are describing a parade that passed before you, you could describe each element of the parade in chronological order.

The best pattern is often dictated by the subject itself. For example, if you are describing a house, you might use an outside-to-inside pattern. If you are describing a landscape, however, it would be more appropriate to use a near-to-far or left-to-right pattern. Once you select a pattern, list in your outline your details in that order. Follow your outline as you write to avoid jumping around. Particularly in descriptions, readers must understand the details' arrangement in order to create a mental picture.

As you write descriptions, use transitions that help your reader understand how the details are related. The following list includes common spatial transitions:

above	to the left, to the right	overhead
below	nearby	underneath
under	in the distance	between
inside	on top	among
outside	at the bottom	across
toward	in the center	next to
away	close by	far away
in front	in back	up
down		

Notice in the following paragraph how the spatial transitions and information, which are highlighted, help you organize the details in your mind and form a mental picture of the subject:

Our house was on a piece of land that rose **about four feet up from heavily trafficked Vermont Avenue.** The yard sloped down to the street, and three steps and a short walkway led up **the middle of the grass to our front door.** There was a similar house **immediately to the south of us. Next to it** was Carmen's Barber Shop. **Next to Carmen's** was a junk store where, one summer, I made a little money polishing brass and rewiring old lamps. **Then came** a dilapidated[1] real estate office, a Mexican restaurant, an empty lot, and an appliance store owned by the father of Keith Grateful, the streetwise, chubby boy who would become my best friend. **Right to the north of us** was a record shop, a barber shop presided[2] over by old Mr. Graff, Walt's Malts, a shoe repair shop, a third barber shop, and a brake shop. **Behind our house** was an unpaved alley that passed, **just to the north,** a power plant the length of a city block. **Across the street** was a huge garage, a tiny hotdog stand run by a reclusive[3] man named Freddie, and a bowling alley.*

EXERCISE 21.3   **Organizing Details in Descriptive Paragraphs**

On your own paper, prewrite to generate ideas, and then complete each of the following topic sentences by filling in the blank. Then, on the other blanks provided, prepare an informal outline by listing the major details with an appropriate type of spatial order.

1. An object that is special or precious to me is _____.

   _____

   _____

   _____

   _____

2. My first car was a _____.

   _____

   _____

   _____

   _____

1. **dilapidated:** shabby; run-down   3. **reclusive:** withdrawn from society
2. **presided:** acted as president

*Source: Adapted with the permission of The Free Press, a division of Simon & Schuster Adult Publishing Group, from *Lives on the Boundary: The Struggles and Achievements of America's Underprepared* by Mike Rose. Copyright © 1989 by Mike Rose. All rights reserved.

3. My favorite room in the house is _____.

_____

_____

_____

_____

_____

EXERCISE 21.4   **Recognizing Spatial Transitions**

Circle all of the transitions and space-related information in the following paragraph.

Let me tell you about our house. If you entered
the front door and turned right, you would see
a small living room with a couch along the east
wall and one along the west wall—one couch
was purple, the other tan, both bought used
and both well worn. A television set was placed
at the end of the purple couch, right at arm
level. An old Philco radio sat next to the TV,
its speaker covered with gold lamé.[1] There was
a small coffee table in the center of the room
on which sat a murky[2] fish-bowl occupied by
two listless[3] guppies.[4] If, on entering, you
turned left, you would see a green Formica[5]
dinner table with four chairs, a cedar chest
given as a wedding present to my mother by

1. lamé: fabric interwoven with threads of metal

2. murky: not clear; cloudy

3. listless: lacking interest or enthusiasm

4. guppies: a type of small fish

5. Formica: a brand of plastic covering

her mother, a painted statue of the Blessed

Virgin Mary, and a black trunk. It also had

a plastic chaise longue[1] between the door

and the table. I would lie on this and watch

television.*

EXERCISE 21.5   **Writing a Descriptive Paragraph That Includes Transitions**

Choose one of the topic sentences and outlines you prepared in Exercise 21.3. Write the paragraph, including transitions that indicate how the details are arranged in space.

Using Vivid Language

In Chapter 20, you learned how to include specific words, factual and sensory details, and action-oriented verbs in your writing. The first two types of vivid language are particularly important in descriptive paragraphs like the following one:

> The wreck of the *Titanic,* which sank on April 15, 1912, killing more than 1,500 people, is located in 12,600 feet (more than 2.33 miles) of water about 1,000 miles due east of Boston, Massachusetts. Discovered in 1985 by Robert Ballard and French explorer Jean Louis Michel, the ship lies on the cold, dark ocean floor in two pieces 1,970 feet apart from each other, and the bow is buried 60 feet below the ocean floor. The ship sank after colliding with an iceberg, and even today, nature continues to take its toll. In particular, bacteria are feeding on the ship's steel, forming "rusticles" that appear to drip from railings and flow down the sides of the wreck. Now, after more than ninety years in its watery grave, the ship is heavily corroded.[2] Also, the pressure of the extreme depth is crushing the ship's walls.

1. **chaise longue:** a long reclining chair   2. **corroded:** destroyed

*Source: Adapted with the permission of The Free Press, a division of Simon & Schuster Adult Publishing Group, from *Lives on the Boundary: The Struggles and Achievements of America's Underprepared* by Mike Rose. Copyright © 1989 by Mike Rose. All rights reserved.

Notice how the author paints the scene by including specific words. Instead of saying that *part of the ship* is buried, for example, she says the *bow* is buried. She also provides numerous facts, such as specific names, dates, and measurements, and sensory information about colors and temperature.

EXERCISE 21.6   **Writing with Vivid Language**

Rewrite each of the following sentences to substitute more specific words and add factual and sensory details.

1. The place was very peaceful.

   _____

2. The view from there is great.

   _____

3. We smelled something bad.

   _____

4. The room was a mess.

   _____

5. Her outfit was unusual.

   _____

In Summary: Steps in Writing Descriptive Paragraphs

1. **Prewrite to generate ideas and to determine a main idea.**
2. **Select relevant details,** including only information that is essential to understanding the main idea, and create an outline using an appropriate type of spatial order.
3. **As you write, include space-related transitions and information.** Also, use vivid language, including specific words and factual and sensory details.

WRITING FOR SUCCESS

Uses of Description

You might not be writing many descriptions of special people, places, and things outside of your English classes; however, you *will* incorporate elements of good descriptions into all of the other kinds of writing you do. Think of anything you have read—a novel, a magazine article, even a textbook passage—that was clear and interesting, and chances are good that it included descriptive detail. In fact, description helps breathe life into all kinds of writing. It often goes hand in hand with narration, for example. As you relate a series of events, you must re-create the scene by using descriptive details. Writers also provide descriptive details to help readers understand examples or explanations.

Writing descriptions also hones your word-choice skills. To create a mental image for a reader that exactly matches the image in your own mind, you must select just the right words. Therefore, writing good descriptions will provide you with valuable practice in finding the best language to express your thoughts and ideas, a skill that will improve everything else that you write.

CHAPTER 21 REVIEW

Fill in the blanks in the following statements.

1. _____ provides details about what something or someone looks like, sounds like, smells like, and so on.

2. When you generate ideas for description, the _____ method of prewriting is especially useful.

3. The _____ is the essential quality that you want to convey about the subject you are describing.

4. The _____ that you include in your paragraph must match or contribute to the dominant impression that you want to convey.

5. _____ organization patterns such as front-to-back, left-to-right, and inside-to-outside help orient the specific details for the reader by explaining how those details relate to one another in space.

6. _____ such as specific words and factual and sensory details are important to include in descriptions.

Topic Ideas for Descriptions

Exercise 21.1 includes topic ideas that you may want to develop into narrative paragraphs or essays. Here are some additional ideas:

- My favorite place to relax
- An awe-inspiring place
- A beautiful creature
- My favorite hangout
- An interesting celebrity
- A childhood friend
- My hometown
- The crowd at a concert
- A place that did not live up to my expectations
- An expensive thing that I own
- A wonder of the world
- A popular but silly fashion
- The scene in the following photograph:

© Philip and Karen Smith/Iconica/Getty Images

WebWork

To practice your descriptive skills, conduct a search of a place that you love to visit. Find a good photograph of that place, one that includes people. Write a description of the scene in that photograph, including details that draw on as many senses as possible.

Online Study Center   For more information and practice with space order, go to the Online Study Center that accompanies this book, at **http://www .college.hmco.com/pic/dolphinwriterone.**

Giving Examples: Illustration

GOALS FOR CHAPTER 22

▶ Define the term *illustration*.

▶ Describe the steps in writing an illustration paragraph.

▶ Write an illustration paragraph.

Some paragraphs need to be developed with specific examples. Illustrating ideas with examples is a valuable way to help readers understand ideas. We often make general or vague statements or use abstract terms that readers will not be able to understand or correctly interpret if we do not provide some examples. Look, for instance, at the following statement:

Many companies have begun encouraging their customers to use self-service.

To fully understand this statement, you probably need additional clarification and explanation. If the writer provides some examples, this idea will become much clearer:

Self-service is not just for gas pumps and ATMs anymore. Many companies have begun encouraging their customers to use self-service. Starwood hotels has placed kiosks[1] in many of its Sheraton hotels and is in the process of installing them in the rest of that chain's nearly two hundred locations. Guests can visit these kiosks to check in, check out, or upgrade rooms. In a number of cities, CVS, Osco, and Sav-on drug stores are trying out kiosks that let customers scan their items and then pay a machine. In several different states, McDonald's and Burger King fast-food restaurants have set up kiosks that allow customers to order, get food, and pay all by themselves.*

1. **kiosks:** small areas surrounded by walls

*Adapted from Barbara Kiviat, "May You Help You?" *Time,* September 6, 2004.

321

In this paragraph, the author provides multiple examples to illustrate her point that self-service is becoming an option at more types of businesses.

Writing an Illustration Paragraph

Some topic sentences will need to be illustrated with specific examples. When you develop a paragraph using illustration, you give specific instances that back up the claim you make in your main idea.

Determining a Main Idea and Writing a Topic Sentence

A topic sentence that will need to be developed with one or more examples usually states a general observation or opinion, as the following three examples do:

> Some of today's popular fashions are downright painful.
> Most of the jobs in the helping professions do not pay very well.
> Cheating seems to be becoming more common in our society.

To prove that the observation in each topic sentence is valid, each paragraph would need to be developed with some examples.

EXERCISE 22.1   **Writing Topic Sentences for Illustration Paragraphs**

For each of the following topics, use some prewriting techniques to generate ideas on your own paper, and then write a topic sentence you could use for an illustration paragraph.

1. Someone who has helped me

   Topic sentence: _____

2. A great vacation spot

   Topic sentence: _____

3. One of today's most talented performers

   Topic sentence: _____

4. A specific habit of good students

   Topic sentence: _____

5. A certain weight-loss technique

   Topic sentence: _____

Selecting Relevant Examples

In Chapter 21, you learned to convey a dominant impression in a description by carefully choosing the right details. Similarly, illustration must incorporate only those examples that develop the main idea. Whether you choose to include one example or several, all examples must directly relate to the point you are trying to make. Therefore, if you are trying to illustrate that almost everyone you know has at least one unhealthy habit, you would choose several examples of people with unhealthy habits. You might mention one friend who never exercises, a relative who smokes, and a coworker who eats fast food every day. You would not bring up people who do not have unhealthy habits.

To discover the best examples, begin by prewriting. Then, weed out any example that does not exactly match your main point.

 **EXERCISE 22.2**   **Selecting Relevant Examples**

For each of the following topic sentences, circle the letter of the example in the list that would not develop the topic sentence.

1. Topic sentence: Joe often procrastinates, or puts off, getting things done.
   a. He does not begin tackling his school assignments until the night before they are due.
   b. He does not start working on his tax return until April 14.
   c. He never remembers where he put his car keys.

2. Topic sentence: Our town is changing in positive ways.
   a. New businesses, such as a clothing store and a bookstore, have opened in the downtown area.
   b. The flooding from this past summer's hurricanes was not as bad in our town as it was in other towns.
   c. The old children's park is being renovated with all new equipment.

3. Topic sentence: The college I attend is ethnically diverse.
   a. The Spanish language courses are very popular and fill up fast.
   b. India is the native country of about 12 percent of our student body.
   c. Many Asian students from places like Korea and Laos have enrolled at our college.

4. My mother is very superstitious.
   a. Friday the thirteenth makes her nervous.
   b. She always buys the same brand of cat food.
   c. She is terrified of breaking a mirror for fear of bringing about seven years of bad luck.

5. A sense of humor is an essential quality of an effective teacher.
   a. My history professor, Mr. Robertson, kept his lectures interesting by sprinkling them with jokes and amusing stories.
   b. My math teacher used laughter in the classroom to help relieve his students' tension, anxiety, and frustration.
   c. My English professor wrote and published two books of poetry.

Including Adequate Examples

After prewriting to generate the examples you want to include, consider whether or not you are providing an adequate number of examples. Readers will not be able to understand or agree with your point if they do not feel as though they have been given enough information. In the case of a controversial idea, or one that is difficult to believe, you will have to provide sufficient examples to get the reader to accept that idea. For example, if you are trying to convince readers that miracles really do happen, you will need to provide several examples of these unexplained miracles to persuade the skeptical reader that this opinion is valid. If you give only one example of a particular occurrence, you will probably not have offered enough evidence in support of your point.

EXERCISE 22.3   Adding Examples

Read the following paragraph. Then, on the blanks provided, list two or three additional examples the writer could add to better support the paragraph's main idea.

I have seen people do some very dangerous things while driving. I saw one man actually reading a magazine as he drove sixty-five miles an hour down the highway. He would glance from the page to the road and then back to the page as he sped along.

Additional examples:

_____

_____

_____

Organizing Details and Using Transitions

If you include several examples in support of your main idea, you will need to decide on the best order in which to present them. Sometimes, the order will not matter. If all of your examples are equal in importance, you can arrange them in any order. At other times, though, some examples are more significant than others. In that case, you need to decide if you should present the most important examples first or save them for last. In that paragraph about miracles, for instance, you might want to present your strongest example first so that the reader will not dismiss your point out of hand and stop reading. Then, save the weaker evidence for later in the paragraph, after you have convinced your reader that your claim is possible.

After you have decided on the best order for your examples, list them in that order in an outline. Then, as you write, make sure you include transitions to help readers follow your organization and progression of thought. Some common illustration transition phrases are

for example	an illustration of this is
for instance	one example
to illustrate	another example (or instance)
in one case	a case in point is

EXERCISE 22.4 **Organizing Details in Illustration Paragraphs**

On your own paper, prewrite to generate ideas, and then complete each of the following topic sentences by filling in the blank. Then, on the other blanks provided, prepare an informal outline by listing the examples you would include in an appropriate order.

1. Many medical advances have greatly improved the quality and length of our lives.

_____

_____

_____

_____

_____

2. People who _____ are usually successful in life.

_____

_____

_____

_____

3. Being happy is a matter of _____.

_____

_____

_____

_____

EXERCISE 22.5   **Recognizing Illustration Transitions**

Circle all of the illustration transitions in the following paragraph.

Inventors have registered dozens of patents for strange and weird products. For example, three-legged pantyhose allow the wearer to tuck the spare leg away until a run occurs, and then it can be rotated into action. Another example of a wacky invention is toilet landing lights, waterproof lights that can be mounted under a toilet seat to guide nighttime bathroom visitors. A third example is the alarm fork, which is equipped with a light that turns red after the diner takes a bite. He or she is supposed to wait to take another bite until the fork light turns green. And then there is the gourd[1] head, a plastic mold that is slipped over a growing vegetable, shaping produce like squash and eggplants into elves and hearts.*

1. **gourd:** a fruit with a hard outer covering

*Adapted from Anita Manning, "New Meaning to 'Patently Absurd,'" *USA Today,* July 30, 2001, p. 8D.

WRITING FOR SUCCESS

Uses of Illustration

The ability to provide relevant examples is a skill that you will use in many areas of your life. For example, let's say that you want to visit a certain place with your family members, but they are reluctant to go. You could convince them to change their minds, perhaps, if you provide examples of activities or sights that will interest them.

You may also need good illustration skills on the job. If you want to argue for a certain change that will improve a procedure or a working condition, you can provide your supervisor with specific examples to illustrate why the current circumstances are not as effective as they could be. Obviously, illustration can be a valuable persuasive tool.

 **EXERCISE 22.6** **Writing an Illustration Paragraph That Includes Transitions**

Choose one of the topic sentences and outlines that you prepared in Exercise 22.4. Write the paragraph, including transitions that indicate how the details are related.

Developing an Illustration Paragraph

If you have decided to develop your illustration paragraph with several shorter examples, you will probably only briefly mention each one. Thus, you will probably write just one to three sentences to explain each example.

In Summary: Steps in Writing Illustration Paragraphs

1. **Select relevant examples.** Make sure that each example matches your main idea or thesis.
2. **Plan to include a sufficient number of examples.**
3. **Organize your examples.** Decide if some of them are more important than others, and arrange them accordingly.
4. **As you write, develop each example with a sentence or two.**

CHAPTER 22 REVIEW

Fill in the blanks in the following statements.

1. _____ is providing specific examples to help readers understand general or vague statements or abstract terms.

2. Using illustration to develop a paragraph may involve providing one long, extended _____ or several shorter _____.

3. A topic sentence that will need to be developed with one or more examples usually states a general _____.

4. Illustration must incorporate only those examples that develop the _____.

5. Readers will not be able to understand or agree with your point if you do not provide _____ examples.

6. If all of your examples are _____ in importance, you can arrange them in any order.

7. If some of your examples are more significant than others, you might want to present the _____ example first.

8. Common illustration _____ include *for example, for instance,* and *in one case.*

Topic Ideas for Illustration

Exercise 22.1 includes topic ideas that you may want to develop into illustration paragraphs or essays. Here are some additional ideas:

- A bad date (or a good one)
- Funny or effective television commercials
- A quality of today's young people
- Unattractive or unflattering fashion trends
- Famous people who are not very talented
- _____ is the _____ (kindest, boldest, most patriotic, and so on) person I know
- Great presidents

- Dangerous jobs
- Great places to go _____ (fishing, dancing, shopping, people watching, and so on)
- A great era for _____ (music, films, fashion, a specific sport, and so on)

WebWork

Search the Internet for examples to develop a particular topic. Choose one of the topics in the "Topic Ideas for Illustration" list or in Exercise 22.1. Using a search engine such as Google (www.google.com) or Yahoo! (www.yahoo.com), type in your topic. In the list of search results, find three to five good examples you could use, and write them down.

Online Study Center   For more information and practice with illustration, go to the Online Study Center that accompanies this book, at **http://www .college.hmco.com/pic/dolphinwriterone**.

23

Comparison and Contrast

▶ Define the terms *comparison* and *contrast*.

▶ Describe the steps in writing a comparison/contrast paragraph.

▶ Write a comparison/contrast paragraph.

▶ Recognize the features of a comparison/contrast essay.

When you *compare* two things, you examine the similarities between them. When you *contrast* two things, you examine the differences between them. Comparison, contrast, or a combination of both is useful for developing ideas in compositions. A study of how two people, places, things, or ideas are alike or different is a good way to help your readers understand something about the two subjects. For example, read the following paragraph:

> Staying single and getting married both have their advantages and disadvantages. Single people, of course, usually have more freedom and independence than married people do. Single people can generally do what they want without taking into consideration the needs or desires of another person. Married people cannot always spend their time the way they would like to spend it. However, marriage does bring financial benefits. Not only does a married couple often have two sources of income for one household, but they are often also better off when it comes to taxes and benefits. Being married also means having constant companionship and affection. There is always someone to talk to or turn to for help or support. Single people, on the other hand, often face loneliness.

This paragraph contrasts staying single and getting married. After reading this paragraph, we understand the main advantages and disadvantages of these two options.

Comparison and contrast are also useful for persuading readers to favor or choose one thing over another.

> Leasing a car often looks like a good deal. With leases, drivers get brand-new cars for much less than they would pay if they bought the cars. But for most people, buying is usually the most cost-effective option in the long run. A lease is basically just an extended rental contract, so at the end of the lease, the driver has nothing to show for all of those monthly payments. When buying a car, however, drivers usually have thousands of dollars in value left in the vehicle when they finish paying for it. At the end of the lease, a driver can look forward to more monthly payments on another vehicle. After paying off a loan for a purchased car, though, the driver can look forward to years of no monthly payments while driving his or her paid-off vehicle. Plus, there can be additional costs involved in leasing that end up raising the cost more than people expect. Buying a car allows a driver to put an unlimited number of miles on it. Leasing a car, on the other hand, forces the driver to stay within certain mileage limits or pay extra for the additional miles. Leases also typically come with thousands of dollars of up-front fees that do not accompany a loan for a purchased car.

This paragraph compares leasing a car and buying a car, focusing on why buying is better for most people. Therefore, it is designed to persuade readers that buying is the better choice of the two.

To write effective comparison/contrast paragraphs, follow the principles presented in the next sections.

Writing a Comparison/Contrast Paragraph

Comparison and contrast are ways of understanding something in relation to its similarities to or differences with something else. To write an effective comparison/contrast paragraph, you need to determine your points of comparison, decide on the best order for presenting those points, and develop each point with descriptive details and examples.

Determining the Points of Comparison and the Main Idea and Writing a Topic Sentence

To write an effective comparison/contrast paragraph, it is important, first of all, to decide *why* you are comparing and/or contrasting your two subjects. Do you want readers to understand one of the subjects by seeing how it resembles something with which they are already familiar? Do you want to show that the two subjects are more different than readers think they are? Do you want to prove that one of the subjects is better than or preferable to the other subject? Your answers to these questions will lead you to decide on your purpose, which will affect how you formulate your topic sentence. For example, the following topic sentence focuses on how two subjects are very different:

> Attending a community college and attending a university are two completely different experiences.

This topic sentence suggests that an informative and relatively objective comparison will follow. If you want to persuade your reader that one is better than the other, though, the topic sentence would need to change:

> Attending a community college *is better than* attending a university.

After you write a working topic sentence, decide which features of the two subjects would be most appropriate for proving your main point. In proving the first previous topic sentence, you would probably need to examine the different aspects of the two educational experiences, such as cost, quality of teaching, class size, and overall atmosphere. A discussion of the two institutions' layouts or history, though, would probably not be relevant to this thesis.

In the paragraph about leasing or buying a car, the writer wants to persuade the reader that buying is the better choice. In order to accomplish that, the writer compares the monthly payments, the amount of equity or value of the car, and additional costs.

After deciding on the right points of comparison, you will need to make sure that you examine both subjects in terms of those points. Therefore, in a paragraph about attending a community college and attending a university, you would need to discuss the cost, class size, quality of teaching, and overall atmosphere at a community college, and then you would need to devote equal attention to the cost, class size, quality of teaching, and overall atmosphere at a university. You would not compare the cost of a community college to the quality of teaching at a university. Doing so would be "comparing apples and oranges," as the saying goes, and you would not truly be contrasting the two subjects. To avoid this type of faulty comparison, it is important to outline your ideas, the topic of the next section.

EXERCISE 23.1   **Determining Points of Comparison**

For each of the following topics, determine three points of comparison and write those points on the blanks provided. Then, write down the main idea that would arise from your comparison of these points.

1. Topic: Two instructors of mine

   Points of comparison: _____

   _____

   _____

   Main idea: _____

2. Topic: Two brands of the same product (two computers, two digital music players, two cars, two soft drinks, and so on)

   Points of comparison: _____

   _____

   _____

   Main idea: _____

3. Topic: City versus small town

   Points of comparison: _____

   _____

   _____

   Main idea: _____

EXERCISE 23.2   **Writing Topic Sentences for Comparison/Contrast Paragraphs**

For each of the following topics, use some prewriting techniques to generate ideas on your own paper, and then write a topic sentence you could use for a comparison/contrast paragraph.

1. Two friends of mine

   Topic sentence: _____

2. Two types of music

Topic sentence: _____

3. A choice I need to make

Topic sentence: _____

4. Two types of vehicle (car, van, truck, sport-utility vehicle)

Topic sentence: _____

5. Two places I have lived or two schools I have attended

Topic sentence: _____

Organizing Points of Comparison and Using Transitions

Organization is especially important in comparison/contrast paragraphs because when you are juggling two different subjects and examining several features of each of those subjects, a reader can become lost easily if the composition is not clearly organized. Therefore, after you have chosen your points of comparison, you must give careful thought to how you will arrange your discussion of these points to help readers follow your ideas. There are two major patterns to choose from when organizing the points of a comparison/contrast paragraph.

Whole-by-Whole Pattern of Organization

The first pattern, whole-by-whole, looks at all of the points of comparison for one whole subject, and then it turns to a discussion of those same points of comparison for the other subject. An outline of this pattern looks like this:

I. Comparison of Subject A and Subject B
   A. Subject A
      1. Point of comparison #1
      2. Point of comparison #2
      3. Point of comparison #3
   B. Subject B
      1. Point of comparison #1
      2. Point of comparison #2
      3. Point of comparison #3

The advantages of this pattern are mostly for the writer because he or she has to concentrate on only one subject at a time. However, it often asks more of readers, who are burdened with the task of remembering what was said about the first subject as they read about the second subject. Often, this pattern also requires readers to make necessary connections or distinctions between the two subjects on their own. The other pattern of organization, however, eliminates these problems.

Point-by-Point Pattern of Organization

In a point-by-point organization pattern, the writer alternates back and forth between his two subjects, arranging his or her composition according to the points of comparison. An outline of this pattern looks like this:

I. Comparison of Subject A and Subject B
    A. Point of comparison #1
        1. Subject A
        2. Subject B
    B. Point of comparison #2
        1. Subject A
        2. Subject B
    C. Point of comparison #3
        1. Subject A
        2. Subject B

This pattern usually makes it easier for the reader to see the similarities and/or differences between two subjects. Also, it allows the writer to make clearer, more explicit connections for the reader about the two subjects. However, it does require the writer, who is switching back and forth from one subject to the other, to be more attentive to thought progression. In addition to dividing the information into distinct paragraphs, another way for the writer to prevent the reader from getting lost is to use clear transitions to signal similarities, differences, or the movement from one subject to another. The following lists include many of the common comparison and contrast transitions:

Comparison transitions

also	similarly	similar to
too	in like manner	in the same way
likewise	just like, just as	along the same line

Contrast transitions

however	nevertheless	in contrast
but	on the one hand/on the other hand	conversely
yet	unlike	even though
although	rather	still
instead	on the contrary	nonetheless
in opposition	actually	whereas
in spite of	despite	in reality
just the opposite	while	as opposed to
though	unfortunately	

EXERCISE 23.3   **Organizing Details in Comparison/Contrast Paragraphs**

On your own paper, prewrite to generate ideas, and then complete each of the following topic sentences by filling in the blank. Then, on the other blanks provided, prepare an informal outline by listing the points that you would include in an appropriate order.

1. _____ and _____ are similar in some ways and different in others.

   _____

   _____

   _____

   _____

2. _____ is better than _____.

   _____

   _____

   _____

   _____

3. Although _____ and _____ seem similar, they are really quite different.

   _____

   _____

   _____

   _____

 **EXERCISE 23.4** · **Recognizing Comparison/Contrast Transitions**

Circle all of the comparison/contrast transitions in the following paragraph.

Should you work for someone else or own your own business? Being self-employed is better in some respects but worse in others. When you work for someone else, you usually have to take orders from someone else. However, when you work for yourself, you are in control and make all of the decisions affecting your business. The working hours will be longer, though. When you work for a company you do not own, you can often limit your work hours to nine to five o'clock, five days a week. When you are self-employed, on the other hand, your hours can be far longer and less regular. Self-employed people usually work more and harder. Plus, they assume much more financial risk. A regular job usually comes with a paycheck that you can count on. In contrast, working for yourself may mean coping with a more uncertain amount of income, at least at first. In addition, you will have to give up paid vacations and other benefits, such as paid health insurance and a retirement plan. Nevertheless, owning your own business may help you make a lot more money than you would make by working for someone else.

 **EXERCISE 23.5** · **Writing a Comparison/Contrast Paragraph That Includes Transitions**

Choose one of the topic sentences and outlines you prepared in Exercise 23.3. Write the paragraph, including transitions that indicate how the points are related.

Developing the Points in a Comparison/Contrast Paragraph

Because comparison/contrast paragraphs examine the features of two subjects to show how they are alike and/or different, you will often use descriptive details and examples to develop each point of comparison. For example, if you were to write the paragraph about attending a community college versus attending a university, you would want to add specific descriptive details when you describe the atmosphere at each institution. You might describe the look and feel of two representative campuses. When you explained the differences in cost, you would want to provide factual information about the cost of tuition, books, and fees. In explaining the difference in the quality of teaching, you might present two examples of instructors from your own or someone else's experience. These kinds of details will help the reader understand each point better.

WRITING FOR SUCCESS

Using Comparison/Contrast for Problem Solving

Learning how to compare and contrast two subjects can also improve your ability to solve problems or evaluate choices in the other areas of your life. If you face an important decision, or if you have to choose between two different paths or options, you can use what you have learned about comparison/contrast to help you evaluate the possibilities. For example, if you needed to decide whether to keep your old car or buy a new one, you would first determine your points of comparison. You might decide to consider the cost, dependability, and safety of the two vehicles. You could brainstorm ideas in the form of a list or chart. Or you might want to examine the pros and cons of each option, again jotting down your ideas for easier comparison. Once your thoughts are side by side on paper, the better choice may become more apparent. Try this technique with a choice that you need to make right now.

In Summary: Steps in Writing Comparison/Contrast

1. **Determine a main idea and points of comparison.** Decide on the point of your comparison, and then select relevant points of comparison. Make sure that you apply these points to both subjects.

2. **Choose an organizing pattern for the points of comparison.** Use either a whole-by-whole or point-by-point pattern for arranging ideas, and include transitions to help the reader follow these ideas.

3. **Develop each point of comparison.** Use descriptions, examples, or any other kind of details that explain each point.

Fill in the blanks in the following statements.

1. When you _____ two things, you examine the similarities between them.

   When you _____ two things, you examine the differences between them.

2. The first step in comparison/contrast is determining the _____ of your comparison.

3. After you write your topic sentence, decide on the best _____, the features of the two subjects that would be most appropriate to proving your main point.

4. Two major comparison/contrast patterns of organization are the _____ pattern and the _____ pattern.

5. Common comparison/contrast _____ include *also, similarly, however,* and *on the contrary.*

6. Comparison/contrast paragraphs are often developed with _____ and _____.

Topic Ideas for Comparison/Contrast

Exercises 23.1 and 23.2 include topic ideas that you may want to develop into comparison/contrast paragraphs or essays. Here are some additional ideas:

- Walking versus riding

- Two ways of doing something (losing weight, doing a household chore, kicking a bad habit, and so on)

- One of my relatives and I (or two of my relatives)

- Two restaurants

- Two similar books, films, or television shows

- High school and college

- Two religions

- Men and women

- Two regions of the United States (or two states)

- Expectations versus actual experience

- Two athletes, celebrities, politicians, or historical figures (such as two presidents, two military leaders, or two inventors)

- Two works by the same artist (singer, musician, author, poet, painter, and so on)

- Two options or solutions to a problem

- The present versus the past

- The two people who would select the meals pictured in the following photograph:

© Getty Images

WebWork

When comparing or contrasting, filling in a grid of information about your two subjects is an effective way to determine points of comparison and supporting details. For sample grids, go to **http://www.rscc.cc.tn.us/owl&writingcenter/OWL/Com_Con .html** and **www.fno.org/oct97/grids.html**.

Online Study Center   For additional information and practice with writing comparison/ contrast paragraphs and essays, go to the Online Study Center that accompanies this book, at **http://www.college.hmco.com/pic/ dolphinwriterone**.

Order of Importance: Argument

GOALS FOR CHAPTER 24

▶ Define the term *order of importance.*

▶ List some of the uses of the order of importance pattern.

▶ Define the term *argumentative paragraph.*

▶ Describe the steps in writing an argumentative paragraph.

▶ Write an argumentative paragraph.

One final pattern for organizing the development of a paragraph is order of importance. In **order of importance** paragraphs, the ideas are in order from least to most important or most to least important. In many paragraphs, you will develop the main idea with a series, or list, of points. This series is often best arranged in the order of each point's greatness in size, extent, or significance. For example, if you are writing about some of your resolutions for the New Year, you might want to arrange the ideas according to how big each change will be. You might begin with the smallest or easiest change and end with the biggest or most difficult change. For example, you could order the ideas as follows:

1. Change my hairstyle
2. Put fifty dollars a month in my savings account
3. Lose fifty pounds

If you are writing about different groups of something, you might want to arrange the ideas according to the size of the group.

Voters are usually placed in one of four different categories. The two largest groups of people who vote in elections are the thirty-to-forty-four-year-olds and the forty-four-to-fifty-nine-year-olds. During the 2004 presidential election, each

341

of these groups made up 32 percent of all voters, for a total of 64 percent. The next largest group includes citizens over sixty, who made up 19 percent of voters in 2004. The smallest group of voters is the people under thirty. In 2004, they accounted for just 17 percent of all voters.

If you are writing about the costs of items, you might want to arrange the ideas according to how much each thing costs, usually from smallest to largest.

If you will not quit smoking for your health, do it to save yourself a lot of money. You will, first of all, save hundreds of dollars that you now spend on cigarettes. If you are a pack-a-day smoker, at $2 per pack, you will save yourself $730 per year if you kick the habit. Second, you may save yourself thousands of dollars in medical insurance costs. Smokers are charged more for insurance than non-smokers, so quitting can significantly lower the cost of your monthly premiums. But most of all, if you give up smoking, you might save yourself and your family hundreds of thousands of dollars in medical costs down the road. Smoking-related diseases like cancer and emphysema are expensive to treat, but they will also rob you of wages when you are lying in a hospital bed instead of out earning money.

Another common use for order of importance is within paragraphs that present reasons in support of a specific opinion or viewpoint. These paragraphs are **argumentative** because they argue for or against something. Their goal is to persuade the reader to agree with the writer's viewpoint.

The following paragraph, for example, argues against the death penalty:

A number of reasons form a powerful argument against the death penalty. First of all, the death penalty reflects the assumption that the wrongdoer is beyond rehabilitation.[1] Perhaps some individuals cannot be rehabilitated, but others definitely can. How can anyone make that determination? Second, the death penalty is not equitable.[2] It is unfair to black Americans because blacks are sentenced to death more often than whites are. But last and most importantly, capital punishment cannot be reversed if the person is later found to be innocent. If just one person is put to death by mistake, that is too many. And this has occurred many times.*

1. **rehabilitation:** restoring someone to a useful place in society

2. **equitable:** equal and fair to everyone

*Adapted from Coretta Scott King, "The Death Penalty Is a Step Back," in Mary Lou Conlin, *Patterns Plus,* 7th ed. (Boston: Houghton Mifflin, 2002), p. 284.

In this paragraph, the author provides three reasons why the death penalty is a bad idea. The reasons are presented in order of importance. The author gives the least important reason first and then builds to the most important reason, strengthening her case with each new point. In other paragraphs, beginning with the most important reason might be more appropriate.

Writing an Argumentative Paragraph

Arguing for or against something involves offering convincing reasons in support of your position. To write an effective argumentative paragraph, you need to consider your audience's needs and goals, write a persuasive topic sentence, select relevant reasons, acknowledge opposing arguments, and develop your reasons with sufficient logical or emotional evidence.

Thinking About Your Audience

Many of the other modes for development usually focus either on the writer and his or her thoughts and experiences (narration, description) or on the subject itself (comparison/contrast, cause/effect, definition, and so on). Argumentative writing, in contrast, focuses on the *reader*. Because the whole purpose of persuasive writing is to persuade, or convince, the reader, the whole essay revolves around the kinds of reasons and evidence the reader will need in order to accept the idea presented in the writer's topic sentence.

Thus, the first step in planning an argumentative paragraph is to carefully consider the targeted reader. Whether this is one person or many, remember that arguments are not directed at people who agree with the writer; writing a paragraph for those who already concur with the thesis would be a waste of time. Instead, argumentative paragraphs are directed at readers who either disagree with the writer's viewpoint or have not yet made up their minds.

Once you have determined exactly who needs to be persuaded to accept your opinion, then spend some time thinking about the needs, goals, and potential objections of that reader (or readers). At this point, at least informally analyze your readers. What do they probably believe now? What do you think their goals and priorities are? To what parts of your argument will they object? Can you think of ways to overcome these objections? As you plan and write your paragraph, you will return often to this analysis to guide you in making decisions about *what* to include and *how* to include it.

 **EXERCISE 24.1**   **Considering Your Audience**

For each of the following argumentative topic sentences, consider who the best audience would be. On the blanks provided, identify the most likely audience members and briefly describe their needs, goals, and potential objections.

1. You should take a computer skills course.

_____

_____

_____

2. The national minimum wage should be increased.

_____

_____

_____

3. No teenager should drop out of high school.

_____

_____

_____

4. I deserve a pay raise.

_____

_____

_____

5. America should send astronauts to Mars.

_____

_____

_____

Determining Your Topic Sentence and Relevant Reasons

Your analysis of your readers will affect, first of all, your choice of a topic sentence and supporting reasons. It will also help you determine how to refute those readers' objections to your ideas.

The Persuasive Topic Sentence

Persuasive topic sentences usually have two important characteristics:

1. Persuasive topic sentences often state exactly who should make or bring about the recommended change. For example, read the following topic sentences:

> Our state legislature needs to lower the highway speed limit to sixty miles per hour.

> College professors should not make class attendance mandatory.

> Pet owners must spay or neuter their cats and dogs.

In the previous statements, the state legislature, college professors, and pet owners are the ones being asked to alter either a belief or a behavior.

2. As the three previous statements illustrate, persuasive topic sentences also clearly state the behavior or belief they want the reader to adopt after reading the paragraph. And to reflect their persuasive purpose, these types of topic sentences often include words and phrases like *should, must, ought to,* and *have to.*

EXERCISE 24.2   **Writing Topic Sentences for Argumentative Paragraphs**

For each of the following topics, use some prewriting techniques to generate ideas on your own paper, and then write a topic sentence you could use for an argumentative paragraph.

1. An animal that makes a great pet

   Topic sentence: _____

2. Cell phones or cell phone users

   Topic sentence: _____

3. A needed improvement at this college

    Topic sentence: _____

4. Violence on television or in video games

    Topic sentence: _____

5. Mandatory physical education classes

    Topic sentence: _____

Supporting Reasons

Just as a consideration of your reader determined your thesis statement, your analysis of your audience should guide your choice of supporting points. Often, there are many different reasons in support of a particular opinion. However, not all of these reasons may be *relevant* to your target audience. Therefore, in the planning stages of writing your paragraph, you will need to decide which reasons most closely match your readers' priorities and goals.

For example, if you intend to argue to drivers that they should not buy a sport-utility vehicle, you would need to consider these readers' priorities. Typical motorists want a vehicle that is safe, trustworthy, stylish, enjoyable, and affordable. Thus, they will respond to reasons that relate to accident statistics, costs, driving ease, and image. These readers would be less likely to be convinced by reasons—such as environmental issues—that are unrelated to their main concerns, so the writer can leave those points out.

EXERCISE 24.3   **Selecting Relevant Supporting Reasons**

For each of the argumentative topic sentences you wrote for Exercise 24.2, identify the target audience on the corresponding blank that follows, and then list two or three supporting reasons that would be relevant to that audience.

1. Audience: _____

    Supporting reasons:

    _____

    _____

    _____

2. Audience: _____

Supporting reasons:

_____

_____

_____

3. Audience: _____

Supporting reasons:

_____

_____

_____

4. Audience: _____

Supporting reasons:

_____

_____

_____

5. Audience: _____

Supporting reasons:

_____

_____

_____

Organizing an Argumentative Paragraph and Using Transitions

After you decide on the reasons you will offer in support of your argument, your next major consideration will be the order in which to present these reasons. Order of importance is the most common pattern for arranging reasons. Therefore, rank each of your reasons in importance, and then let your analysis of your readers guide you in your decision about whether to discuss them in the order from most important to least important or vice versa, from least important to most important. If your readers are very busy decision-makers, consider beginning with your strongest, most important reason, the one that will be most likely to persuade them. If you are reasonably sure that your readers will be willing to read the entire paragraph, giving your argument careful consideration, consider saving your strongest reason for last so it will be the one they remember best after they have finished reading.

As you write, do not forget to include transitions that will help readers follow you from one point to the next. Some of the most common argumentative transitions are

first, second, third
one reason, another reason, and so on
most important
for one thing
next
last
finally
another
in addition
furthermore
also

EXERCISE 24.4   **Organizing Reasons in Argumentative Paragraphs**

On your own paper, prewrite to generate ideas, and then complete each of the following topic sentences by filling in the blank. Then, on the other blanks provided, prepare an informal outline by listing the reasons you would include in an appropriate order.

1. _____ should not be mandatory.

   _____

   _____

   _____

2. _____ should be outlawed once
   and for all.

   _____

   _____

   _____

3. _____ is a complete waste of money.

_____

_____

_____

_____

 **EXERCISE 24.5**   **Recognizing Argumentative Transitions**

Circle all of the argumentative transitions in the following paragraph.

For academic, professional, and personal reasons, all college students should study a foreign language. One important reason to study a foreign language is to improve your cognitive[1] and critical thinking abilities. Several studies have shown that bilingual people score higher than their one-language peers on tests of verbal and nonverbal intelligence, creativity, and problem-solving. Another good reason to learn about other cultures is to increase your professional qualifications. Recent surveys indicate that more than eighty agencies of the federal government rely on professionals with intermediate to high-level competence[2] in foreign languages. American multinational corporations and nongovernmental organizations, too, need employees who can communicate in foreign languages and understand other cultures. An employer will see you as a bridge to new clients if you know those clients' language. Perhaps the most important reason to study a foreign language, though, is to expand your personal horizons. Studying a new language, communicating with people in their own language, and learning about their culture can be a source of both pleasure and personal enrichment. Also, knowledge of other cultures may actually help you keep your country safer for yourself and your loved ones. American citizens' knowledge of foreign languages is vital for the U.S. government to effectively meet twenty-first-century security challenges by better understanding the languages and cultures of its allies and enemies.*

1. **cognitive:** related to thinking or mental activity

2. **competence:** ability

*Adapted from Languages of the World, **http://www.nvtc.gov/lotw/months/november/WhystudyFL.htm.**

EXERCISE 24.6   **Writing an Argumentative Paragraph That Includes Transitions**

Choose one of the topic sentences and outlines that you prepared for Exercise 24.4. Write the paragraph, including transitions that indicate how the reasons are related.

Developing Your Reasons with Evidence

As you present the reasons that support your thesis, make sure to develop each one with plenty of evidence. Evidence can take the form of your own personal observations or experiences, but be careful not to make unfair generalizations based on what you alone have witnessed. More reliable forms of evidence include facts, statistics, expert opinion, and examples. You may need to gather this information in your library or on the Internet.

In Summary: Steps in Writing Argumentative Paragraphs

1. **Consider your reader.** An analysis of your reader will drive all of the other decisions you will make as you plan and write your paragraph or essay.

2. **Write a persuasive main idea statement that takes your audience into consideration.** Write a topic sentence that clearly expresses what you want your reader to do or to believe.

3. **Match your supporting reasons to your reader's priorities and goals.** Include only those reasons that are relevant to your reader.

4. **Determine the best order for your reasons.** Decide whether you should arrange your reasons from most important to least important, or vice versa. Include transitions to help the reader follow you from one point to the next.

5. **Develop each reason with evidence.** Use personal observations and experiences, facts, statistics, expert opinion, and examples to provide support for each reason you give.

WRITING FOR SUCCESS

Argumentation in Your Personal and Professional Life

Good argumentative writing skills are useful not only for your college courses but also for personal and professional situations. In your personal life, you may need to write a letter to a company arguing for or against something. For example, you may need to write a letter to your congressional representative to express your opinion about a law or political situation. You may need to write a letter of recommendation for someone. Or you may want to express your views about a current event or social issue by writing a letter to your newspaper's editor. You will need a knowledge of argumentation to express your views effectively in all of these situations.

On the job, you will have many occasions to use your argumentative skills. In letters, memorandums, and reports, you will argue that you deserve a pay raise, that some procedure needs to be changed, or that some piece of new equipment needs to be purchased. Your powers of argument can help you get ahead in your career.

CHAPTER 24 REVIEW

Fill in the blanks in the following statements.

1. In order of importance paragraphs, the ideas are in order from _____ important or _____ important.

2. Series of ideas are often best arranged in order of each point's relative _____ in size, extent, or significance.

3. Argumentative paragraphs present reasons in support of a specific _____ _____. Their goal is to _____ the reader to agree with the writer's viewpoint.

4. While the other modes of development focus on the writer's thoughts or experiences or on the subject itself, argumentative writing focuses on the _____.

5. The first step in planning an argumentative paragraph is to carefully consider the _____, _____, and _____ of the targeted reader.

6. Persuasive topic sentences often include the _____ who should make or bring about the change.

7. Persuasive _____ clearly state the behavior or belief they want the reader to adopt after reading the paragraph, and they often include words and phrases like *should, must, ought to,* and *have to.*

8. In the planning stages of writing an argumentative paragraph, the writer needs to decide which reasons are most _____ to the target audience.

9. _____ is the most common pattern for arranging reasons in an argumentative paragraph.

10. Common argumentative _____ include *first, second, third, most important,* and *finally.*

11. Writers should support each of their reasons with _____, which includes personal observations and experiences, facts, statistics, expert opinion, and examples.

Topic Ideas for Argument

Exercises 24.1 and 24.2 include topic ideas you may want to develop into argumentative paragraphs or essays. Here are some additional ideas:

- Something that should be banned
- Something that should be changed
- Something that I should do (exercise more, watch less TV, get my own apartment, and so on)
- A needed improvement
- A worthy cause
- Gun control
- Health care in America
- Mandatory military service
- The legal drinking age
- People who deserve to make more money
- Why college students should attend a community college instead of a university
- Smoking in public places

WebWork

Search online for the Web site of your local newspaper, or go to the Web site for *USA Today* (**www.usatoday.com**), the *New York Daily News* (**www.nydailynews.com**), or the *New York Times* (**www.nytimes.com**). Read some of the editorials or letters to the editor, and select one that you believe is particularly effective. Why do you think this editorial is effective? How did the writer make his or her argument convincing?

Online Study Center   For more information and practice with order of importance, go to the Online Study Center that accompanies this book, at **http://www.college.hmco.com/pic/dolphinwriterone**.

Reading Selections

An IQ Contest

By Stephen Juan

1   Are dolphins smarter than humans? Scientists agree that dolphins are extremely intelligent. A dolphin's brain, in proportion to body size, is larger than a human brain. It has two brain hemispheres, just like the human brain. But unlike the human brain, the dolphin's brain hemispheres work independently of each other. We don't know exactly what this means, but complicated thought beyond that of human thought is a possibility.

2   Humans have hands with opposable thumbs and fingers, making tool production and other technological creations possible. Dolphins do not have this, so even if they can "invent" with their brains, they can't build without hands.

3   Humans have a more complicated voice-producing apparatus, allowing the most sophisticated verbal language known in nature. Dolphins communicate, too, but in different ways. They use high-pitched clicks, whistles and other sounds, but obviously not words. Their clicks bounce off objects in their path. By listening to the echo and judging the time it takes for the echo to return, the dolphin can estimate the size of the object and its distance.

4   This dolphin form of sonar is superior and more complicated than the sonar invented by humans for use in submarines. Human sonar utilizes a single sound frequency and has a limited range. Dolphin sonar emits clicks spanning low to high frequencies. It may be heard by other dolphins many miles away. Through its sonar, a bottlenosed dolphin can detect a piece of metal only 13 thousandths of an inch in size.

5   Although dolphins cannot speak like humans, they can understand simple human sentences when spoken to. Neurophysiologist Dr. John Lilly argued in "Man and Dolphin" (1961) that dolphin behavior indicates a very intelligent, creative and self-aware mind at work. He maintained that, compared with humans, dolphins were equal or perhaps greater in intelligence. If they had hands and fingers and if they lived on land, they would prove it.

6   He suggested that on this planet, high intelligence evolved twice: In the human and in the dolphin. Some individuals have gone so far as to assert that dolphins were brought here by aliens visiting Earth and thus represent an "alien intelligence" different from but equal to the intelligence of humans. As experiments with dolphins continue, most scientists today would probably agree that dolphins exhibit great intelligence, but not greater intelligence than humans. However, if dolphins were asked the same question, maybe they'd say the opposite. ■

Source: Stephen Juan, "Are Dolphins Smarter than Humans?" *New York Daily News*, Body & Soul Section, Wednesday, July 27, 2005, p. 6. Reprinted by permission of the author.

Vocabulary

Answer the following questions about some of the vocabulary words from "An IQ Contest." Circle the letter of the correct answer.

1. What is a *hemisphere* (paragraph 1)?

   a. half of anything globe-shaped
   b. a round object
   c. the size of the earth
   d. another name for the solar system

2. In this context, what does *apparatus* (paragraph 3) mean?

   a. system
   b. contraption
   c. vocal cords
   d. communication

3. What does it mean to *assert* (paragraph 6) something?

   a. give up
   b. rebel
   c. disobey
   d. claim

Checking Comprehension

Circle the letter of the correct answer.

1. According to this selection, how is the dolphin brain different from the human brain?

   a. It is smaller.
   b. The dolphin's brain hemispheres work independently of each other.
   c. It is larger.
   d. The dolphin's brain hemispheres work together.

2. What of the following can be said about dolphin sonar?

   a. It is not as sophisticated as that of the humpback whale.
   b. It is pretty unsophisticated, which is unusual, given dolphins' ability to communicate with each other.
   c. It is highly sophisticated and more complicated than submarine sonar.
   d. Dolphins do not have sonar.

3. Which of the following statements is true, based on your reading of this selection?

   a. Dolphins travel in packs.
   b. Dolphins have unsophisticated sonar.
   c. Dolphins can understand simple human sentences when spoken to.
   d. Dolphins do not live very long.

4. According to Dr. John Lilly, what would dolphins need in order to prove that at one time, they had intelligence equal to or greater than that of humans?

   a. hands and fingers
   b. a more sophisticated communication system
   c. tools
   d. the ability to breathe out of the water

Mode and Skill Check

Circle the letter of the correct answer or write your answer on the blanks provided.

1. What is the main idea of this selection?

   a. Dolphins are not as smart as humans.
   b. Dolphins are almost as smart as humans.
   c. Dolphins have great intelligence but are not as smart as humans.
   d. Dolphins communicate via a series of clicks and whistles.

2. What are the predominant modes of development used to organize the details in paragraph 3?

   a. narration and description
   b. comparison/contrast and process
   c. argument and illustration
   d. illustration and process

3. Which of the following paragraphs begins with a contrast transition?

   a. paragraph 1
   b. paragraph 3
   c. paragraph 4
   d. paragraph 5

Questions for Discussion and Writing

1. Based on the information in this selection, write a one paragraph summary about the ways that dolphins and humans are alike and different.

2. Are there other animals that exhibit great intelligence? If you do not know, do some research online. Summarize your findings.

3. What do you think about explanations that involve aliens visiting Earth? Do you agree with people who believe in aliens? Why or why not?

My Roving Barcalounger

By Michelle Cottle

1   We did it. With less than two months to go until our second child is scheduled to arrive, my husband and I swallowed our pride, plundered our savings and joined the much ridiculed ranks of minivan owners. It had to be done. Neither of our old vehicles had what it takes to handle two car seats, two parents, the odd grandparent and the sheer tonnage of baby paraphernalia required for even quick trips to the grocery. Still, it took multiple visits to the dealership before I came to terms with the sociological enormity of what we were about to do. In America, you are what you drive. And as everyone knows, cruising around in a shiny new minivan definitely announces to your fellow road warriors, "I am an unabashed suburban breeder."

2   But, hey, I'm a big girl. I can sacrifice a little hipness for the sake of my offspring. Besides, whatever my new midnight-blue ride lacks in exterior flash it more than makes up for with interior luxuries: huge leather seats, lightning-quick seat warmers, individual climate control, DVD player, satellite radio, five-CD changer, three power outlets for my cell phone, "conversation mirror" (to facilitate chats with backseat passengers), voice-activated navigation system and, of course, 15 cup holders for those mornings when I feel the need for several different flavors of Frappuccino. Throw in a wet bar and a shower massage, and I can't foresee the need to leave my vehicle ever again.

3   But as snug as I feel in my rolling rec room, I have started to wonder if maybe it offers a few more bells and whistles than are prudent. Should there really be a mirror designed to shift my gaze from the road to my traveling companions? And while the DVD player takes the edge off long trips with my 2-year-old son, I can't shake this feeling that it's only a matter of time before I plow into a busload of schoolkids while struggling to cue up *SpongeBob SquarePants*. My navigation system, meanwhile, not only can locate the five nearest Chinese restaurants from any point in the continental U.S. but will also remind me that I have a noon dental appointment and that I need to pick up the cat's antifungal cream before the vet closes at 6. Cool? Absolutely. But also utterly distracting.

4   As if Americans weren't scary enough behind the wheel, our cars are becoming as diversion-packed as our homes. Customizers have started installing TV screens in the front

Source: Michelle Cottle, "My Roving Barcalounger," *Time*, Aug. 1, 2005. © Time, Inc. Reprinted by permission.

seat of vehicles, allowing drivers to watch movies as they weave in and out of rush-hour traffic. If you think some jerky lawyer yammering on his cell phone is a road hazard, just imagine how deadly he'll be while watching *Braveheart* at the same time.

5   While it's still too early to gauge the precise safety impact of such high-tech amusements, there's ample evidence that the driving public already pays far too little attention to the road. In June, researchers at the Virginia Tech Transportation Institute released the results of a yearlong study showing that driver distractions—including such low-tech basics as eating, chatting with passengers and fiddling with the radio—account for nearly 80% of crashes. The AAA Foundation for Traffic Safety has released similar reports detailing the link between various distractions and vehicular crack-ups. And the *British Medical Journal* added to the mound of data about the dangers of dialing while driving when it reported last month that gabbing on a cell phone (even the hands-free variety) quadruples your risk of getting into an accident requiring a trip to the hospital.

6   Of course, each year also brings new reports on the ballooning number of hours Americans spend commuting and chauffeuring the kids between soccer, ballet, T-ball, karate and tuba lessons. Because we can't be at home, kicking back in the Barcalounger with a tall cold one, we're dead set on making our motoring experience feel like the next best thing. But driving a car—particularly the supersize models—really should demand more concentration than, say, slouching slack-jawed in front of the wide screen in your den. And who knows? Maybe if we were a little less content to veg out in our wombs-on-wheels, we might work a little harder on ways to spend less time on the road.

7   Contemplating the downsides of so much vehicular comfort and entertainment, I find myself getting anxious all over again about having taken the minivan plunge. Maybe I should call the dealer and see if it's too late to swap my new blue marvel for a stripped-down subcompact with no AC, no stereo and bad suspension—just to be safe. ▪

Vocabulary

Answer the following questions about some of the vocabulary words in "My Roving Barcalounger." Circle the letter of the correct answer.

1. What does *plundered* (paragraph 1) mean?

   a. spoiled
   b. stolen
   c. despaired
   d. driven

2. What does it mean to be *prudent* (paragraph 3)?

   a. careful
   b. reckless

c. unknowing
d. disobedient

3. What does it mean to *yammer* (paragraph 4)?

a. whisper
b. call
c. talk loudly
d. cry

Checking Comprehension

Circle the letter of the correct response.

1. What made the author and her husband buy a minivan?

a. the desire for more "bells and whistles" in their vehicle
b. the upcoming birth of their second child
c. the need for a second car
d. the birth of twins

2. What does the author think of the vehicle's numerous "bells and whistles"?

a. She loves them.
b. She wonders if there should be fewer, since she thinks they might distract a driver.
c. She thinks that the vehicle is missing some.
d. She did not comment on the things that came with the minivan.

3. Of the following, which is NOT one of the things that the author describes her minivan as being like?

a. a tuna can
b. a rolling rec room
c. a Barcalounger
d. a womb-on-wheels

4. According to the Virginia Tech Transportation Institute, what percentage of accidents are caused by driver distractions?

a. 75
b. 80
c. 90
d. 100

Mode and Skill Check

Write your answer on the blanks provided, or circle the letter of the correct answer.

1. In the space below, write the main idea of this selection in your own words.

   _____

   _____

   _____

2. The predominant mode of development used in paragraph 5 is

   a. narration
   b. illustration
   c. comparison/contrast
   d. description

3. The predominant mode of development used in paragraph 2 is

   a. illustration
   b. narration
   c. process
   d. comparison/contrast

Questions for Discussion and Writing

1. Do you agree with Cottle that if we had fewer "bells and whistles" in our vehicles we would "work a little harder on ways to spend less time on the road"? Write a brief response.

2. Do the amenities you have in your vehicle, such as your radio and/or CD player, make the time you spend driving more enjoyable? What additional amenities would make that time even more enjoyable?

3. Do you agree with the author that "in America, you are what you drive" (paragraph 1)? Illustrate your answer with specific examples.

E-mail: The Future of the Family Feud?

By Candy Schulman

1   A few months ago I had my first e-mail argument. I've heard about e-mail romances, but I didn't know how common e-mail fighting is—until I mentioned it to friends, who readily confessed their own online tiffs. My foray into Internet madness began with a disagreement between one of my relatives and me. We had never bickered before. As our barbs zapped through cyberspace, I became increasingly alarmed at how modern technology is affecting human relationships.

2   My twentysomething relative, a.k.a. quarrel2000@gripemail.com, was born A.C. (after computers) with a mouse in his hand. I am a bit of a technophobe[1], viewing computers with trepidation but knowing I must log on if I am to move forward in this fast-changing world.

3   Our fight was a misunderstanding involving ego, self-esteem, you-hurt-my-feelings, I'm-right-you're-wrong. The altercation[2] began over the antiquated[3] telephone. We both hung up in a huff. Disturbed that issues were unresolved, I transferred our argument onto the Internet, where our family does almost everything these days, from sending birthday cards to sharing recipes.

4   We all know that e-mail makes communication immediate, but in the modern e-mail argument, discourse is actually slowed down—with painful consequences. When my first e-mail went unanswered, I wrote a sec-ond the next day. No new mail! Then a third, with a plea, "I can't believe we can't talk about this. I've been crying every night."

5   I couldn't know whether quarrel2000's lack of response meant he was angrier than I'd imagined. Or was he simply nonplused about my hurt feelings? Or had my e-mail disappeared someplace in cyberspace and not even reached its destination?

6   And then, I logged on at 12:06 P.M. and there was mail from quarrel2000! My fingers shook as I clicked on READ NEW MAIL. Quarrel wrote, "This isn't something to cry over. I don't even care anymore." "You don't care about my hurt feelings?" I typed. SEND MAIL. Click.

7   Eighteen hours later: "I meant I don't care about whatever it is we were fighting about. I'm over it. You should be too."

8   Oh. Misunderstandings and days of delay before clarifications[4] can be heard make these conversations (if I dare to call them that) very unsatisfying. As a writing professor, I've often felt optimistic about e-mail because it makes writers out of everyone, renewing our enthusiasm for the moribund written word. But as a family member with hurt feelings, I can't always read messages with emotional clarity. Not to mention the risk of screen words' being misinterpreted. Is the writer of this e-mail argument taking on an angry tone? An ironic one? Conciliatory[5]? Only the most highly skilled writers can make these nuances[6] clear.

1. **technophobe:** person who fears technology
2. **altercation:** fight or disagreement
3. **antiquated:** old
4. **clarifications:** explanations
5. **conciliatory:** peace-making
6. **nuances:** shades of meaning

Source: Candy Schulman, "E-mail: The Future of the Family Feud?" From *Newsweek,* December 18, 2000. All rights reserved. Reprinted by permission.

9   When arguments occur face to face, we're more likely to hear each other, sit through silences and think about what's transpired. I don't know if quarrel2000 ever read my lengthy e-mails trying to justify my actions and words—he might have said, "Oh, no! Not another angry e-mail from my obstinate relative!" and simply pressed DELETE.

10   I've watched people's interpersonal skills steadily decline since the advent of answering machines. Rather than having conversations with each other, we leave one-way messages, never risking retribution[1]. Talk into a recording and you expediently[2] do the job: cancel a dinner reservation, terminate an employee, send a message of condolence[3] after a death. Nobody says "It's Susan, call me back" anymore. Now it's "I can't go out with you Saturday night . . ." Beep! End of message.

11   And now, we don't even fight in person anymore. I can imagine a new dot-com company being launched to sell accouterments[4] to online arguments: written scripts to download into your computer with guarantees to prove your point of view, flower services for making up with your loved one.

12   Right now, my online argument with Q2000 is in remission[5]. We e-mail each other in polite, concise, guarded messages. Our altercation briefly spread, however, through our family on the Web, as other family members heard about our feud and began sending their own commentaries back and forth to one another. As our disagreement catapulted[6] into a multigenerational group e-mail debate, its original premise became increasingly unclear, even distorted.

13   As we move farther away from human interaction, I am making a resolution that the next time words between relatives or friends explode in anger, I'm going to demand that, whenever possible, we climb in the ring together and spar it out in person. It might sting, but there's a prize at the end of the match: we can hear each other say "I'm sorry," then fall into each other's arms in a reassuring, forgiving hug. ■

Vocabulary

Answer the following questions about some of the vocabulary words in "E-mail: The Future of the Family Feud." Circle the letter of the correct response.

1. What is a *foray* (paragraph 1)?

   a. venture
   b. hazard
   c. risk
   d. volunteer

1. **retribution:** revenge
2. **expediently:** promoting one's own self-interest
3. **condolence:** sympathy
4. **accouterments:** equipment
5. **remission:** a resting period
6. **catapulted:** launched

2. What does *trepidation* (paragraph 2) mean?

a. forgiveness
b. happiness
c. fear
d. longing

3. What is *discourse* (paragraph 4)?

a. writing
b. communication
c. e-mail messages
d. a delivery

4. In this context, to be *nonplused* (paragraph 5) means to be

a. confused
b. affected
c. mystified
d. overwhelmed

5. What does *moribund* (paragraph 8) mean?

a. mysterious
b. healthy
c. thriving
d. nearly dead

6. Someone who is *obstinate* (paragraph 9) is

a. satisfied.
b. obedient.
c. stubborn.
d. flexible.

Checking Comprehension

Circle the letter of the correct answer.

1. According to Schulman, what has happened to people's interpersonal skills since they started communicating via e-mail?

a. Their interpersonal skills have declined.
b. Their interpersonal skills have gotten better.
c. Nothing has happened.
d. Their interpersonal skills have become more aggressive.

2. Where did the argument between Schulman and quarrel2000 begin?

   a. in e-mail messages
   b. via letter
   c. over the telephone
   d. in person

3. What does Schulman think happens to discourse as a result of e-mail?

   a. It is sped up.
   b. It is slowed down.
   c. It is unaffected.
   d. It is more immediate.

4. The next time she needs to resolve an argument, what will Schulman do?

   a. resolve it in e-mail messages
   b. resolve it via letter
   c. resolve it in person
   d. resolve it over the phone

Mode and Skill Check

Circle the letter of the correct response or write your answer on the blanks provided.

1. In the space below, write the main idea of this selection in your own words.

   _____

   _____

   _____

2. What are the two predominant modes used in this selection?

   a. argument
   b. narration/description and argument
   c. cause/effect
   d. comparison/contrast

3. What is the predominant mode of development in paragraphs 10–11?

   a. narration
   b. process
   c. illustration
   d. argument

Questions for Discussion and Writing

1. Do you agree or disagree with the author that "modern technology is affect-ing human relationships" in an adverse way (paragraph 1)? Why or why not?

2. Have you had an experience similar to the author's? If so, write a paragraph describing what happened and whether it was resolved.

3. In your opinion, what are the best uses for e-mail? What should *never* be handled via e-mail messages?

The Curly Cue

By Kevin Sintumuang

1   It started on my first day of kindergarten, at Lindeneau School in central New Jersey. I was sitting on the floor stacking building blocks with the other kids and shamefully pretending to drink out of a carton of milk (I'm lactose intolerant[1], a common condition among Asians) when my teacher, the rotund yet cheerless Ms. S., came and took me by the hand. She escorted me from her classroom and into another one with decidedly less "Romper Room[2]"-esque decor, where a second teacher sat me at a desk and started quizzing me with a series of flashcards. What color is this? What kind of animal is this? Can you count to 10?

2   I answered all of the questions correctly. *This kindergarten stuff is cake! Bring on first grade!* Then I looked around. There were older kids here—first- and second-graders. About a dozen of them. All Latino. All speaking Spanish.

3   This was an ESL class. I'd been brought here to be tested on how well I could understand English—which happened to be my first language. Another Asian American kid might have wondered why he alone—not, say, any of the Korean Americans in the class—had been shuffled off for testing. But I, even at age 5, looked around and knew.

4   It was my hair. Tightly curled, like that on an idealized Greek statue or, frankly, a poodle, it had clearly said "Latino" to my kindergarten teacher. Or, at the very least, it had stated, "Not Asian!" and left Latino as a default. (Why that automatically meant a trip to the ESL room, I'll leave for someone else's essay.)

5   I hadn't even taken a nap yet, and my hair was already causing identity havoc. It couldn't have been the first time. And it certainly wouldn't be the last.

6   At a college party, someone once described me as looking "vaguely pan-ethnic[3]." In fact, both my parents are from Thailand, which makes me 100 percent Asian American. But riding public transportation, I've seen enough people staring above my forehead to gather that most don't expect to see

1. **lactose intolerant:** an inability to digest the sugars contained in milk and other dairy products
2. **Romper Room:** a television show for preschoolers that aired in the 1950s and 1960s

3. **pan-ethnic:** comprised of many different ethnicities

Source: Kevin Sintumuang, "The Curly Cue," from *The Washington Post*, November 12, 2006. Reprinted by permission of the author.

Shirley Temple[1] locks above an Asian-looking face. At parties, my hair is often a topic of discussion—an ice-breaker. Not a month goes by without someone asking permission to feel it, what hair products I use or whether I've gotten it permed. My hair is fairly novel[2]—even to me. Until I was 7, the only other Asian with curly hair I knew was my father. Then I met my grandfather.

7   If I were white, Latino or black, the texture of my hair—curly, wavy or straight—wouldn't be such a defining feature. But a big part of being identified as Asian is being plunked into a box labeled "You guys all look alike." My slight deviations from what people expect—eyes slightly rounder than those of most Asians, skin slightly darker and, most visibly, the hair—have been enough to turn me ethnically ambiguous in people's eyes. About 25 percent of the time, when they guess my ethnicity, they're completely off the mark: They think I'm Latino or native Hawaiian. Another 65 percent of the time, they figure I've got to be mixed: half black, half Asian, for example. Only 10 percent of the time has anyone pegged me for Thai.

8   Of course, it wasn't always this way.

9   Back in the late '80s and early '90s, when people were less ethnicity-savvy, they seemed to have no doubts about what I looked like: I looked Chinese American, just like Asian celebrity du jour[3] Michael Chang.

10   At the time, Chang was burning up the tennis courts. In 1989, he was the first American to win the French Open since 1955. He was everywhere. I'm sure any Asian American guy doing anything athletic back then was, at some point, called Michael Chang by his

friends. That I didn't mind. What I did mind: when people said I actually looked like Chang.

11   "It's a compliment. Michael Chang is very good-looking," a friend's aunt explained. That would have been reassuring—had I looked anything at all like Michael Chang.

12   The real Chinese American kids in my community seemed to agree with me. I'd say one-third of my high school class was Asian, with the Chinese and Korean kids forming pretty tight cliques[4]. But I was never really accepted in them. I only had one Asian friend growing up. As for Edison, N.J.'s, Thai community—at the time, my family was the Thai community. There were no other Thais for miles.

13   Frankly, even if there had been, they might not have offered the sense of belonging I sought. In the summer of 1993, when I was 14, I traveled to Thailand with my mother. Walking around with her, I realized pretty quickly that I wouldn't be able to pass for native. In her hometown of Chumphon, a small coastal town about 300 miles from Bangkok, a department store saleswoman asked my mother if my father is black. My mother thinks the saleswoman imagined a black American GI[5] who had left my mother alone with a son. And when we ran into my mother's old friends, they also asked her whether she'd married a Thai.

14   There is one moment in my teenage years when I remember being ethnically accepted. I was shopping for a television with my father at Price Club[6], when one of the salespeople, who was Latina, mistook us for her peers and graciously—in Spanish—told us that the TV we were interested in would be on sale in two

---

1. **Shirley Temple:** a 1930s/1940s child actress who wore her hair in ringlets
2. **novel:** unusual or different
3. **celebrity du jour:** the celebrity of the moment; a celebrity who is very popular at the time

4. **cliques:** exclusive groups
5. **GI:** a soldier
6. **Price Club:** a warehouse store that sells many items in bulk

weeks. It seemed as though she was giving us the inside scoop[1] because we were comrades, members of the same club. Luckily, I'd taken about five years' worth of Spanish, so I got the gist of what she was saying. We came back in two weeks and got the TV for 15 percent off. And it felt great.

15   For most of my early life, the questions about my ethnicity were pretty binary: Was I Asian or Latino? Was my father Asian or black? All that changed in the late '90s, with the ascent of Tiger Woods.

16   Never heard of him? Let me give you a brief bio. Aside from being a golfer, Tiger is also famous for being pan-ethnic. He's only one-quarter Thai, but there's enough fame in that quarter to make him the most famous Thai person in the world.

17   In 1997, Tiger had just become the youngest player to win the Masters[2]. For me, it was the beginning of freshmen orientation at Johns Hopkins University. Orientation at Hopkins, as at other schools, was an orgy[3] of awkward getting-to-know-you events. They included viewing and discussing a play about relationship abuse, a massive game of "Twister" (which seemed to nullify[4] everything you learned in the play), and a humongous speed-meeting session on the lacrosse field, in which you shook hands with up to 100 people and remembered none of their names. The typical conversation I had with my anonymous classmates went like this:

18   "What's your nationality?"

19   "American. Do you mean ethnicity?"

20   "Sure."

21   "I'm Thai."

22   "Like Tiger! What else are you?"

23   Oh, the pressure. Not only did I rarely break 100 as a golfer, I was expected to be more ethnically diverse than I am.

24   From that time on, I've sometimes felt I was disappointing people by telling them that I'm just Thai. Making something up—something like the globe-spanning mix of ethnicities they've come to expect from exotic fashion models and MTV veejays[5]—would be a relief. It would make me seem much cooler and put an end to all of my explaining: Yes, some Asians have curly hair. No, I'm not the only one; my dad and grandfather have curly hair. No, I'm not lying.

25   In the past few years, I've been traveling a lot, and one thing to note is that in many places outside of the United States, the big "You guys all look alike" box is still the norm. In Poland, schoolchildren on a field trip made slanty-eyed faces at me as I walked past them. In Cuba, they called me Jackie Chan[6]; one kid threw a rock at my head. In Belgium, I was billed for a Japanese person's hotel room—the manager apologized and explained that it was an honest mistake, because we all look the same.

26   All of these things made for one very angry Asian. That big box is depressingly deep, narrow and hard to climb out of. For that reason, today, I've found that it's more comfortable for me to be misidentified as multiracial or Latino than it is to be labeled entirely Asian. Not only do fewer people throw things at my head, but my world feels as though it has more flexibility. I've gotten comfortable being unique. My sister thinks the celebrity I most resemble is New York Yankee Bernie Williams. I get John Legend[7] a

---

1. **scoop:** a slang term for inside information or details
2. **the Masters:** a professional golf tournament
3. **orgy:** uncontrolled participation in an activity
4. **nullify:** cancel out, invalidate

5. **MTV veejays:** people who introduce music videos on the MTV television channel
6. **Jackie Chan:** an Asian martial-arts movie star
7. **John Legend:** an American singer

lot, too. Both comparisons feel much less re-ductive, more mysterious and ripe with pos-sibilities than arguing over a Japanese man's hotel bill.

27   If we're being honest, cutting my hair short would probably put an end to all the confusion. But then I'd just blend in; I wouldn't be noticed as much. And if I'd cut my hair, I would have never landed my first date out of college.

28   In 2001, when I lived in my first apart-ment, I used to pass a movie theater on my way to work every day. At a party a few months after I moved in, this cute, arty girl with black-dyed hair came up to me and said, "You're that guy who walks past the movie theater every morning."

29   It turned out she worked there; she saw me every day. So how did she remember me out of hundreds of other passersby?

30   Just as back in kindergarten, I knew instantly.

31   It was the hair. ▨

Vocabulary

Answer the following questions about some of the vocabulary words in the reading selection. Circle the letter of the correct answer.

1. What does *rotund* mean (paragraph 1)?

   a. unhappy
   b. tall
   c. overweight
   d. smiling

2. What does *havoc* (paragraph 5) mean?

   a. chaos
   b. interest
   c. understanding
   d. discouragement

3. What does *deviations* (paragraph 7) mean?

   a. similarities
   b. troubles
   c. differences
   d. movements

4. What does *ambiguous* (paragraph 7) mean?

   a. same
   b. mixed
   c. clear
   d. unclear

5. What does *gist* (paragraph 14) mean?

a. general idea
b. opposite
c. cost
d. definition

6. What does *binary* (paragraph 15) mean?

a. having two parts
b. rude
c. in thirds
d. confusing

7. What does *humongous* (paragraph 17) mean?

a. massive
b. tiny
c. square
d. round

8. What does *reductive* (paragraph 26) mean?

a. complex
b. confusing
c. oversimplifying
d. large

Checking Comprehension

Circle the letter of the correct answer.

1. What is Kevin Sintumuang's actual ethnic background?

a. Korean
b. Thai
c. Chinese
d. Japanese

2. Why did the saleswoman at Price Club tell the author and his father about the upcoming sale on televisions?

a. She thought they were Latino and wanted to give them a special advantage.
b. She thought they were shoplifters and wanted them to leave the store.
c. She thought they were poor.
d. She thought she knew them.

3. According to Kevin Sintumuang, why are people confused when it comes to his ethnicity?

a. because he is light-skinned
b. because of his hair
c. because of the way he speaks
d. because of the way he dresses

4. How does Sintumuang feel about the confusion surrounding his ethnicity?

a. He does not care about it.
b. It amuses him.
c. It makes him angry.
d. He feels sad about it.

Mode and Skill Check

Circle the letter of the correct answer or write your answer on the blanks provided.

1. What is the topic of this selection?

a. family
b. ethnicity
c. Thailand
d. Tiger Woods

2. On the lines below, write the main idea of this selection in your own words.

_____

_____

_____

3. What are the two predominant modes of development?

a. narration and comparison/contrast
b. description and illustration
c. narration and argument
d. argument and process

4. What mode of development is dominant in paragraphs 1–2 and 14?

a. comparison/contrast
b. process
c. argument
d. narration

Questions for Discussion and Writing

1. Would you consider yourself representative—looks-wise—of your ethnicity? Why or why not? Write a paragraph or two describing yourself and why either you look like other people in your ethnic group or you don't.

2. Why do people care so much about pinning down others' specific ethnicities? What are the advantages and disadvantages of doing so? Do you think that, in the future, this interest in ethnicity will increase, decrease, or stay the same? Why?

3. Write a letter to Kevin Sintumuang to convince him that he should (or should not) cut his hair.

When the Boss Is the Problem

By Carolyn Kepcher

1   It's not easy, but at some point in our lives, necessary. I, like many, have had the pleasure of working under a supportive boss and unfortunately, a difficult one. Believe it or not, it is a great experience to have worked under both.

2   Supportive bosses can advance your career and allow you to make decisions without fear. Difficult bosses, if you can detect them, can make you stronger and teach you valuable lessons along the way—such as what NOT to do.

3   Of all the relationships you develop on the job, the one you have with your boss is by far the most important and, more often than not, either the most taxing[1] or the most rewarding.

4   After speaking with many people in my life and reflecting on my own experiences, I've found that bosses come in many shapes and sizes. Let's categorize some of them:

- The weak, indecisive and insecure. He (or she) is afraid to make a decision and yet criticizes your decisions when you're not in the room.
- Those who manage by fear, as opposed to motivation. He gains his power and authority through intimidation.
- Those who know how to reduce you to a trembling mass of low self-esteem. In his presence he can make you feel tongue-tied and inarticulate. He carefully and strategically disarms you with a subtle put-down.
- Those who make a point of keeping tabs on everyone and everything. He forms alliances with people he can

1. **taxing:** difficult, wearing

manipulate. His greatest skill is cutting you off from any ally[1] who might be able to resist him, even from your ultimate superior, to whom he's terrified you'll rat him out.

■ The micromanager[2] and egomaniac. They need to control everything and take credit. They are quick to point the finger when something fails.

5   In my experience, difficult bosses frequently mix and match their abusive styles according to the opportunity and situation.

6   I can't explain how some individuals who are not qualified to lead are given the chance. The best type of boss is one who leads by example but, more importantly, inspires you and allows you to make mistakes.

7   The worst type is the kind who scares you into making the wrong decision or taking risks. The result: progress is halted and he might as well hire mere paper pushers. Creativity also is hindered. The concept of thinking outside the box is diminished and overall morale is cut. All employees should be encouraged to take appropriate risks and know there is a safety net attached to those decisions. Realize, of course, a safety net can only hold so much weight.

8   Take the Trump organization[3], where executives and managers were given, to a certain degree, the freedom to make decisions and take risks—as long as they're profitable. I'm obviously kidding, but the ultimate goal

in taking risks is for the overall success of the company.

9   I certainly have taken some risks at times; some have paid off and some, let's just say, didn't increase the bottom line.

10   Since not all bosses are good leaders, how do we deal with them as an employee?

11   As a manager, I also believed in the philosophy that we manage personalities and not people. But sometimes we have to manage our managers. Try to get inside our bosses' head, even though some are not always easy to read. Try to dissect the decisions he makes in order to get a better understanding of his thought process. The best thing you can do in dealing with a difficult boss is to try to anticipate his next move, as opposed to chalking his decision up to what you may think is stupidity.

12   If you are lucky enough to be in a situation where you can change things, by all means, do so. That means if you're lucky enough to work in a company where there are outlets and resources to share your frustrations without the fear of a backlash[4], use them. These companies are in tune with good management. If those resources aren't available to you—and unfortunately that's typically the case—by anticipating your boss' reaction to different situations and understanding his decision making (wrong or right), he will not only increase your productivity but make your life easier.

---

1. **ally:** friend, partner
2. **micromanager:** a boss who manages every aspect of his employees' work down to the most minute detail
3. **the Trump organization:** run by Donald Trump, the Trump organization is mostly a real estate

company but conducts other business ventures as well
4. **backlash:** a reaction to an action or event

13   Here's a word of advice to those in executive positions. Be thoughtful and considerate when promoting and hiring people as managers. Remember, the title Manager refers to managing people and situations. Some employees can excel in their positions but do not know how to manage properly. Take the top sales person in a corporation who had a banner year. Often, the next obvious step is to promote him to manager. But be careful—you may have just set him up for failure. He has the proper skill set[1] to sell, yet he may not be trained or have the tools for managing "personalities." ■

Vocabulary

Answer the following questions about some of the vocabulary words in the reading selection. Circle the letter of the correct answer.

1. What does *intimidation* (paragraph 4) mean?

   a. fear
   b. supportiveness
   c. eagerness
   d. productivity

2. What does *inarticulate* (paragraph 4) mean?

   a. clear
   b. powerful
   c. speechless
   d. truthful

3. What is an *egomaniac* (paragraph 4)?

   a. someone who cares about others
   b. someone who is obsessed with himself or herself
   c. a great boss
   d. someone who is mentally ill

4. What does *hindered* (paragraph 7) mean?

   a. sped up
   b. expanded
   c. reversed
   d. blocked

---

1. **skill set:** collection of skills or talents

5. What does *dissect* (paragraph 11) mean?

    a. analyze
    b. avoid
    c. oppose
    d. organize

Checking Comprehension

Circle the letter of the correct answer.

1. How does Carolyn Kepcher feel about the experience of working for a bad boss?

    a. She does not think it has any merit.
    b. She thinks it can be a great learning experience.
    c. She does not say in this selection.
    d. She would rather work for a bad boss than a good one.

2. How does the best type of boss lead, according to Kepcher?

    a. by intimidation
    b. by micromanagement
    c. by example
    d. by always being right

3. According to Carolyn Kepcher, what is the best thing to do when dealing with a difficult boss?

    a. Manipulate him or her.
    b. Try to anticipate his or her next move.
    c. Bring him or her coffee.
    d. Quit.

4. Kepcher thinks that employees who excel in their positions

    a. always make great managers.
    b. may not know how to manage properly.
    c. make great employees for a strict boss.
    d. should always get promoted.

Mode and Skill Check

Circle the letter of the correct answer or write your answer on the blank provided.

1. What is the topic of this selection?

   a. working
   b. bosses
   c. Carolyn Kepcher
   d. Donald Trump

2. On the lines below, write the main idea of this selection in your own words.

   _____

   _____

   _____

3. What paragraphs are developed with the process mode?

   a. paragraphs 1–3
   b. paragraph 4
   c. paragraphs 5–7
   d. paragraphs 11–12

4. Which paragraph is developed with illustration?

   a. paragraph 4
   b. paragraph 7
   c. paragraph 8
   d. paragraph 12

Questions for Discussion and Writing

1. Who was the best boss you have ever had? What made him or her so great, in your opinion? Write a few paragraphs describing this person and your experience working for this person.

2. Do you have management experience? If so, what kind of boss are you? If you do not have management experience, what kind of boss do you think you will be one day?

3. Would you add any other types of bad bosses to Kepcher's list in paragraph 4? Describe these other types and provide at least one example to illustrate each type.

This Is Where the Rubber Meets the Road Rage

By Dave Barry

1   Here's the problem: If you stop 100 people at random and ask them to evaluate their driving ability, every single one will say "above average."

2   It is a scientific fact that all drivers, including those who are going the wrong way on interstate highways, believe they are above average. Obviously, this is impossible: Some drivers have to be below average. Not me, of course. I am currently ranked fourth among the top drivers in world history, between Mario Andretti[1] and Spartacus[2]. But there are many incompetent people out there on the roads, changing speed and direction without warning or drifting along in the left, or "passing," lane at 23 mph, blinking their turn signals, which they never turn off, even in the garage.

3   These people make me crazy, which is why I am so excited about the car harpoon.

4   I found out about the car harpoon from an Associated Press item, sent to me by many alert readers, concerning the police in the town of Oulu, Finland.

5   You might think that the biggest traffic menace in Finland would be unlicensed reindeer, but the Oulu police have a problem with speeders and drunken drivers who refuse to stop. That's why police Sgt. Markku Limingoja invented the car harpoon. This is a missile-shaped object, equipped with hydraulically activated barbs[3], that sticks several feet out from the front bumper of the police car.

6   The idea is that if the police are chasing somebody, they ram the harpoon into the fleeing car's trunk, activate the barbs to keep the two cars stuck together, then use their brakes to stop both vehicles.

7   We definitely need the car harpoon over here. Of course, we'd have to modify the concept slightly, as follows:

8   1. It would not be limited to police cars. It would also be available as an option on cars operated by qualified civilian drivers such as (needless to say) yourself.

9   2. The civilian model car harpoon—which I assume would be marketed under the name "Carpoon"—would contain additional features, including a powerful public-address system[4].

10   The Carpoon would greatly enhance the driving experience. Envision this scenario: You're behind a bad driver stopped at a traffic light.

11   The light turns green, but the bad driver does not move. He was completely unprepared for the fact that red would be followed by green. He's sitting there, baffled, like a person watching a drive-in movie with a very complicated plot. You honk your horn, but this has no effect on the bad driver; peo-

1. **Mario Andretti:** a famous race-car driver
2. **Spartacus:** a gladiator who led a slave revolt in ancient Rome
3. **hydraulically activated barbs:** arrow points activated by fluid

4. **public-address system:** a system that is used to transmit sound to a large group or to a large space

Source: Dave Barry, "This Is Where the Rubber Meets the Road Rage," as found in the *New York Daily News,* January 13, 2007. © Tribune Media Services, Inc. All rights reserved. Reprinted with permission.

ple are always honking at him, and he never knows why. Suddenly—WHAM—the bad driver feels a jolt. Then he hears a very loud voice—your voice—coming from inside his car, saying: "Excuse me! The light is green! You can go now!" This announcement would be followed, after a courtesy interval[1] of one-10th of a second, by tear gas[2].

12   As a motorist, I want a Carpoon now. And I'll tell you what else I want: a Tire Assault Vehicle. This is a real device that was featured in a publication called NASA Tech Briefs, sent in by alert reader Robert Stolpe.

13   The Tire Assault Vehicle, or TAV, is designed to protect humans from high-pressure aircraft tires that might explode. Basically, the TAV is a remote-controlled model tank that has been modified to incorporate a video camera on top and an electric drill sticking

out the front. The operator, from a safe distance, drives the TAV up to an aircraft tire and drills a hole in it, safely letting out the air.

14   You know how sometimes you're trying to find a space in a crowded parking lot, and you come to a car that some jerk has deliberately parked diagonally[3] across two spaces?

15   Can you imagine the satisfaction you'd experience if, without even having to leave the comfort and safety of your car, you could drill holes in the jerk's tires?

16   Wouldn't that be great? That's why you need to tell your federal government to stop nattering[4] about air bags and start providing you, the above-average driver, with the Tire Assault Vehicle, the Carpoon and other technology. So don't wait! Write to your congressperson now! Also, press the accelerator, okay? The light is green. ■

Vocabulary

Answer the following questions about some of the vocabulary words in the reading selection. Circle the letter of the correct answer.

1. What does the phrase *at random* (paragraph 1) mean in this context?

   a. on purpose
   b. carelessly
   c. irregularly
   d. without reason

2. In paragraph 2, what does *incompetent* mean?

   a. useful
   b. unskilled
   c. purposeful
   d. on target

1. **interval:** time period
2. **tear gas:** a chemical agent that irritates eyes, often used by law enforcement to control a crowd or unruly mob

3. **diagonally:** slantwise or crosswise
4. **nattering:** chattering

3. What is a *harpoon* (paragraph 3)?

    a. a spear-like weapon
    b. someone who spears fish
    c. a glass of beer
    d. a car jack

4. If you *envision* (paragraph 10) something, you

    a. imagine it.
    b. shop for it.
    c. make it happen.
    d. do not think about it.

Checking Comprehension

Circle the letter of the correct answer.

1. According to Dave Barry, if you stop 100 people and ask them to evaluate their driving ability, every single one will say

    a. "average."
    b. "below average."
    c. "above average."
    d. none of the above; most will not answer.

2. The police department in Oulu, Finland, came up with the car harpoon to combat

    a. bad teenage drivers.
    b. speeders and drunk drivers.
    c. unlicensed reindeer.
    d. people who take up two parking spaces.

3. Barry thinks that the car harpoon should be used in the United States. But his version would be available to civilians and include

    a. a fuel-generated rocket.
    b. a hydraulically activated rocket.
    c. flames painted on it.
    d. a public-address system.

4. The Tire Assault Vehicle was designed to protect humans from

    a. exploding aircraft tires.
    b. exploding bicycle tires.
    c. exploding car tires.
    d. reckless drivers.

Mode and Skill Check

Circle the letter of the correct answer or write your answer on the blank provided.

1. What is the topic of this selection?

   a. bad drivers
   b. the Carpoon and the Tire Assault Vehicle
   c. driving in Finland
   d. Finnish car accessories

2. On the lines below, write the main idea of this selection in your own words.

   _____

   _____

   _____

3. What is the dominant mode of development in paragraphs 10–11?

   a. argument
   b. narration
   c. comparison/contrast
   d. illustration

Questions for Discussion and Writing

1. Write a paragraph describing what irritates you about other drivers on the road.

2. Write a paragraph describing an accessory that you would like to have in your car to combat the bad drivers you see when you drive.

3. How would you rate yourself as a driver? Provide examples to support your opinion of your own driving.

I'm Not Fat, I'm Latina

By Christy Haubegger

1   I recently read a newspaper article that reported that nearly 40 percent of Hispanic and African-American women are overweight. At least I am in good company. Because according to even the most generous height and weight charts at the doctor's office, I am a good 25 pounds overweight. And I am still looking for the panty-hose chart that has me on it (according to Hanes[1], I don't exist).

2   But I am happy to report that in the Latino community, my community, I fit right in.

3   Latinas in this country live in two worlds. People who do not know us may think we are fat. At home, we are called *bien cuidadas* (well cared for).

4   I love to go dancing at Cesar's Latin Palace here in the Mission District of San Francisco. At this hot all-night salsa[2] club, it is the curvier bodies like mine that turn heads. I am the one on the dance floor all night while some of my thinner friends spend more time waiting along the walls. Come to think of it, I would not trade my body for any of theirs.

5   But I did not always feel this way. I remember being in high school and noticing that none of the magazines showed models in bathing suits with bodies like mine. Handsome movie heroes were never hoping to find a chubby damsel[3] in distress. The fact that I had plenty of attention from Latino boys was not enough. Real self-esteem cannot come from male attention alone.

6   My turning point came a few years later. When I was in college, I made a trip to Mexico, and I brought back much more than sterling-silver bargains and colorful blankets.

7   I remember hiking through the awesome ruins of the Maya and the Aztecs, civilizations that created pyramids as large as the ones in Egypt. I loved walking through temple doorways whose clearance was only two inches above my head, and I realized that I must be a direct descendant of those ancient priestesses for whom those doorways had originally been built.

8   For the first time in my life, I was in a place where people like me were the beautiful ones. And I began to accept, and even like, the body that I have.

9   I know that medical experts say that Latinas are twice as likely as the rest of the population to be overweight. And yes, I know about the health problems that often accompany severe weight problems. But most of us are not in the danger zone, we are just *bien cuidadas*. Even the researchers who found that nearly 40 percent of us are overweight noted that there is a greater "cultural acceptance" of being overweight within Hispanic communities. But the article also commented on the cultural-acceptance factor as if it were something unfortunate, because it keeps Hispanic women from becoming healthier. I am not so convinced that we are the ones with the problem.

1. **Hanes:** a manufacturer of pantyhose and stockings
2. **salsa:** a popular form of Latin-American dance music

3. **damsel:** a young woman or girl

Source: Christy Haubegger, "I'm Not Fat, I'm Latina," © 1994 by Christy Haubegger. Reprinted by permission of the author.

10 If the medical experts were to try and get to the root of this so-called problem, they would probably find that it is part genetics[1], part enchiladas. Whether we are Cuban-American, Mexican-American, Puerto Rican or Dominican, food is a central part of Hispanic culture. While our food varies from fried plantains[2] to tamales[3], what does not change is its role in our lives. You feed people you care for, and so if you are well cared for, bien cuidada, you have been fed well.

11 I remember when I used to be envious of a Latina friend of mine who had always been on the skinny side. When I confided this to her a while ago, she laughed. It turns out that when she was growing up, she had always wanted to look more like me. She had

trouble getting dates with Latinos in high school, the same boys that I dated. When she was little, the other kids in the neighborhood had even given her a cruel nickname: la seca, "the dry one." I am glad I never had any of those problems.

12 Our community has always been accepting of us well-cared-for women. So why don't we feel beautiful? You only have to flip through a magazine or watch a movie to realize that beautiful for most of this country still means tall, blond and underfed. But now we know it is the magazines that are wrong. I, for one, am going to do what I can to make sure that mis hijas, my daughters, will not feel the way I did. ■

Vocabulary

Answer the following questions about some of the vocabulary words in the reading selection. Circle the letter of the correct answer.

1. In paragraph 7, what does *clearance* mean?

   a. permission
   b. decoration
   c. empty space
   d. color

2. What is a *descendant* (paragraph 7)?

   a. a relative
   b. a parent
   c. a believer
   d. an employee

1. **genetics:** heredity, or the inheritance of certain characteristics or tendencies
2. **plantain:** a fruit like a banana; a staple food in many tropical countries
3. **tamale:** a Mexican dish made of fried chopped meat and crushed peppers wrapped in cornhusks and steamed

3. What does *envious of* (paragraph 11) mean?

   a. happy for
   b. sad about
   c. full of pity for
   d. jealous of

Checking Comprehension

Circle the letter of the correct answer.

1. According to the newspaper article that Christy Haubegger read, what percentage of Hispanic and African-American women are overweight?

   a. 20
   b. 30
   c. 40
   d. 50

2. Which of the following statements is true?

   a. The author has always been comfortable with her body.
   b. The author has become comfortable with her body.
   c. The author was once comfortable with her body, but she is dissatisfied now.
   d. The author became comfortable with her body only when she lost weight and became as skinny as her friends.

3. Where was Haubegger when she had her "turning point" concerning her body?

   a. She was hiking in the ruins of the Maya and the Aztecs.
   b. She was eating a traditional Hispanic meal of plantains and tamales.
   c. She was in high school flipping through magazines.
   d. She was dancing in a nightclub in San Francisco.

4. What did the kids in her neighborhood call Haubegger's thin friend when they were growing up?

   a. the skinny one
   b. the underfed one
   c. the curvy one
   d. the dry one

Mode and Skill Check

Circle the letter of the correct answer or write your answer on the blank provided.

1. What is the topic of this selection?

   a. Latinas
   b. the Latina body type
   c. Hispanic culture
   d. food

2. On the lines below, write the main idea of this selection in your own words.

   _____

   _____

   _____

3. What is the most dominant mode of development in this reading selection?

   a. description
   b. process
   c. illustration
   d. argument

Questions for Discussion and Writing

1. What role does food play in your culture? Describe a typical family dinner and the types of foods that are served.

2. Does your culture value thinness, or is it acceptable to be what the "experts" would call overweight? Write a few sentences describing what kind of body type is acceptable in your culture and why.

3. Do you think that the media play a role in shaping how women feel about themselves with regard to their weight and bodies? Write a paragraph discussing your viewpoint.

Becoming a Creative Problem Solver

By Jeffrey S. Nevid

1   The range of problems we face in our personal lives is virtually[1] limitless. Consider some common examples: getting to school or work on time; helping a friend with a personal problem; resolving disputes; juggling school, work, and family responsibilities. Creative problem solvers challenge preconceptions and consider as many alternative solutions to a problem as possible. Were you stumped by the problem about the key that opened no locks but allowed the man to enter? Perhaps it was because you approached the problem from only one vantage point[2]—that the key was a door key. Solving the problem requires that you consider an alternative that may not have seemed obvious at first—that the key was an Enter key on a keyboard. Speaking of keys, here are some key steps toward becoming a creative problem solver.

Adopt a Questioning Attitude

2   Finding creative solutions to problems begins with adopting a questioning attitude. The creative problem solver asks, "What alternatives are available? What has worked in the past? What has not worked? What can I do differently?"

Gather Information

3   Creative problem solvers acquire the information and resources they need to explore possible solutions. People today have a wider range of information sources available than ever before, including newspapers and magazines, college courses, and, of course, the Internet. Want to know more about combating a common problem like insomnia[3]? Why not search the Internet to see what information is available? However, think critically about the information you find.

Avoid Getting Stuck in Mental Sets

4   Here's a question: "If there were three apples and you took two away, how many would you have?" If you answered one, chances are you had a mental set to respond to this type of problem as a subtraction problem. But the question did not ask how many apples were left. The answer is that you would have two apples—the two you took away.

5   To avoid slipping into a mental set that impairs problem-solving efforts, think through each question carefully. Ask yourself:

- What am I required to do?
- What type of problem is this?
- What problem-solving strategy would work best for this type of problem?

6   Put these skills into practice by responding to a few brainteasers[4]:

1. How many two-cent stamps are there in a dozen[5]?

---

1. **virtually:** almost
2. **vantage point:** a position giving a good view; a personal standpoint
3. **insomnia:** inability to sleep
4. **brainteasers:** difficult mind puzzles
5. There are 12 two-cent stamps, since a dozen of anything is 12.

Source: "Becoming a Creative Problem Solver," from Nevid, Jeffrey S., Psychology: Concepts and Applications, 2d ed. Copyright © 2007 by Houghton Mifflin Company. Reprinted with permission.

2. You are holding two U.S. coins that total 55 cents. One of the coins is not a nickel. What are the coins you are holding[1]?

3. A farmer had 18 cows and all but 11 of them died. How many were left[2]?

7 Be on guard against the destructive side of mental set—the tendency to apply a "tried and true" solution even when it no longer applies. The major danger is not the mental set itself, but failing to realize when one is trapped in a fixed way of doing things (Luchins & Luchins, 1994). By remaining aware of this tendency, you can stop yourself every now and then to reflect on whether the strategies you are using are working for or against you.

Generate Alternatives

8 Creative problem solvers generate as many alternative solutions to a problem as possible. They may then decide to return to their original solution. Or they may decide that one of the alternatives works best. Sifting through alternatives can help you rearrange your thinking so that a more workable solution becomes obvious. Here are a few suggestions for generating alternatives:

1. *Practice personal brainstorming.* Alex Osborne (1963) introduced the concept of brainstorming to help business executives and engineers solve problems more creatively. The basic idea is to encourage divergent thinking. Brainstorming encourages people to propose as many solutions to a problem as possible without fear of being judged negatively by others, no matter how far-fetched

their proposals may seem. There are four general rules for brainstorming:

> *Rule 1: Write down as many solutions to the problem as you can think of.* Quantity counts more than quality.
> *Rule 2: Suspend judgment.* Don't evaluate any of the possible solutions or strike them off your list.
> *Rule 3: Seek unusual, remote, or even weird ideas.* Today's strange or oddball idea may turn into tomorrow's brilliant solution.
> *Rule 4: After generating your list, put it aside for a few days.* When you return to it, ask yourself which solutions are worth pursuing. Take into account the resources or additional information you will need to put these solutions into practice.

2. *Find analogies*[3]. Finding a situation analogous[4] to the present problem can lead to a creative solution. Ask yourself how the present problem is similar to problems you've encountered before. What strategies worked in the past? How can they be modified to fit the present problem? This is constructive use of mental set—using past solutions as a guide, not an impediment, to problem solving.

3. *Think outside the box.* Recall the nine-dot problem in Figure 7.3. People have difficulty with this problem because of their tendency to limit the ways they think about it. If you didn't solve the nine-dot problem, you're in good company. In a laboratory test, none of the

1. You are holding a fifty-cent piece and a nickel. One of the two coins (the fifty-cent piece) is not a nickel.

2. There are 11 cows left. All but 11 died.
3. **analogies:** comparisons
4. **analogous:** similar to

research participants who were given several minutes to solve the problem were able to do so (MacGregor, Ormerod, & Chronicle, 2001). The problem is solvable only if you think "outside the box"—literally, as shown in Figure 7.19. Creative problem solvers make an effort to conceptualize problems from different perspectives, steering their problem-solving efforts toward finding new solutions (Ormerod, Mac-Gregor, & Chronicle, 2002).

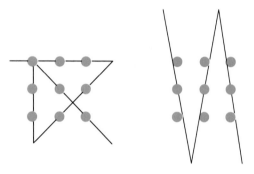

Figure 7.19 **Two Solutions to the Nine-Dot Problem in Figure 7.3***

Sleep on It

9 In cases where people are faced with difficult problems, evidence supports the age-old wisdom of "sleeping on it." For example, some investigators found that research subjects who were challenged with solving challenging math problems did better after they slept (Wagner et al., 2004). Indeed, the cognitive[1] benefits of getting a good night's sleep may account for the experiences of many famous scientists and artists whose inspired ideas occurred shortly upon awakening (Komaroff, 2004).

10   If you are unable to find a solution to a problem, take time away from thinking about it. Allow the problem to "incubate[2]" in your mind. When you return to it, you may have a fresh perspective that will help you discover a workable solution.

Try It Out

11 Try out possible solutions to see how they work. Gather information that will help you evaluate what you need to do differently to achieve a better solution.

12   However you arrive at a possible solution, test it out to see how it works. Even if it doesn't succeed, you may be able to gather additional information that can help you evaluate what you need to do differently to achieve a better solution. ■

Vocabulary

Answer the following questions about some of the vocabulary words in the reading selection. Circle the letter of the correct answer.

1. What are *preconceptions* (paragraph 1)?

   a. ideas formed in advance
   b. mistakes

---

1. **cognitive:** relating to thought

2. **incubate:** develop

*The original nine-dot problem referred to in this textbook excerpt can be found on the student website for this book, in Prepare for Class: http://www.college.hmco.com/pic/dolphinwriterone.

c. facts

d. opposing arguments

2. What does *impair* mean (paragraph 5)?

a. improve

b. expose

c. weaken

d. expand

3. What is a *tendency* (paragraph 7)?

a. a movement toward

b. a hobby

c. a motivation

d. a time

4. When you *sift* (paragraph 8) through something, what are you doing?

a. washing it

b. sorting through it

c. breaking it into pieces

d. imagining it

5. *Divergent* (paragraph 8) means

a. similar.

b. colorful.

c. logical.

d. different.

6. To *conceptualize* (paragraph 8) means to

a. form thoughts.

b. dream.

c. forget.

d. disagree.

Checking Comprehension

Circle the letter of the correct answer.

1. According to the author of this selection, finding creative solutions to problems begins with

a. gathering information.

b. avoiding getting stuck in mental sets.

c. adopting a questioning attitude.

d. generating alternatives.

2. Which of the following is a question you should ask yourself to avoid slipping into a mental set that impairs your problem-solving efforts?

   a. What am I required to do?
   b. What type of problem is this?
   c. What problem-solving strategy would work best for this type of problem?
   d. All of the above.

3. True or false: Creative problem solvers generate as many alternative solutions to a problem as possible.

   a. true
   b. false

4. Complete the following sentence: _____ encourages people to propose as many solutions to a problem as possible without fear of being judged negatively by others, no matter how far-fetched their proposals may seem.

   a. Generating alternatives
   b. Synthesizing
   c. Brainstorming
   d. Freewriting

5. True or false: If you are unable to find a solution to a problem, taking a nap or getting a good night's sleep can help.

   a. true
   b. false

Mode and Skill Check

Circle the letter of the correct answer or write your answer on the blank provided.

1. What is the topic of this selection?

   a. thinking outside the box
   b. generating alternatives
   c. gathering information
   d. becoming a creative problem solver

2. On the lines below, write the main idea of this selection in your own words.

   _____

   _____

   _____

3. What is the predominant mode of development in this selection?

   a. narration
   b. example/illustration
   c. process
   d. description

Questions for Discussion and Writing

1. Do you consider yourself a good problem solver? Write a paragraph describing what you do to solve problems. Do you use any of the skills or strategies contained in this selection?

2. Tell a story about a time when you faced a difficult problem. What steps did you take to solve this problem? What was the outcome?

3. How can the information in this selection help you become a better problem solver? Now that you have read the author's advice, what skills or strategies will you use to solve problems from now on?

Music This Beautiful Is Something to Share

By Leo Harris

1   In 1926, when I was 6 years old, I moved from Kansas City, Mo., to Chicago to live with my aunt and uncle. Until then the only radio I had ever seen was my older brother's crystal set with its accompanying earphones. Now I was pleased to find that my uncle had an Atwater Kent Battery Radio.

2   One day as I was listening to it, I heard a symphony orchestra perform Mozart's "Serenade K. 525" ("Eine Kleine Nachtmusik"). I ran excitedly through the rooming house and begged all of our neighbors to come and hear this wonderful music. They gathered around and then gave me a puzzled look as if to say, "What is wrong with you?" I had an innate love for classical music.

3   As a teenager I attended as many concerts as I could afford. When I was 14, a small orchestra of black musicians played at my church and I fell in love with the melodic sound of the cello. The cellist, a dentist by profession, agreed to teach me how to play. I worked in a grocery store two days a week to earn the money to pay him—$1 per lesson. Two years later I was good enough to study with the first-chair cellist of the Chicago Women's Symphony Orchestra.

Source: Leo Harris, "Music This Beautiful Is Something to Share," from *Newsweek,* June 9, 2003, © Newsweek, Inc. All rights reserved. Reprinted by permission.

4   In those days, it was almost impossible for a black man to make a living as a classical musician, so when I graduated from high school, I became an air-conditioning and heating engineer and pursued music in my spare time. When I was 22, I got married and started a family. My kids absorbed my love of classical music and learned to play the piano and other instruments. Even my wife took up the piano so she could give our children extra coaching. Consequently my family had two violinists, a violist, a cellist and a pianist, and we formed the South Side Family Chamber Orchestra.

5   Over the years my children have left the group and other musicians have joined, but my goal has remained the same: to bring classical music to African-American kids who would otherwise never hear it. We give free concerts in housing projects and schools all over Chicago. We operate on a limited budget, but we do our best to provide lessons and instruments to young people who show a passion for it. We have seen how the discipline of learning classical music can transform even the most excitable kids into calm and interested students.

6   Just as rewarding are the reactions from the adults who hear us play. A few years ago, my chamber orchestra was scheduled to perform at a state college. One of the featured selections was a work by composer Jacques Offenbach titled "Orpheus in the Underworld," which includes a major harp solo. My neighbor, an African-American man in his late 60s, agreed to use his station wagon to transport the harpist and her harp to and from the school. It was the first time he had ever attended an orchestral performance. Afterward he told me how much he had enjoyed himself. He was astounded by his natural love of classical music.

7   It was a wonderful moment, but I wished he could have had this realization years before. My own kids have made music a central part of their lives. My son and daughter still play the violin and the piano, and my oldest son, who played viola in our family ensemble, is now a high-profile keyboard artist who plays contemporary music.

8   My grandchildren are getting in on the act as well. My grandson gives clarinet lessons to children, my granddaughter is perfecting Beethoven's "Moonlight Sonata" on the piano and my great-granddaughter took advantage of our youth music project to study the cello. Several months ago I picked up my 14-year-old great-grandson in the car. I assumed he didn't want to hear the classical music that I had been listening to, but when I reached for the radio dial he asked me not to switch the station.

9   Unfortunately, my family is the exception in the black community. Even young African-Americans who are lucky enough to be exposed to classical music often feel uncomfortable expressing their appreciation, largely because the media often define "black" music as hip-hop or rap. But I see signs of progress. Several weeks ago I accompanied my college-age string quartet to a conference for young African-American musicians and was thrilled to hear the advanced playing level of the participants. The Chicago Symphony Orchestra has started a diversity program to encourage minorities to audition, and last year it hired its first black permanent musician. Recently a young man who occasionally plays with my group applied for a position in its violin section. If he makes it, he will have done something I could only dream about. ■

Vocabulary

Answer the following questions about some of the words in the reading selection. Circle the letter of the correct answer.

1. In paragraph 2, *innate* means

   a. natural.
   b. hurried.
   c. huge.
   d. sad.

2. *Melodic* (paragraph 3) means

   a. extremely loud.
   b. pleasant-sounding or musical.
   c. strange.
   d. bird-like.

3. To *pursue* something (paragraph 4) means to

   a. ignore.
   b. run around with.
   c. believe.
   d. work at.

Checking Comprehension

Circle the letter of the correct answer

1. Why did Harris become an air-conditioning and heating engineer after high school?

   a. because he loved the work
   b. because in those days, it was almost impossible for a black man to make a living as a musician
   c. because heating and air-conditioning was his family's business
   d. because that was what he had trained to do

2. What is Harris's goal in life?

   a. to raise musicians in his own family
   b. to raise money for instruments
   c. to grow his heating and air-conditioning business
   d. to bring classical music to African-American kids

3. According to Harris, what do the media often define as "black" music?

   a. disco
   b. hip-hop or rap
   c. Motown
   d. soul

4. What has the Chicago Symphony Orchestra done to encourage minorities to audition?

   a. It starts music programs in predominantly black schools.
   b. It gives free instruments to black children who want them.
   c. It started a diversity program.
   d. It encourages black musicians to teach music to black children.

5. What is one thing that Harris and his family do to promote love of classical music among black children?

   a. They give free concerts in housing projects and schools all around Chicago.
   b. They collect money to donate instruments to schools.
   c. They give free violin lessons.
   d. They pass out free tickets to Chicago Symphony Orchestra concerts.

Mode and Skill Check

Circle the letter of the correct answer or write your answer on the blanks provided.

1. The topic of this selection is

   a. love of classical music
   b. children.
   c. a history of classical music
   d. orchestras.

2. In your own words, write the main idea of this selection below in your own words.

   _____

   _____

   _____

3. What is the predominant mode used in this selection?

    a. narration
    b. description
    c. example/illustration
    d. comparison/contrast

Questions for Discussion and Writing

1. Harris writes of a moment that changed his life—when he heard a Mozart serenade performed. Have you had a similar, life-changing moment in your life? If so, write a paragraph in which you describe it.

2. Do you think that music is something to which all children should be exposed? Why or why not? Write a paragraph discussing—and defending—your position.

3. Do you excel at something in particular? Is it a sport? Playing an instrument? Cooking? Describe your passion. Or, if you do not feel as though you excel at something, describe something you would like to learn how to do, outlining what it will take for you to excel at it.

I Want Constantine's Murderer to Die

By Olga Polites

1   I was the one who was home on that Tuesday afternoon in 2000, just having gotten back from a jog. Since my husband was walking in the door from work, I was the one who answered the phone when my sister-in-law called to tell us that her 22-year-old cousin had been brutally murdered in a robbery attempt gone awry. Nearly hysterical, she kept repeating, "We have lost him. We have lost him." After the young men suspected of the crime were arrested the next day, my husband turned to me and asked, "Are you still opposed to capital punishment?"

2   Since then I have thought a great deal about the death penalty. It is hard not to, and not just because a heinous crime hit so close to home. More recently, lawyers, politicians and even Supreme Court justices are increasingly questioning the role of the death penalty in our justice system. I always thought I knew exactly where I stood on this issue, but now I find myself constantly wavering.

3   My husband's cousin Constantine was living at home while attending Temple University when his newly moved-in next-door neighbors and their friend broke into a second-floor bedroom window, looking for some quick cash. Constantine, who did not have any classes scheduled that day, most likely confronted them. After what police believe was a short struggle, Constantine was tied up with an electrical cord, stabbed 41 times and shot three times in the head. One of the bullets landed in the kitchen sink on the first floor. When his mother came home from work later that afternoon, she found him. Neighbors said her screams could be heard blocks away.

4   Going to the funeral, watching Constantine's parents deal with the aftermath of what had been done to their son, was terribly painful. For months they could not resume working, saying repeatedly that they could not think about the future because as far as they were concerned, theirs had abruptly ended.

5   When the trial took place two years later, all three suspects were convicted, and the prosecutor's office sought the death penalty for the shooter. I was in court for the penalty phase, and as I listened to witnesses testify on his behalf, I was surprised at how indifferent I was to his personal plight. I did not much care that his family had escaped from Vietnam and that he had had problems assimilating to[1] American culture, or that his parents had a difficult time keeping him out of trouble.

6   Before this happened, I likely would have argued that this young defendant had extenuating circumstances beyond his control. But not anymore. Maybe it is because my daughter is almost the same age as Constantine was when he was killed, or maybe it is because the reality of experience trumps[2] theoretical[3] beliefs. Whatever the reason, when I looked at the young man sitting at the defense table, I did not see a victim. All I saw was the man who took my family member's life.

---

1. **assimilating to:** blending in with; getting used to
2. **trumps:** beats or overrides

3. **theoretical:** based on principles

Source: Olga Polites, "I Want Constantine's Murderer to Die," from *Newsweek*, January 22, 2006, © 2006 Newsweek, Inc. All rights reserved. Reprinted by permission.

7   I find it hard now to resist the urge to support the death penalty, especially since it is getting so much attention. Some states, such as Illinois, have placed moratoriums[1] on executions; others have looked into how well defendants are represented at trial. I recognize that there are sound reasons for doing so. The recent use of DNA[2] has proved that some former death-row inmates were unfairly convicted. Locking up the innocent is unacceptable; executing the innocent is unconscionable. And I agree with recent Supreme Court rulings barring the execution of the mentally retarded, the criminally insane and those who committed crimes when they were juveniles.

8   Perhaps a serious review in the way the death penalty is administered will bring about changes that are clearly necessary. Justice John Paul Stevens is right: there are serious flaws in how we apply capital punishment. Intellectually, I can make the argument that it does not deter crime, and that race and class play major roles in determining who ends up on death row. But the truth is that personal involvement with the horrible crime of murder renders[3] the academic arguments for or against capital punishment meaningless. It was easy to have moral objections to an issue that didn't affect me directly.

9   The jury verdict for Constantine's killer was life in prison without parole. Although he will die in jail, there is a part of me that wishes he got the death penalty. I am not proud of this, nor am I sure that next year, or even next month, I will feel this way. What I am sure of is that today, my head still says that capital punishment should be abolished[4], but my heart reminds me of the pain of losing Constantine. ■

Vocabulary

Answer the following questions about some of the vocabulary words in the reading selection. Circle the letter of the correct answer.

1. When something goes *awry* (paragraph 1), it goes

   a. straight.
   b. wrong.
   c. as planned.
   d. perfectly.

2. Something *heinous* (paragraph 2) is

   a. terrible.
   b. minor.
   c. understandable.
   d. famous.

1. **moratoriums:** suspensions of activity
2. **DNA:** substance that contains a biological organism's genetic code

3. **renders:** makes
4. **abolished:** ended, done away with

3. Someone who is *wavering* (paragraph 2)

a. has made up his or her mind.
b. has given up.
c. is running away.
d. feels unsure or indecisive.

4. What is a *plight* (paragraph 5)?

a. an achievement
b. the future
c. a bad or unfortunate situation
d. an illness

5. In paragraph 6, *extenuating* means

a. excellent.
b. excusing.
c. untrue.
d. hidden.

6. Something *unconscionable* (paragraph 7) is

a. evil and unfair.
b. unavoidable.
c. sad but necessary.
d. impossible.

Checking Comprehension

Circle the letter of the correct answer.

1. How did the author's cousin die?

a. He was killed during a robbery attempt.
b. He was killed during a fight between two gangs.
c. He died in an auto accident.
d. He died of cancer.

2. What happened to the person responsible for Constantine's death?

a. He was never caught.
b. He was tried and found innocent.
c. He was convicted and sentenced to life in prison.
d. He was convicted and sentenced to death.

3. How did the author feel about the people responsible for Constantine's death?

    a. She felt sorry for them.
    b. She did not see them as victims.
    c. She thought that they should be deported back to their homeland.
    d. She forgave them for what they did.

Mode and Skill Check

Circle the letter of the correct answer or write your answer on the blank provided.

1. What is the topic of this selection?

    a. crime
    b. violence in America
    c. the death penalty
    d. the prison system

2. On the lines below, write the main idea of this selection in your own words.

    _____

    _____

    _____

3. What are the two predominant modes of development?

    a. narration and comparison/contrast
    b. description and process
    c. narration and argument
    d. argument and process

Questions for Discussion and Writing

1. Write a paragraph arguing for or against the death penalty.

2. In your opinion, what are the main causes of violent crime in America? Write a paragraph to explain your answer.

3. Besides the death penalty, what is something else in America that many people consider to be seriously flawed? In an illustration paragraph, give examples of these flaws.

Additional Practice for Multilingual Writers

English differs from other languages in certain aspects of grammar and sentence construction. For writers whose native language is not English, this appendix addresses some of those issues.

Countable and Noncountable Nouns

Many nouns in the English language are **countable.** That is, they refer to things—such as dollars, birds, compact discs, and waves—that are separate units. Therefore, they can be counted, and they have both singular and plural forms:

Singular	*Plural*
boat	boats
message	messages
potato chip	potato chips
child	children

Other nouns in English, however, are **noncountable.** They name ideas, emotions, or other things that cannot be divided into separate parts or pieces. Some examples of noncountable nouns follow:

Abstract ideas: honesty, bravery, happiness, patience

Activities: homework, housework, football, surfing, chess, sleeping

Things made up of small particles or grains: oatmeal, salt, sugar, flour, dust

Liquids: blood, soup, paint, coffee, water, milk, gravy, oil

Certain foods: bread, popcorn, butter, cheese, ham, beef, bacon

Gases: air, steam, hydrogen, oxygen, smoke, pollution

Things with individual parts that are thought of as a whole: furniture, garbage, luggage, jewelry, food, clothing, money

Weather and other natural phenomena: snow, rain, thunder, sunshine, fog, gravity

Materials: cotton, glass, concrete, copper, steel, wood

Subjects or fields: biology, photography, English, math, computer science

Noncountable nouns do not have a plural form. Adding an *–s* to the noncountable noun *fun*, for example, is not appropriate. *Fun* does not have a plural form, so *funs* would be incorrect.

Some nouns have both a countable and a noncountable meaning. The context determines which meaning is specific, and therefore countable, or more general, and therefore noncountable.

Countable: She accidentally broke two wine **glasses.**
Noncountable: The window is made of **glass.**

Countable: He was charged with two **crimes.**
Noncountable: **Crime** does not pay.

EXERCISE 1

Write the correct form of the noun in parentheses in each blank.

1. Frank possesses great _____. (*wisdom*)

2. Did you and Mark ride _____ on vacation? (*bicycle*)

3. The _____ were bending in the wind. (*tree*)

4. Could you pass the _____? (*bacon*)

5. To serve in the Armed Forces, you must have _____. (*courage*)

6. The dresses were made of _____. (*cotton*)

7. My children have both finished their _____. (*homework*)

8. That book costs three _____. (*dollar*)

9. They bought new _____ for their living room. (*furniture*)

10. She put too much _____ in their _____. (*sugar, coffee*)

Articles

The is a definite article, a kind of adjective that refers to one or more specific things. It is used before singular and plural countable nouns.

the zoo
the salesclerk
the organizations
the feelings

The can sometimes be used before noncountable nouns if the noun is specifically identified.

She was surprised by **the** patience that he displayed.
I was able to find **the** information you need.

A and *an* are indefinite articles that refer to one nonspecific thing. They are used before singular countable nouns.

a teacher
a promise
an ability
an orange

A and *an* are never used before noncountable nouns.

EXERCISE 2

Circle any article that is used incorrectly. If the use of articles in the sentence is correct, write *Correct* on the blank.

1. Our father is a member of the association. _____

2. I have an information for you. _____

3. I feel the joy every time I sing. _____

4. You should never take the life for granted. _____

5. She put a butter and a salt on her corn. _____

6. Jim ate an orange for breakfast. _____

7. I am majoring in the biology. _____

8. Do you enjoy an art? _____

9. I would like a soup for lunch. _____

10. Did you bring money? _____

Order of Verbs in Verb Phrases

There are twelve verb tenses, which are listed and illustrated in the following chart.

SIMPLE TENSES indicate a past, present, or future action.

Present tense	He walks to school every day.
Past tense	He walked to school last year.
Future tense	He will walk to school next year.

PERFECT TENSES indicate that an action was or will be completed before another time or action.

Present perfect tense	He has walked to school every day for the last three years.
Past perfect tense	He had walked to school once or twice in the past.
Future perfect tense	By the time he graduates, he will have walked to school for three years.

PROGRESSIVE TENSES indicate continuing action at a specific time.

Present progressive tense	He is walking to school right now.
Past progressive tense	He was walking to school at 7:30 yesterday.
Future progressive tense	He will be walking to school at 7:30 tomorrow morning.
Present perfect progressive tense	He has been walking to school for twenty minutes now.
Past perfect progressive tense	He had been walking for twenty minutes when he realized that he did not have his backpack.
Future perfect progressive tense	When the clock strikes eight, he will have been walking for thirty minutes.

As you can see from this chart, different combinations of helping (or auxillary) verbs and main verbs allow speakers of English to indicate different times and qualities of verbs. The components of verbs must occur in a specific order:

MODAL* + BASE FORM OF VERB
I must write.
He can write.
They must write.

Has/have/had + PAST PARTICIPLE OF VERB
I have written.
He has written.
They had written.

Is/are/was/were + PRESENT PARTICIPLE (–ING FORM) OF VERB
I am writing.
He is writing.
They are writing.

MODAL + has/have + PAST PARTICIPLE FORM OF VERB
I might have written.
He should have written.
They could have written.

MODAL + be + PRESENT PARTICIPLE OF VERB
I could be writing.
He will be writing.
They may be writing.

MODAL + has/have + been + PRESENT PARTICIPLE OF VERB
I will have been writing.
He must have been writing.
They may have been writing.

*The modals are *can, could, may, might, must, will, would, shall,* and *should.*

Fill in the blank with the words in parentheses in the order that correctly expresses the tense.

1. On Friday, they _____ to Florida. (*driving will be*)

2. Jim _____ the train to New York. (*must taken have*)

3. He _____ in that house for twenty years. (*been had living*)

4. Shawn _____ you a message tomorrow. (*be sending will*)

5. Ann and Mike _____ on the next plane. (*be arriving may*)

6. You _____ sooner. (*have could come*)

7. On their next anniversary, they _____ husband and wife for twenty years. (*been have will*)

8. You _____. (*been must dancing have*)

9. The board _____ this matter at the next meeting. (*be will discussing*)

10. At the end of the day, they _____. (*stopping will be*)

For additional practice with verbs and verb tense, see the Parts of Speech section of the Handbook.

Verbs with Gerunds and Infinitives

Some verbs are followed by a gerund (*a verbal,* a verb form that functions as another part of speech in a sentence), and others are followed by an infinitive, another verbal. A **gerund** is the *-ing* form of a verb that acts as a noun in a sentence.

> **Dancing** is great exercise.
> She enjoys **reading** and **traveling.**

The following verbs are usually followed by a gerund:

admit	discuss	finish	practice	resist
avoid	dislike	imagine	put off	risk
consider	enjoy	miss	quit	stop
deny	escape	postpone	recall	suggest

You would not write *He practiced **to hit** the ball*. Instead, you would write *He practiced **hitting** the ball*.

An **infinitive** is made up of the word *to* plus the base form of a verb. It most often functions as a noun in a sentence (but can also be an adjective or an adverb). The following infinitives (nouns) are direct objects:

He asked her **to dance.**
She likes **to read.**

The following verbs are usually followed by an infinitive acting as a noun (direct object):

afford	fail	mean	offer
agree	forget	need	refuse
appear	hesitate	neglect	remember
begin	hope	plan	start
continue	intend	prefer	try
decide	learn	pretend	wait
expect		promise	

You would not write: *She cannot afford **buying** a new car* (gerund phrase). Instead, you would write *She cannot afford **to buy** a new car*. Notice that gerunds and infinitives can take objects to form gerund or infinitive phrases. When that happens, the whole verbal phrase functions as the sentence element (direct objects in these examples).

EXERCISE 4

Circle the correct word or words for each sentence.

1. She practiced (reciting, to recite) the poem.

2. They enjoy (walking, to walk) their dog.

3. He agrees (paying, to pay) for the damage.

4. The boys like (playing, to play) football.

5. I could not resist (buying, to buy) the dress.

6. We need (saving, to save) more money.

7. We considered (postponing, to postpone) our trip.

8. The dog learned (catching, to catch) a Frisbee.

9. I hope (singing, to sing) the National Anthem on July Fourth.

10. I just finished (eating, to eat).

Verbs with Prepositions

Prepositions are often used with verbs to express certain meanings. For example, notice how the verb *wait* is paired with different prepositions in the following examples:

> I waited **for** an hour.
> I waited **on** the customers.
> I waited **at** the bus stop.
> I waited **in** the waiting room.

These prepositions are not interchangeable, for they express different meanings.

Consult a dictionary when you are unsure of the right preposition to use with a particular verb.

EXERCISE 5

Circle the correct preposition for each sentence.

1. She would not comment (on, for) the problem.

2. Bob was charged (with, on) extortion.

3. Will Lori wait (in, for) me?

4. We were asked to participate (on, in) the session.

5. You need to adapt (on, to) changing times.

6. I am completely dissatisfied (on, with) your work.

7. Pay attention (to, with) the teacher.

8. You can use this card to pay (with, for) your items.

9. I waited (at, in) home for three hours.

10. We differ (from, about) the best solution to the problem.

The Prepositions *in, at,* and *on*

For expressions related to time and place, the prepositions *in, at,* and *on* have specific meanings.

Use *in*

- before a month, year, season, century, or period: *in June, in 2003, in spring, in the nineteenth century, in a week*
- before a city, state, country, or continent: *in Seattle, in California, in France, in South America*
- to mean "into" or "inside of": *in the kitchen, in the lake*

Use *at*

- before an actual clock time: *at five o'clock*
- before a specific place or address: *at the post office, at 1612 Oak Street*

Use *on*

- before a day or date: *on Thursday, on April 5*
- before holidays: *on Thanksgiving, on Labor Day*
- to mean "supported by," "on top of," or "at a certain place": *on the bench, on the table, on Oak Street*

EXERCISE 6

Circle the correct preposition for each sentence.

1. Marie will see you (in, at, on) Saturday.
2. I will meet you (in, at, on) 205 Oak Street.
3. Jessica will arrive (in, at, on) 8:00.
4. The store is (in, at, on) the mall.
5. The store is (in, at, on) Lexington Avenue.
6. They jumped (in, on) the bed.

7. They swam (in, on) the lake.

8. The dinner dance is (in, at, on) July.

9. The dinner dance is (in, at, on) July third.

10. I bought this china (in, at, on) France.

Unnecessary Repetition of Subjects

In some languages, some parts of sentences are repeated. Resist in particular the repetition of the subject of a sentence. It is unnecessary to state the subject and then refer with a pronoun to it again, as in the following sentences:

> Mrs. Rodriguez **she** is an excellent teacher.
> Her raise in pay **it** was not enough.
> The employees at the factory **they** work in shifts.

To correct each of these sentences, simply eliminate the bold pronoun.

EXERCISE 7

In each of the following sentences, circle pronouns that unnecessarily repeat the subject. If there are no unnecessary pronouns, write *Correct* on the blank beside the sentence.

1. The gate it was open. _____

2. The professor he was on time for the lecture. _____

3. Jennifer and he plan on going on vacation together. _____

4. I drove by, but she was not at home. _____

5. The shoes under her bed they were dusty. _____

6. Unlike Mary, she never goes out. _____

7. The pilot he landed the plane. _____

8. They talked, and they ate. _____

9. The woman on Tenth Avenue she was a performer. _____

10. The nurses at that hospital they are underpaid. _____

Index

Rhetorical Index

417

Order of Importance and Argument